D0915257

When a Writer Can't Write

Perspectives in Writing Research

LINDA S. FLOWER AND JOHN R. HAYES, EDITORS

When a Writer Can't Write: Studies in Writer's Block and Other Composing-Process Problems
MIKE ROSE, EDITOR

New Directions in Composition Research
RICHARD BEACH AND LILLIAN S. BRIDWELL, EDITORS

Forthcoming

Writing in Nonacademic Settings
LEE ODELL AND DIXIE GOSWAMI, EDITORS

Protocol Analysis
LINDA S. FLOWER AND JOHN R. HAYES

When a Writer Can't Write

STUDIES IN WRITER'S BLOCK AND OTHER COMPOSING-PROCESS PROBLEMS

EDITED BY

Mike Rose

UNIVERSITY OF CALIFORNIA, LOS ANGELES

The Guilford Press

NEW YORK LONDON

A Division of Guilford Publications, Inc.
200 Park Avenue South, New York, N.Y. 10003

Printed in the United States of America

LIBRARY OF CONGRESS CATALOGING IN PUBLICATION DATA
Main entry under title:

When a writer can't write.

(Perspectives in writing research)
Includes index.
1. Writer's block—Addresses, essays, lectures. I. Rose, Mike. II. Series.
PN171.W74W48 1985 808'.001'9 84-19304
ISBN 0-89862-251-4
ISBN 0-89862-904-7(pbk)

To all the Meraglio uncles and aunts

Anna
Frank and Mary
Joan and Eddie
Joe and Mariam
Sammy and Ann
Russ and Anna Mae

their stories
their memories

Contributors

DAVID BARTHOLOMAE, PhD, Department of English, University of Pittsburgh, Pittsburgh, Pennsylvania

LYNN Z. BLOOM, PhD, Department of English, Virginia Commonwealth University, Richmond, Virginia

ROBERT BOICE, PhD, Department of Psychology, State University of New York, Albany, New York

JOHN A. DALY, PhD, College of Communication, University of Texas, Austin, Texas

DONALD A. GRAVES, PhD, Department of Education, University of New Hampshire, Durham, New Hampshire

MURIEL HARRIS, PhD, Department of English, Purdue University, West Lafayette, Indiana

STAN JONES, PhD, Department of Linguistics, Carleton University, Ottawa, Ontario, Canada

REED LARSON, PhD, Laboratory for the Study of Adolescence, Michael Reese Hospital and Medical Center, and Department of Psychiatry, University of Chicago, Chicago, Illinois

DONALD M. MURRAY, AB, The English Department, University of New Hampshire, Durham, New Hampshire

MIKE ROSE, PhD, Freshman Writing Program, University of California, Los Angeles, California

CYNTHIA L. SELFE, PhD, Humanities Department, Michigan Technological University, Houghton, Michigan

Preface

No one writes effortlessly. Our composing is marked by pauses, false starts, gnawing feelings of inadequacy, crumpled paper. Many of these dead ends are necessary; they occur when we've come up short on information or hit a knotty conceptual problem, when we can't quite arrive at the most effective way to organize material or we're trying to go beyond staid and stereotypic phrasing. Would that more writers understood such tangles for what they are: signs that they've hit a critical moment in composing. And would that more writers honored these moments—took the time to struggle with the conceptual or rhetorical challenge they present. Our reading would be made sweeter by their efforts.

But some writers with some tasks seem unduly vexed. Thoughts won't come, and when they do they evanesce as the writer tries to work them into written language. Pauses become longer and longer and transmogrify into avoidances. Inner conflicts manifest themselves in jumbled syntax and unclear diction. The demands of one's life and the ways one has been taught to deal with them interfere again and again with writing. The conventions of a genre or a discipline baffle and intimidate rather than guide. The very way one composes contains within it narrow or rigid assumptions and procedures that stymie production. And so goes the painful litany.

Distinguishing the necessary, productive dead end from the intractable composing-process problem is difficult and is ultimately a judgment that must be made after some consideration of an individual's writing history and current practice. There is no quick definition of writer's block, no facile description of the stymied writer. It is into this uncertain territory that the authors in this volume venture; and while no single author arrives at an easy formula, together they provide the reader with a good sense of what can go wrong as the writer writes.

This volume marks an attempt, the first of its kind really, to bring together a number of investigations focusing on composing-process problems. The essays address various cognitive and emotional dimensions of disrupted composing and describe some of the situational variables that can contribute to it. One of the strengths of the collection is the variety of methods the investigations include: naturalistic inquiry, survey procedures, tracing of cognitive process, clinical–experimental techniques, text analysis, and literary analysis. These investigations involve children, adolescents, college students, and academic and professional writers and are concerned with both theory and practice.

Let me summarize each chapter and introduce the authors.

Donald Graves directs the Writing Process Laboratory at the University of New Hampshire's School of Education and has spent most of his professional career conducting naturalistic observation studies of elementary school writers. His observations demonstrate that children will write energetically, the focus of their attention shifting with growth from the basic formal and mechanical conventions of written language to more sophisticated concerns about audience and revision. What Graves suggests is that children will naturally concentrate on the concerns of the moment and that they might well get stuck on them, but that the response of parents or teachers will determine whether or not they resolve and move beyond their difficulties to new challenges or fixate—truly block—and remain limited as writers.

Reed Larson, a developmental psychologist affiliated with the Laboratory for the Study of Adolescence at Chicago's Michael Reese Hospital and with the Department of Psychiatry at the University of Chicago, offers a series of exploratory studies on the complex relation between emotion and writing. Working with adolescents involved in writing ambitious research papers, Larson monitored the emotional states that co-occurred with planning, drafting, and revising. From those surveys, he has derived a set of rich illustrations of emotion and cognition interacting in optimal as well as debilitating ways.

John Daly, a professor of communication studies at the University of Texas at Austin, summarizes the considerable body of empirical research on writing apprehension. He offers a questionnaire to assess writing apprehension and discusses at length the relation of writing apprehension to other cognitive and emotional traits, to details of educational history, and to various measures of the quality of writing. He also speculates on the development as well as the amelioration of writing apprehension and concludes with a call for a theoretical framework that would consider the full range of cognitive and emotional variables that are related to this negative response to composing.

Cynthia Selfe, a former student of Daly's and now with the Humanities Department at Michigan Technological University, provides us with a detailed case study to complement Daly's survey and other correlational studies of writing apprehension. The college student whom Selfe has chosen is not a good writer by university standards; and, as the young woman's story unfolds, we see the ways in which apprehension can further limit a writer's already limited skills.

Stan Jones, an applied linguist at Carleton University who specializes in second language acquisition, turns our attention to the composing-process problems of people writing in a nonnative language. Relying on "monitor theory," a set of assumptions about the development and use of skill in a second language, Jones presents two studies: one of a writer who relies on consciously learned grammar rules as she composes; and another of a writer who composes more spontaneously, worrying about grammatical correctness after the fact. The differences in composing styles are dramatic and have important implications for instruction.

Lynn Bloom of Virginia Commonwealth University has been conducting workshops for student and professional writers for nearly a decade and draws on that experience to give us two case studies, both of female graduate students struggling with dissertations. Bloom's investigations show how very skilled writers can be limited by the circumstances of their jobs and families and by the roles they have been socialized into assuming.

David Bartholomae, Director of Composition at the University of Pittsburgh, relies on textual analysis informed by recent Continental literary theory to argue that any piece of writing is produced within a particular linguistic–rhetorical context, a context that places profound constraints on a writer's composing process. When writers write, they must work within a history of conventions associated with the kind of essay they're composing. These conventions—their history as well as their current incarnations—range from stylistic tricks to commonplace ways of addressing a particular topic. Bartholomae uses student essays to illustrate various levels of failure or success at accommodating this complex linguistic–rhetorical context and speculates about what occurs in students' prose as they struggle to place themselves within that context.

Muriel Harris, Director of the Writing Center at Purdue University, attempts to bridge the gap between research and teaching by applying the researcher's tools and procedures directly to student writing problems. By analyzing the way her student writers compose, Harris has been able to uncover and then correct the ineffective planning, production, and reviewing strategies that limit the effectiveness of their work.

Robert Boice is an experimental psychologist at the State University of New York at Albany who for over a decade has been working with writers who are unable to meet their deadlines. As a skilled methodologist, Boice has relied on a wide variety of treatments and designs to aid his clients and to document the results of his interventions. In his essay he surveys the history of writing-process problems and their treatments, from the psychoanalytic to the behaviorist, and presents evidence of his own clinical success with each kind of treatment. He concludes with speculations on ways not only to remedy but also to forestall stymied composing.

Donald Murray at the University of New Hampshire, a novelist, essayist, poet, and Pulitzer Prize-winning journalist, raises a cautionary voice. Relying on his own rich experience and a wealth of anecdotes from professional writers, Murray reminds us that to write is also to wait. While delays and dead ends may signal nonproductive disruptions in composing, they can also represent those necessary periods during which writers must struggle with the shape of material, elusive connections, and the accuracy of vision.

In the final chapter, I summarize my earlier studies of the cognitive dimension of writer's block and suggest that researchers can investigate such complex writing problems by using multiple and converging methods drawn from a variety of orientations and disciplines. Such eclectic inquiry involves some philosophical difficulties, and I attempt to resolve those. I also offer a research framework that honors the emotional and situational, as well as the cognitive, dimensions of the writing act and illustrate its use with a brief case study.

The authors and I worked closely together on this volume. For nearly two years we wrestled with the issues and with ways to present our theories and our findings. I'm sure there were times when I became overbearing, when the authors' temptation to snip the phone cord was enticing, delicious. But no one did. The authors were most cooperative. I thank them both for their intellectual integrity and for their good humor. And I especially thank them for the stimulation our collaboration provided me.

One more person deserves mention. Linda Flower guided me through this first crack at editing. I can testify that she is as patient as she is wise.

MIKE ROSE

Contents

1.
Blocking and the Young Writer
Donald H. Graves 1

2.
Emotional Scenarios in the Writing Process: An Examination of Young Writers' Affective Experiences
Reed Larson 19

3.
Writing Apprehension
John A. Daly 43

4.
An Apprehensive Writer Composes
Cynthia L. Selfe 83

5.
Problems with Monitor Use in Second Language Composing
Stan Jones 96

6.
Anxious Writers in Context: Graduate School and Beyond
Lynn Z. Bloom 119

7.
Inventing the University
David Bartholomae 134

8.
Diagnosing Writing-Process Problems: A Pedagogical Application of Speaking-Aloud Protocol Analysis
Muriel Harris 166

9.
Psychotherapies for Writing Blocks
Robert Boice 182

10.
The Essential Delay: When Writer's Block Isn't
Donald M. Murray 219

11.
Complexity, Rigor, Evolving Method, and the Puzzle of Writer's Block: Thoughts on Composing-Process Research
Mike Rose 227

Name Index 261

Subject Index 267

Blocking and the Young Writer 1

DONALD H. GRAVES

Adam couldn't write. "Teacher, I can't spell 'horse.' Help me." He often waited as long as 15 minutes for his teacher to arrive with the correct spelling. Adam's parents expected his papers to be perfect even though he was only 6 years old and just starting first grade.

Sarah wrote two and one-half six-page booklets each day until she realized at 7 years of age that the other children felt differently about her books. Now Sarah only writes at night on the backs of old booklets under the covers at home.

John writes a line, "The cars was going fast." "Arrgh, that's dumb," he bellows. John is 9 and the line doesn't measure up to his intention. He makes a ball of the paper and throws it in the basket. "Can I have another piece of paper?" he asks his teacher.

The term "writer's block" is foreign to each of these children. Yet each is thwarted by a complex interaction of his or her own development as a writer and the environment in which he or she lives. Adam is blocked by a concern for spelling and by parental expectations; Sarah has discovered the idea of an audience for the first time, yet is intimidated by new responses from the other children; John senses a gap between his intention and what he places on the paper, but lacks the experience to know how to resee his piece.

Most children outgrow the kinds of blocks illustrated by the cases of Adam, Sarah, and John. Suppose, however, that Adam's spelling problem persisted. He could be suffering visual memory problems, while his teachers are continually calling attention to his spelling deficiencies. Adam might well become a self-diagnosed poor speller and,

Donald H. Graves. Department of Education, University of New Hampshire, Durham, New Hampshire.

worse yet, connect his inability to spell with a generic inability to get access to information worth sharing. He simply says, "I can't write."

It is difficult to attribute blocking problems to purely developmental issues. In some cases the block is a natural event in the normal course of growing up as a writer. In other instances, environmental factors (teachers, parents, other children) cause normal blocks to become more aggravated and lead children to the syndrome of diagnosing themselves as having generic inabilities—"I can't write." Blocking is rarely the result of a single variable; rather, it represents a combination of developmental and environmental variables.

"Development" is defined in this chapter as changes in a writer, changes that take place when a child notes a discrepancy or disequilibrium and seeks to right the imbalance. When the child rights the imbalance, new schemas, new conceptual orders are created. Mary composes the word "liked." She writes "lt." She starts to compose the next word but senses something is missing. She sounds the word again, hears a medial "k" sound, erases the letters, and writes "lct." Jason realizes his lead has little to do with the main force of his piece, so he rights the imbalance by rewriting the lead. Both writers develop new schemas, new strategies, new internal structures that help them deal with problems. In some cases they fail; in others they are successful. But whatever the case, there is growth.

Writer's block arises out of children's development as writers. The data that reveal this were gathered during a study, funded by the National Institute of Education (NIE), of the writing processes of 6-, 7-, 8-, and 9-year-old children over a two-year period. Three researchers observed children full-time in classrooms. Case study was the principal methodology with detailed data gathered on a core of 16 children, with other data gathered on another 30 children, and in some instances with data gathered on a larger group of 120. Data were gathered through interviews with children and with teachers, through direct observation of children composing, while conversing with other children in the classroom, and conference, and through all of the children's written products.

Three categories, particularly rich for observing children's development, have been chosen from the data as a framework for discussing blocking in the writing process:

1. *Conceptual sequences:* How do children change their concepts of what is important to them in the writing process?

2. *Use of page, process and information:* How do children change their use of page, process, and information?
3. *Audience:* How do children change their understanding of audience?

As children change in each of these categories, they experience different types of blocking; their different kinds of blocking arise according to how their development occurs in combination with the influence of their environments.

Conceptual Sequences and the Order of Blocks in Development

Blocking in the writing process seems to signal children's concepts of what is important to them. They show what is important by what they revise and talk about with others. The data suggest that there is a general developmental order to children's concerns from the day they first start to write to when they move to higher order revisions of their work. The order follows the problems children have to solve in order to grow as writers:

1. Spelling
2. Motor–aesthetic problems: handwriting and the appearance of the page
3. Conventions: marking off meaning units, capitalizing, etc.
4. Topic–information
5. Revision: changing the substance and order of the content

These problem-solving categories are common to any act of writing, and when children first begin to write they function in all of them. The children are unaware of most of the problems they solve. For example, when a child revises information extensively, he is usually unaware that he is spelling words. Revision is an order of functioning higher than spelling. Spelling during revision, then, is more of a subconscious activity.

Figure 1-1 shows the sequence of problem-solving categories and the relationship of unconscious to conscious activity. The diagonal lines indicate when a category is dominant or part of a child's consciousness. The white areas show when that activity is "underground" or unconscious. There are no ages associated with these categories because age has been found to be irrelevant. There is evidence that some 6-year-

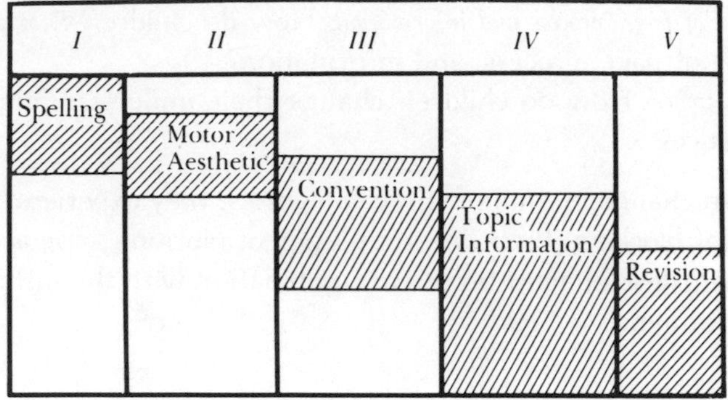

Figure 1-1. The sequence of problem-solving emphases during the writing process.

olds may go as far as category V in one year; while, on the other hand, some writers, because of developmental variables or environmental variables such as what the teacher emphasizes, may never get beyond the first three categories in four years.

Teachers who have not written or who have had little help with the teaching of writing teach as they were taught. They stress only the mechanical components contained in categories I through III. They have little experience with topic choice or the rethinking and revising of information. Parents are often in the same predicament. As a result of responding to these environmental influences, the self-diagnosed poor speller or penman may go a lifetime experiencing blocks in those two categories. This type of child is not only blocked in the course of composing but is often blocked from composing at all.

Examples of blocks in each of these categories are given in the following statements by children or their behaviors. In each of these instances the writer is thwarted in original intention or even abandons the writing.

SPELLING

- "Teacher, I can spell 'grenade.'" The child sits and does not write.
- Donald wants to write about the tooth fairy. After four attempts to arrive at a spelling of "tooth," Donald is so dissatisfied with his crude spelling that he decides to write about "My Dog," a topic that involves words more easily spelled.

MOTOR-AESTHETIC PROBLEMS

- The child is so dissatisfied with the rips and smudges he has caused by changing words that he loses interest in the piece. He may not be able to get another piece of paper, or he may simply not wish to "copy over" what he has already written. He abandons the piece.
- The child is afraid to have others see the appearance of her handwriting.
- Many children will not revise because they must break aesthetic conventions by, for example, placing words in lines in unorthodox fashion. They will not line out, draw arrows, or insert information because of the messy appearance of their changes.
- A child may not believe that the reader will tolerate the separation of information between the bottom of the page and the top even though an arrow connects the parts: "This looks dumb; this part is down here and this part is up here."

CONVENTIONS

- "I don't know where to put the period."
- "When you have a whole buncha stuff, you're supposed to put in a thing [comma in a series], but I can't think what it is. I don't know what to do."

TOPIC AND INFORMATION

When children first wrestle with issues of spelling, the motor-aesthetic, and basic conventions, their attention is so much on these issues that the mere placement of printing on the page is enough to establish their own sense of authority on the subjects they write about. But since children's concern for conventions leads them to realize that other people need punctuation or capitalizations to help them understand the text, the power of audience begins to assert itself. The children may now observe that their audiences accept or reject their pieces, or question their information. Thus blocks on topics and information are born.

- "I can't think of anything good to write about." Up to this point, if the child has written she has had no daily difficulty in choosing topics.

- "This is good because it is about war. This one is stupid because it is about chickens." The topic determines the quality of a piece.
- "This is good because it is long. This one here is crummy because it doesn't have much stuff. I've got to keep putting stuff in here because until I get to the bottom of the page it won't be good. But I can't think of anything more to say."
- "I have so much stuff I don't know where to begin."

REVISION

When children have an abundance of information and see words as temporary and changeable, they cite revision as an important part of the writing process. Children no longer see words as fixed on a page after one draft. They know when they begin to explore a subject that changes will be made in subsequent drafts. When the child knows his subject and the topic is well chosen, he becomes more aware of the discrepancy between his intention and what he puts on the page; blocks appear like those manifest in the following statements.

- "I should never have started it that way. The real interesting part is over here on page 4. I don't feel like doing it over again."
- "I've done over this lead about five times, and it still isn't right. Help!"
- "I know what I should say, but I just can't say it. It isn't here."
- "I used to be able to write in third grade, but this year I'm stuck. I think a lot, but I never finish anything."
- "This piece could go in three directions, and I just don't know which one to take."

This is the general order of children's blocks. Teachers of children ought to expect blocking as a natural event as children progress through each of the five categories. Blocks naturally accompany any struggle, whether it is spelling or the revision of text, and the blocks should be regarded as only temporary. When Mr. Foley focuses only on Anthony's spelling problem and ignores the student's good information and knowledge of a subject, Anthony becomes a self-diagnosed poor speller. As Anthony grows older, he tends to say, "Never could spell; never could write either." In this event the blocking becomes a lifelong problem. Anthony is afraid to write because he believes that his bad spelling will make his information appear worthless.

Teachers and parents need to be wary of sustained focus on one problem at the expense of the child's outer strengths. When Anthony's information is ignored and more mechanical problems are stressed, he loses out on the important struggles of topic choice, the uses of information, and the rearrangement of his text for stronger meaning. These are the normal struggles of writers who believe they have something to say. They struggle to match text with intentions.

Environment has much to do with how humans develop. When teachers provide for daily writing and focus on information versus spelling and conventions, it is not unusual to see some 6- and 7-year-olds block as they revise. This is progress of the highest order! The blocks naturally follow from what children feel is important in the writing process.

How Blocking Changes with Use of Page, Process, and Information

When this second category of growth is examined, children's development becomes more visible and new blocks in the writing process are seen. By examining in tandem how children use the page, the processes of their writing, and how they use information, we have arrived at some of our most fruitful understanding of our data on the writing of young children.

THE PAGE

The writer's struggles are revealed on the page where he or she first learns, then breaks, conventions. At first children use the page in unconventional ways. They may start in the lower right-hand corner and move, column fashion, up the right margin. Then when they run out of space at the top of the page, they may continue across the top edge from right to left. Convention is partially followed since words do follow words, but the usual space of the page is not used from left to right. Children are seldom blocked until they realize that their approach to the page does not fit the acceptance of others or meet with their understanding. Gradually the children learn to compose from left to right, to spell words in conventional fashion, and to place punctuation in appropriate locations.

Children work toward order from the beginning. Placement of writing on the page, formation of letters, the ordering of the message become concerns as they move toward orthodoxy. The feel and appearance of the page is a built-in schema that grows throughout the writer's life. We observe children cleaning blank pages by brushing them with the hands or by erasing small specks and smudges before they begin composing, as they compose, and after they have finished.

Not long after the child masters basic conventions of the page, they must be broken. New information, incorrect spellings, reorganizations of the text demand new uses of the page. For a long time children rub out errors or, in order to change a single error, copy entire selections over again. Children seek to maintain an aesthetic equilibrium. Quite apart from the tedium of copying over, children do not like the appearance of texts that are lined out or of new information written up the side of the paper. The messy appearance bothers them. In addition, the marring of the page suggests that the information is temporary, still under construction, while they wish the piece were completed.

When children cease to rub out or erase errors and begin lining out words and writing in margins, they show a changing view of information. Information is no longer fixed when it goes down on the page, but occupies only a temporary existence in draft form. Usually each stage of a child's development demands the breaking of an older convention such as the orthodox appearance of a page. The convention that needs to be broken can be the source of a *temporary* block to the child.

PROCESS

When most children first write at 6 years of age, composing behaviors are similar to play behaviors. The child composes as he or she builds with blocks, deciding on the spot what to build. Mary walks into the classroom writing center muttering, almost singing, "What'll I write today? Let's see. Oh, I know: the wedding. My aunt's wedding. I'll do the wedding." She quickly draws her aunt coming down the aisle. Beneath the picture she writes, "My aunt got married. She was pretty." The composing episode is over in about 9 minutes. Six minutes are given to the drawing; 3 minutes to the writing. Blocking is seldom observed at this level of composing. The drawing is the more important feature to Mary; the words are only an extension of the drawing. If there is blocking, it is more likely related to drawing the figure's hairstyle or jewelry correctly.

If a child in the midst of composing is asked what he or she will do next, the child usually answers in terms only of the very next step. "I'll draw the people. I'll put her hair on." There is little discussion of how the part under construction relates to the larger whole. Protected by the cloak of egocentricity, the child confidently builds into the future, though only one step at a time. The child works for himself or herself, for the moment, and is not worried about audience. There is little discrepancy between the child's intention and what goes down on the paper, and therefore blocking is seldom seen. If there is blocking, it arises from problems with aesthetics and mechanical functions. Rarely is content an issue, with the exception of the issue of property exhibiting content in drawings.

Development for the beginning writer is characterized by occurring in episodic fashion. It is an oral, externalized event, with the writer evolving one step at a time into an uncertain future. The past is also indistinct. Ask the beginning writer what he or she has done to this point. The child reports only the last sentence or the last touch to the drawing, not the arrival at the writing area, or the process of deciding what to write about, or the particulars of word choice. The past hardly exists and neither does the future. Until there is a past, a plan or a sense of process and course of action, the future will not have options.

The following is an example of how one teacher's, Mary Ellen Giacobbe's, first-grade child responded to her questions in December, then in June, about what he would write about.

> *December*: "School—writing, and building, and all that. Math, science, art."
>
> *June*: "Chicks . . . I like what I know about chicks and I might write that one just hatched at about eleven past ten. I might write the day that it hatched. I might write that a chick just hatched a couple of days ago—that a chick hatched last night. I'll keep on thinking about it and I'll just think and I'll find out what I'm going to write."

In December the child comes up with a list. Mark is rather definite about what he will do, though he offers only a rough connection between components rather than a logical sequence. By June, on the other hand, Mark has a sense of options. The future is rich with possibilities. While he experienced little blocking in December, June is another story. Now Mark is much more sensitive to the possibilities in his piece, and his decision level will be heightened. On a good day the options will serve as dessert. On others they will be downright poisonous; the choices are likely to paralyze him, especially if (as is usually the case by this point) he begins dealing simultaneously with audience.

By June, Mark's composing process is much more elaborate. He may compose over several days. He talks over his piece with friends and his teacher. If asked how he goes about composing a piece, he is much more elaborative and aware of what he is doing. Note the difference between Mark's responses to questions in December and in June about how he chose his subject.

> *December*: "I just wanted to write that. 'Cause I like school. It just came to my head."
>
> *June*: "I just thought about what we've done. I thought about dinosaurs first. And I thought about butterflies and chicks. We studied about food and shells. Then I decided the chick one."

Even though Mark is only 7, by the end of the school year he regularly adds information to his pieces; occasionally he even deletes pages he feels are irrelevant. Though his composing is still a series of episodes, rarely done in just one sitting, there is evidence that Mark and other children his age think about their composing when they are not writing. This means that the process has been expanded and the process components have become more differentiated. The child is no longer building one step at a time; rather, the behaviors show a constant revisiting of past composing through rereading, insertion and deletion of information. The child's focus in the writing process has moved from mechanical, aesthetic centering to concern for information and for the reassembling of that information as it relates to his intention. Once again, as the process becomes more elaborate and the choice load increases, the opportunities for blocking increase. But in a healthy learning climate, the options for dealing with problems also increase.

When children revise, they show us what they see. When they are thwarted in their attempts to change something, we then see the nature of their blocks. Lucy Calkins, research colleague on the NIE study, analyzed the writing of 8-year-olds and came up with four categories of revising strategies (1980). These categories show what children see, their concepts of the writing process, and their views about information.

Category I: These children seldom revise. The actual amount of time spent writing is short. The child writes to an uncertain future. He builds it one block at a time. Ask this child what will occur next. Little is said beyond the next small information component. The child seldom rereads or changes anything. The child has little concept of option either in process or information. The language is absolute, not tentative.

Category II: This child rereads a piece but only to refine. This kind of refinement is usually of a mechanical nature—changes spellings, put in capitalizations, periods and commas. Information is immutable, fixed. If the child attempts to revise, he cannot regard the first draft in relation to the second draft. Rather, he turns the first draft over, writes from scratch on the second. He cannot deal with two time-space dimensions simultaneously. If he discovers new information he only adds it at the end of a piece. It is not integrated into the main text.

Category III: This child has a different view of information and process than is found in the second or first categories. He knows there is a process to change things and often has information that he would like to put in the text. He has the concept that information is clay-like and manipulable. But he seems to be either torn by the fact that something new is needed but can't think of what it is, or lacks the necessary tools to integrate it into the main text. His reading skills have progressed to the point that he can identify discrepancies or needed changes, but the critic seems to be more powerful and devastating than the producer within him. Many children who seldom have the chance to write fall within the third category, particularly children who have their skills in reading developed without corresponding development in writing and the writing process.

Category IV: Children within this category see information as flexible and manipulable. They move back and forth in their process of writing, rereading from the beginning in order to sense where the part under construction fits into the whole. They discover, experiment, and are responsive to the dictates of their information. If there is blocking, it is sometimes because they are overwhelmed by options; they struggle for simplicity, for what to exclude. Usually their dry periods are of shorter duration (if they write regularly) since they have a broader repertoire to deal with problems. They struggle to realize the clarity of their intentions. They can be blocked at the point of finding their own voice. They won't settle for writing that doesn't have it and can be blocked in trying to find it.

Children show us potential blocks in what they attempt to change in their writing. A child who is only able to work with one draft at a time can block when he or she must look back and forth from one page to another. The child in transition in category III is able to recognize a problem when reading it, but is unable to come forth with solutions. The child in category IV is so filled with possibilities that he or she is blocked by alternatives.

INFORMATION

When 6-year-old children first write, they rarely experience a block related to their use of information. They are sure they know their subjects. They are self-appointed authorities on most anything. If an audience questions, the audience has a problem; they do not. Blocking related to use of information usually appears after children have put the challenges of spelling, handwriting aesthetics, and subject choice behind them. This shift in development can be seen when children begin to lessen their sounding of letters, subvocalizations, drawing prior to writing, and extensive conversations with friends during composing. They now engage in more planning, thinking through of topic options, and brainstorming before actually starting formal composing. When these rehearsals appear, the child is doing more internal thinking and the process of selecting information is accelerated.

Writers of all ages and abilities have a common problem: They assume information is in their texts that is simply not there. Egocentricity is the lifelong problem of any writer. Writers need to be both the self and the other, both writer and reader, simultaneously. Young children assign false understandings to others in most of their activities, and writing is no exception. Six-year-old Mary assumes that her aunt's entire wedding event is contained in these lines: "There were lots of people there. Aunt Ruth was pretty. We had lots of cake and ice cream."

As Mary advances in her understanding of the writing process and in her ability to recall information, new dilemmas arise: how and where to put the new data. Once mechanical and aesthetic problems connected with inserting information have been overcome, problems concerning the logical placement of new information remain. At first children add information at the end. The latest information, regardless of the piece's internal logic, goes at the end because it was the last thing to come into the mind of the writer. Latest things go last on the page. Later the child realizes that information dictates a logic within the space that contains it. Thus the first block on logical grounds may arise: "I don't know where this goes! It doesn't seem right."

A block can also arise because the child lacks adequate information. The child knows there is a discrepancy between his or her intention and the information on the page. "This just isn't right. Something's missing and I can't think what it is." The writer has a gut feeling that the piece isn't right but lacks the objectivity or experience to summon the needed information.

Children encounter significant growing pains when they deal with information without the intervention of teachers. When teachers intervene, therefore, through conferences or comments written on papers, they need to be sensitive to the child's level of understanding of process and use of information. Major blocks occur when teachers require or expect information that has little to do with the child's intention or knowledge base.

For the longest time, the addition of information is the child's dominant approach to revision. Much later the addition of information leads to new organizations. Information is added until there arises a need for a paragraph split for the sake of the audience or of logic or both. Children come to a point in their development when they make the transition from telling "everything," more than the reader needs to know, to making more intelligent selections of information for the sake of greater impact on their audiences. A description follows characterizing this stage and the types of blocks children can encounter in the transition.

There is a definite stage when the young writer composes what I call the "bed-to-bed story." This is a complete narrative giving every detail of a day from rising in the morning to retiring in the evening. The main event may be a wedding, being lost on a mountain, or traveling to the emergency room at the hospital, but the child has a problem in telling it. The only way he or she knows how to write about the main event is to begin with getting out of bed in the morning. The text may involve good detail, but each event seems to possess equal value. The wedding or the adventure on the mountain may occupy but three lines in the narrative, equal in treatment to what the child had for breakfast. The child has a traditional process for getting to the important element and only knows how to write a traditional narrative lead by starting at the beginning of the day. The following is an example of a bed-to-bed narrative.

> We got up early in the morning to go to Northampton. Mom said we better eat a big breakfast because there wouldn't be anything to eat until the reception. I got my clothes all laid out, then put them into the suitcase. When my Dad started the car, it wouldn't go. Mom said, "Oh no, not again." They had a big argument. My Dad banged around and it started. We got there just in time for the wedding. There were all kinds of

> cars. My cousin got them parked in the right place. We sat next to my other cousin, Kathy. The music played and Aunt Ruth came down the aisle. She was beautiful. She had on a jeweled band across the front and the gown went way down behind her. My other little cousin walked behind her to see that nothing happened to it. They got married and she and my new Uncle Tom kissed. Then they came down the aisle and they were smiling. Then we had a reception. You could hardly move there. There was lots to eat. I had cake, ice cream, pop, sandwiches, salad. Then more ice cream. It was so hot I had to eat lots of ice cream and coke too. My Dad said, "We've got to go now," and Mom said let's stay. My Dad won and we got into the car. It was a long trip. It was dark when we got home. My Mom said we didn't need anything to eat because we ate so much junk. What a day! I went to bed about ten o'clock.

What is missing is the heightening of what part of the wedding was of particular interest to the storyteller, Mary. The teacher seeks to get Mary to speak about what part interests her most; as Mary recalls details, the teacher listens to her voice for clues to what engages her. Once certain parts are heightened in importance, the process of deletion or selection can usually begin. It is virtually impossible at certain stages of children's writing, however, to get them to delete, for the ability to delete usually follows development of the ability to add. This is the usual order of development: add, heighten, select, delete. If the teacher ignores this order of development and tries to push the child into skipping some steps, the child will produce blocks very quickly.

The essence of art is selection. When children become aware of what they want to select, they fuss with language and organization, with lining out of data. They have an inner sense of sound and meaning, and they cut and paste to match it. But sometimes neither sound nor sense comes in the drafting. The child is frustrated, feels alone with his or her problem, and needs the help of others. Once again, children who are at this stage should have a broader repertoire of processes and tools to solve problems. Still, when the voice is strong, the intention relentless, the child may find it difficult to return to the problem for fear of failing to get the voice in the writing. The words seem impervious to manipulation or replacement. Children who are composing at this stage of development write pieces about weddings that are much shorter than a bed-to-bed story. The wrestling with information occurs at a different level as in the relationship of the child to her newly married aunt. If the same child who wrote the bed-to-bed selection were to advance as a writer, she might write about the wedding in this way:

> Aunt Ruth and I have always been close. As she walked down the aisle, regal in white gown and tiara, I wondered if we would still talk. Just that morning my parents had an argument, not a big one, but enough to remind me I might not have Aunt Ruth to run to anymore.

The writer who advances to this stage of wrestling with information becomes subject to blocking at the point of solving what bothers her most about Aunt Ruth's getting married. She wouldn't be gaining an uncle. Rather, she would be losing a dear aunt whom she couldn't visit as freely. The blocking occurs at the point of writing her way to the truth about what the wedding means. She may have already written about the tension between her parents in both the morning and evening, but the central question she is solving is how to relate to her aunt as well as how to survive in her own home situation. How hard it is to face the meaning of facts, to say nothing of writing through drafts to find the most succinct way to express them—and thereby arrive at the truth of the matter.

Audiences and Blocking

There are general sequences to children's development, orders that reflect their growing sensitivity to the comments of others. These sequences indicate shifts from one stage of sensitivity to audiences to another, and mark points at which children are subject to blocking because of audience reaction.

At first children are so delightfully self-centered that the audience has little effect, save for sustained, deliberately induced discouragement, particularly from adults. The young writers believe they know their subjects and are so fascinated with the process of putting themselves on paper that the miracle of writing carries them along without restraint. Because of this egocentric protection, they make at this time some of the most rapid growth of their entire lives as writers. Later, when other children begin making remarks discrepant from their own opinions about their pieces, the young writers view the other people as having the problem. They do not. They continue to write, feeling that any reasonable person could read their pieces without any difficulty.

Soon, all within the first year, if children are given adequate time for writing, the full meaning of discrepant views is brought home. By this time, the child has usually put many of the mechanical problems of spelling and handwriting behind him and is just beginning to become more sensitive to the information in his piece. The child is also emerging into a time of orthodoxy. He or she realizes the importance of conventions for punctuation and for the orderly placement of words on the page, as well as the orthodoxy of composing a piece that others will understand. It is at this point that the first effects of blocking due to audience are recorded. There is a loss of innocence, a coming to terms with the fact that one must do something if others cannot understand one's work or disagree with one's approach. Most children adjust quickly with help from the teacher. Some do not, as in the case of Sarah at the beginning of this chapter.

From this point on, there is a growing tension between the child's own voice and intention and the child's perception of what is right for the audience. Sometimes children receive a particularly favorable audience reaction to a piece and try to write a new piece that captures the twist and excitement of the first. But the focus on audience is premature. This happened to Brian when he tried to follow a class-pleasing piece with another of the same ilk. In his first piece Brian wrote about boys his age (9 years old) who dealt with some oppressive "big kids" by means of insults and disappearance tactics in the nearby woods. As Brian read the piece, the class cheered him on, delighting in the victory of the smaller boys. With the sound of laughter in his ears and the premature consciousness of audience, Brian tried to repeat his success with another piece. But the new piece wouldn't budge. He couldn't match the tone and substance of the first in the second. He tried to sing a duet with his audience before ke knew the tune himself. Brian was frustrated and blocked because he knew that the writing on the page didn't correspond with the quality of his previous writing. Worse, it was artificial and did not sound like himself.

There is another phase in which the child hears too well the criticisms of an audience. The child is frequently hindered by the criticisms. Children learn to understand audiences by having them. Teachers who work carefully to develop the child's own experience with audience and properly time their own response to a draft do much to help the child avoid blocks and help develop the writer's sense of voice and self. Until this time, a child deals with audiences in rather absolute fashion. He or she either disregards them completely or takes their suggestions too seriously. Whatever the child's reaction, this first listening, first serious listening to audiences as the emerging writer weighs options, can be a frightening experience.

The strong writer who has experience with good critics in a strong classroom can use those comments from the audience that do not deny him or her a voice yet that contribute to the piece. There is a loss of innocence with the composing of *any* piece. Then there are those moments when it seems impossible to return to a piece that in the writer's eyes has been completely misunderstood. Or the writer sees that the critics are right and feels such a sense of personal loss that he or she is powerless to return to the composing.

Closing Reflections

Children grow as writers because they solve problems in composing, and the patterns of that growth are generally predictable. Sometimes the problem is greater than some children can momentarily handle, and progress in writing is blocked. As children get older and more sophisticated in the writing process, the problems and blocks necessarily increase. Eight-year-old Wendy expressed it this way:

> The more you do in life the harder it is to write because you are growing older and do harder things. When you do harder things, the writing gets harder.

Children keep changing the problems they try to solve. At first they are thwarted by the mechanical demands of spelling and motor-aesthetic problems, and by general conventions such as capitalization and punctuation. Once these kinds of problems are behind them, issues of selection, information, and revising follow. Children who do not master mechanical components of the writing process often become self-diagnosed poor spellers, poor handwriters, or misusers of general conventions. Depending on the response of teachers, family, or friends, such self-diagnosis may infect the knowledge base. Children may conclude they have little to say because they can't spell. The child simply says, "I don't know what to write about."

The composing process lengthens; children move back and forth between drafts, reread, relate parts to wholes, match intention to performance. The page reflects the temporary nature of the draft, the working out of intention. As children gain options through experience, they learn to write when they are not writing and become more precise and economical in their choices of information. But such growth is born of imbalances between intention and performance. The vision exceeds the ability to perform. The muscular critical self picks on the shaky performing self. The child is blocked and cannot go on.

Teachers need to know the *general* orders in which children develop because they can then anticipate the types of problems the children will be trying to solve. If problems are anticipated then blocks will be understood. Teachers who understand how children use the page, process, information, and audience categories possess a valuable tool for helping children through their blocks.

Blocking is too often viewed as a negative experience. But blocking is a necessary by-product of any creative endeavor. If the child had neither voice nor strong intention, no desire to be precise with information and language, then there would be no problems to solve and therefore no thwarting in the creation. When children solve their blocking problems or emerge from a three-day or week-long slump, they have new energy and tools to apply to their writing. Teachers who know how writers change can help them through the normal pangs of composing and rejoice with them when they reach the other side of the impasse.

ACKNOWLEDGMENTS

Most of the information in this chapter came from the National Institute of Education Grant No. G-78-0174, Project No. 8-34/9-0963, September 1, 1978–August 31, 1981, *A Case Study Observing the Development of Primary Children's Composing, Spelling, and Motor Behaviors during the Writing Process.*

REFERENCES

Calkins, L. M. (1980). Notes and comments: Children's rewriting strategies. *Research in the Teaching of English, 14*, 331–341.

Emotional Scenarios in the Writing Process: An Examination of Young Writers' Affective Experiences

2

REED LARSON

Introduction

Emotions, according to Immanuel Kant, are "illnesses of the mind" (1798/1978, p. 155). They are blinding; they wreak havoc upon rational thought and action. Indeed the Latin and Greek origins of "emotion" and "passion" denote a condition of being moved by forces outside one's control (Averill, 1980). Anger, fear, depression, even love are states in which a person's thoughts may be distorted and command over mental processes may be impaired.

What is the role of emotions in writing? The writer's task is to assimilate facts and ideas into some form of lucid and compelling order, to shape an intelligent organization of thought on the page. In analyzing a poem, discussing a field of knowledge, or developing a theory, it would seem that writers need to be in full command of their faculties. Processes of prewriting, problem solving, attending to audience, and editing presuppose that a writer be able to exercise controlled and rational thought. Emotions, therefore, would seem inimical to successful writing.

Passion, however, is often valued in writing. As an antidote to Kant's judgment, we might consider Nietzsche's statement: "Of all writings, I love only that which is written with blood" (1885/1964,

Reed Larson. Laboratory for the Study of Adolescence, Michael Reese Hospital and Medical Center, and Department of Psychiatry, University of Chicago, Chicago, Illinois.

p. 67). Emotions can bring a person to life. Rage, excitement, desire are motivating and can transform mechanical text into engaging prose. Emotions, therefore, would appear to have an uncertain status in writers' experiential worlds after all. They may be disruptive or they may be facilitative. Are they obstacles to be avoided or muses to be courted?

The questions I am investigating in this chapter regard the correlation between two sets of mental processes: one, a set of cognitive processes—the rational processes of ordering words and ideas on the page; the second, a set of emotional processes—the feelings, impulses, and drives that co-occur in a writer's experience. How are these two sets of processes related? How do they interact and affect each other? This paper is a very preliminary attempt to structure these issues. I will focus on young writers and use case study data to examine some of the common emotional experiences writers go through.

A Research Approach

My investigations on this topic began with two tactical decisions. First, I decided to work with people involved in major writing projects, projects that stretched out over weeks, because I believed that the emotional disruptions of intellectual work are magnified in major assignments (as often witnessed in the writing of master's theses and doctoral dissertations). Second, I decided to study adolescents, a group that I believed would be relatively more vulnerable to emotional fluctuations than other older age groups would be, because my earlier research had suggested that they are particularly prone to extreme states. Adolescents report experiencing higher highs and lower lows during their daily lives, and their emotions appear to shift more quickly than those of adults (Larson, Csikszentmihalyi, & Graef, 1980). Indeed, research suggests that negative emotional reactions to writing are extremely common in this age group (Daly & Miller, 1975; Hogan, 1980).

The high school students I studied were working on a research paper for English classes, known in their school as the "junior theme." The paper is expected to be six to ten pages long and to incorporate library research. Students are given six to nine weeks to carry it out, and they receive feedback from teachers at several stages along the way. The subject matter is unspecified in most classes; hence students often choose topics that are personally engaging and less likely to be aversive.

I am going to present examples of students who experienced different emotional states in their work and discuss how these states seem to be related to their final products. Examples have been selected that demonstrate points I am trying to make; thus it should be understood that I am developing a hypothesis rather than scientifically proving one to be true.

The examples come from two studies. In one, students were interviewed at about the time when they were completing their papers (Larson & Csikszentmihalyi, 1982). In the other, students filled out questionnaires on repeated occasions before, during, and after their work. For both studies, I asked a colleague in the English Department at the University of Chicago to evaluate the groups' final papers, employing the same criteria he uses to evaluate papers turned in to him. While he was aware of the general purpose of the study, he was unaware of the particular emotional experiences reported by the students. I will compare the students' reports on their experience with these professional evaluations of what they produced.

I will present case studies from two groups of students: those for whom emotions were clearly disruptive, and those whom emotions appeared to help. Before I present these cases, I should mention that the two groups are approximately matched on several measures of cognitive performance. They are similar in their scores on verbal achievement tests, in their school grade point averages, and in the extent of their experience with large writing assignments. Hence the likelihood is reduced that differences between the two groups of students are due to cognitive variables. Rather, I will argue, the differences are more related to the ways these two groups experienced and responded to the assignment.

We will begin by considering the students who had disruptive emotional experiences. These experiences are divisible into those involving overarousal with anxiety being the prototype, and those involving underarousal with boredom being the prototype.

Overarousal: The Anxiety Scenario

CLINICAL PICTURE

Overarousal takes many forms, from nervous agitation to existential dread, from persistent impatience with the assignment to total contempt for what one has done. One can be afraid that one is going to fail or that one cannot capture everything in one's soul on the written page. Students become angry at the teacher, at the school, and at parents or friends who have nothing to do with the assignment. They describe being "flustered," "overwhelmed," "pissed off," and "scared." They report being plagued by inner voices that are critical of everything they write.

At the core of these different experiences is the state of anxiety. Nearly everyone in a sample of 90 students we studied described encountering some version of anxiety at least once while writing the junior theme (Larson, Hecker, & Norem, in press). It was generally episodic; however, for some it became endemic to the task. They could not sit down to work without experiencing apprehension, worry, and distress.

The first example I will present is that of a girl, E. S., who did her paper on "how advertising influences the women's fashion industry." This girl was interested in becoming a fashion designer someday, so it was a topic pertinent to her. She had done a number of similar projects in the past and received As and Bs; hence, there was no particular reason to expect her to have trouble. The information on her experience comes from questionnaires filled out at eight points before, during, and after her work.

Prior to beginning, she reported feeling slightly positive toward the assignment. She was somewhat enthusiastic and anticipated that her paper would be well organized and say something meaningful. However, she was having a hard time making choices and narrowing her focus. She felt unsure of her topic and could not figure out how to combine all of her materials—she wanted to get all the information in. As a result, she began doubting her abilities, and a variety of other negative feelings cropped up in her experience: She felt confused, overwhelmed, and unable to find time to work on her paper.

As the deadline approached, E. S. began feeling so anxious that she was unable to concentrate. At the outlining stage there was a period of excitement; but when she started writing, she was overtaken by anxiety and was unable to focus her thoughts. She reported that she could not find the right words and was confused and extremely unhappy. Only at the last minute, under pressure of the deadline, was she able to pull something together; and when she turned it in, she had no idea whether her paper would deserve a B or C or A. The experience culminated in a state of emotional and cognitive disorder.

The second example I will present, G. J., is that of a boy who did a paper on the architect, Mies van der Rohe. I interviewed him three days after he turned his paper in and found him to be intelligent and articulate. At first he had been unenthused by his topic. But then he had an evening at the library that raised his excitement. He said, "It was like a hot flash. I went through the card catalogue and got as many books as I could. They were all in front of me; I was going through them and was just eating them up." The problem was that in this experience he created very high expectations for his paper. Thus, in subsequent work sessions, he was repeatedly dissatisfied with what he was accomplishing. Stubbornly determined to write a good paper, he would work until he "dropped," even though the sessions were becoming less and less productive. He appeared to have been unable to distance himself from the project and, as he reported, couldn't quite trust it to leave it alone: "I was really intense with it; I'd eat it, sleep it, and drink it." As a result, he went into a state of clinical depression—what he described experiencing as a "sickness"—which cast a pall over his whole life.

Both of these individuals wrestled with expectations for their papers that were greater than they could meet. The girl kept trying to push herself to "try harder," but this just didn't help; and the boy worked himself into a debilitating frenzy. These students lacked the skills to accomplish the grandiose papers they kept imagining, and they were unable to establish expectations for themselves that were consistent with what they could realistically do. Hence they became overwhelmed and lost control of their work; and the writing project turned into a nightmare of worry, frustration, and internal anger. Now let's examine how these internal states were manifested in their final papers.

EFFECTS OF ANXIETY

Physiologically, anxiety is a state of extreme arousal, including increased adrenaline levels, rapid neural firing, increased heart rate, and greater muscle tension (Izard, 1977). In small amounts these changes can aid a person's functioning, but beyond a certain point they become disruptive (Hunt, 1965).

Cognitively, anxiety is associated with diffused and "disintegrated" attention. Research shows that anxiety reduces one's capacity to hold things in short-term memory, thus effectively reducing the amount of information one can juggle and think about simultaneously (Easterbrook, 1959; Izard, 1977). Fear, a state akin to anxiety, is often associated with blindness to anything other than the source of threat (except one's imminent demise). States of anxiety, fear, and anger are also associated with impulsive behavior: People act without thinking; they are less able to discipline their actions and to contain sudden dispositions.

The students I studied reported all of these elements in their writing experiences. Emotions interfered with their concentration and weakened their control over their thoughts. Anxious students reported wanting nothing more than to have the whole thing finished. The effects can be seen in the opening paragraphs of the papers by our two examples, presented in Figure 2-1. (While space allows me to present only the first paragraphs from each student's work in Figure 2-1, the patterns identified in those paragraphs are repeated throughout their papers.)

With our first case, E. S., the influence of anxiety is more than evident in the opening of the paper. Our critic has this to say about the girl's first three paragraphs:

> E. S. seems to understand perfectly well how her introduction should affect the reader: It should first establish a problem or question; it should then give the reader some sense of the specific concerns that the paper will address; and, at the end, it should establish the main topic that will control the organization of the essay. This introduction does all of these things, but in the crudest way imaginable. E. S. tries to create a question in the reader's mind by asking it directly. She announces subtopics by asking still more questions. And she establishes the controlling topic by giving away the whole point of the paper. The immaturity of this writing is evident in its impatient directness and in its aggressive approach to the reader's responses and to the material itself. This kind of aggressiveness toward the material is evident throughout.

She knew what she should do, and she had demonstrated an ability to do it successfully in past papers (she had received As on two such assignments), but in this case she lacked the internal calm to carry it out with any subletly. Lacking the concentration and patience to develop an argument, she obsessively repeats the same point over and over again as though she mistrusts her reader.

About the paper as a whole, our critic writes:

> The essay is completely out of control. E. S. has no command over her material and consistently shows signs that she is overwhelmed by the task at hand and that she cannot separate in her mind the material and her reactions to it. There is little indication in the body of the essay that

E.S.'s paper:

Why do people by certain styles of clothing? Why do you choose the style you do? Do you choose that style because you like it? Or is it because everyone else has it?

What affects your choice of style? Do you want to be different and stand out in the crowd? Or do you want the least amount attention as possible and just blend in? Most people purchase the certain style of clothes, because they want to conform with their favorite group or organization and also because an admired person wears that style, that makes a way of becoming more like him.

But what exactly influences the consumers to purchase the latest fashion styles and product?

G.J.'s paper:

Architectural styles in the past fifty years have changed greatly. They have gone from beauty and ornateness to stark and coldness, one of the reasons is an architect named Ludwig Mies van der Rohe. Mies came to America with a new architectural style and since then architecture hasn't been the same.

Between the years of 1893 and 1920, the architectural style in America was that like the architectural style that was in old Europe, it had some of Europes styles and ideas, but it was not exactly like it. To be specific before Ludwig Mies van der Rohe came to America, there seemed to be a great originality in the design of staircases, loggias, which are the arches that run along ceilings, and roofs.

The main reason that these styles differ from the styles of modern architecture, is ornateness. During this period right before modern architecture, the ornamentation was dictated by the style of the building because ". . . approprate prototypes did not always exist . . ." A good example is for fireplaces, ceilings, and walls there were inventive adaptations of Greek, Egyptian, or Gothic motifs. While all of this was going on, American architecute was going thru a period of revival. This period of revival was happening in two ways, the first way was related to Gothic architecture, what is meant by that is that the structure built in this time resembled some of the Gothic structures in Europe. The second type of revival, which was more acedimac, was inspired by Italian Renaissance, French Renaissance, and Roman Style architecture. The first trend setters included works by Louis Sullivan and Frank Lloyd Wright.

Figure 2-1. Opening paragraphs of anxious students' papers.

> E. S. has made reader-oriented decisions; and when she does consider the reader in the introduction, she manages only to grab him by the scruff of the neck and barrage him with questions.
>
> It's not that E. S. has nothing to say—she has done her homework and has all the pieces for an intelligent essay. It's more that she has too much to say. She has no sense of what the material in her essay comes to, no sense of the essay as a whole. She has not created the distance between herself and her research, between her role as writer and herself, or between the reader and herself.

Her fragmented internal state resulted in a fragmented attempt at communication. Her high expectations prevented her from getting a handle on her ideas and controlling her writing. The result is a diffused jumble of thoughts and ideas.

The boy writing on Mies van der Rohe, G. J., manifests his agitation in a similar way. His paper attempts to cover a broad span of material and thus relies on grand leaps in the attempt to pull things together. There is no clear focus. Furthermore, his paper is full of misspellings, poor grammar, and idiosyncratic metaphors. It is apparent that he became attached to certain wordings and images and was unaware that they would have limited meaning to anyone else.

Let me give you what his high school teacher wrote about this paper:

> Your paper tackles far too much! Your topic is way too broad, and, as a result, you skip around your topic with no thoroughness focused on any major part of Mies's life. Much more care was needed, also, with sentences; run-ons are abundant. The whole theme ends with a fragment. Few words of any length are spelled correctly. Much greater care was needed here in the proofreading than you were willing to give.

What this teacher did not realize was just how much this student actually tried to make this a good paper. He put in lots of time and effort, but his excitement and anxiety kept him from getting any distance on what he was writing. The time and effort were wasted in myopic, agitated states. He could not use his attention effectively, and hence there were major lacunae in what he produced.

Anxiety is a state of overarousal that interferes with concentration and control of attention. Episodes of anxiety may be unavoidable, especially for young writers: It may be inevitable that students will sometimes be overwhelmed, that they will set expectations too high or find themselves facing too many choices. Problems come when these situations—and the accompanying emotions—become inseparable from the assignment, when a student continually feels at odds with the work. Anxiety at best leads to impulsive and poorly controlled writing. At worst, it creates emotional and cognitive havoc that makes writing impossible. Now let us look at a very different emotional situation.

Underarousal: The Boredom Scenario

CLINICAL PICTURE

Underarousal includes states of apathy, disinterest, depression, and particularly boredom. Its prime characteristic is lack of motivation. Students describe their work as "drudgery" or "a real drag." One boy related the feeling as follows: "You're always looking up at the clock, and it's only two minutes. Sometimes you picked a certain time when you want to go to bed; you wait and you look up and see time is sure going slowly, and you want to be done with it as soon as you can."

Boredom seemed to occur most often during the actual writing of the paper. Students felt that once they had finished their reading they were done with the exciting part and there was nothing new to be discovered. One student explained it this way:

> Writing it, that's a bore; because when I have all these notecards it's all there, but it's a job to put it down on paper. I know what I want to say, but having to put it into words was boring. I'm just kind of a robot repeating what other people say.

It is apparent that this student had little idea of opportunities for excitement in the writing process. Boredom occurs when there is no challenge in the task, when a student can see nothing in the work that is personally interesting or engaging.

Let me present two examples of students who had persistent problems with boredom. The first, M. D., was a student who had plans to pursue an MBA and go into business. At first he was going to write his paper on baseball; but everyone did that, so he talked with his teacher and decided to do it on immigrant housing, a topic he had already studied in history class. I interviewed him four days before the paper was due, a point at which he was almost finished.

Asked whether he had had any problems, he said no. "It wasn't a really hard topic where you had to probe into anything, really." He had had to do it, so he did it. It was all straightforward. He worked at the same time every day after school: first systematically accumulating notecards, then sorting them into an order, then writing it all up. He reported no feelings, no excitement, and no personally meaningful challenge. He said, "I just rolled it." One had the impression of a steamroller that flattened everything in its way.

The second example, D. V., is a fellow who did his paper on the draft. Conscription was something that would affect him when he reached 18, so he thought it an important and personal issue. The information about him comes from questionnaires filled out at eight points before, during, and after his work.

At first he reported being interested in the paper. He found materials easily and indicated being deeply absorbed. But with each successive report he became less and less enthusiastic. By the time he began writing, he reported feeling extremely detached and bored. The cause of this problem seems to have been that his topic had become frozen: It was not changing or becoming refined. He was unable or unwilling to play with the ideas. From the very beginning he said that he was doing lots of "polishing" but little or no "inventing." In sum, there was none of what Getzels and Csikszentmihalyi (1976) have called "problem finding." He knew what he wanted to say about the draft. The process of writing it down on paper was therefore a pointless exercise.

For both students the process of writing became nothing more than a mechanical task. They appeared unaware of the possibilities for excitement and challenge in writing. Psychoanalysts sometimes portray boredom as a defense against intolerable internal feelings (Fenichel, 1951). It could be that these two students adopted a mechanical and conventional approach in order to defend themselves against pain, threat, and novelty in their materials; but their reports indicate only that they found the process unchallenging. They had never learned to find excitement in writing.

EFFECTS OF BOREDOM

Laboratory studies indicate that boredom is usually associated with low physiological activation. Adrenaline levels are low; heart rate is slowed; there is a decrease in oxygen consumption. Cognitively, boredom is associated with decreased attentiveness and slower thought processes. People are less able to control their attention; vigilance and performance decline (Smith, 1981; Thackray, 1981).

The relation of boredom to students' work can be seen by looking at the opening paragraphs written by our two students, which are presented in Figure 2-2. Our critic made the following comments on how the paper about immigrant housing begins.

> The introductory segment of the paper is purely factual and exceptionally uninteresting. There is no hint whatsoever of the topic of the main segment (the horrible living conditions of immigrant housing) and no hint of the point to come. M. D. is working hard here to keep himself and his

Figure 2-2. Opening paragraphs of bored students' papers.

M.D.'s paper:

The great influx of immigrants to the United States in the 1920's and 1930's created unique housing problems. Since most of the immigration was into industrial urban areas, single or two-story housing became impractical.

In order to accommodate the greatest number of people into the available space, housing had to be built up, rather than out. Another requirement of this new housing was low and quick construction. The combination of these factors required a common form for the tenement house. The houses that were already there wasted space with such things as alleys, halls and stair wells.

The new tenement housing began ot resemble rectangular blocks. These were called dumbell tenements because they were wide on the top and bottom but narrow in the middle. These buildings were erected on uniform city plots, twenty or twenty-five feet wide and 100 feet deep. The structure took up almost the entire area of the lot. It was attached to its neighbor on either side, leaving only a strip about ten feel deep in the rear.

D.V.'s paper:

For millions of young men, the age of 18 is very critical. These young men can choose either to go to college or to start a career, but if the draft were reinstated their plans could be drastically changed. The government could disrupt their lives by putting them in the armed services. Our country is making a decision now—draft or volunteer army. The United States needs greater manpower than it presently has with the all-volunteer army. Our nation could gain the manpower it needs without the draft and should for the sake of individual rights.

Draft is the random picking of men for the armed services. It originated in France in 1793 and has been used in the United States since the Civil War. It has been used during all major U.S. wars since that time, but has generally been opposed during peacetime. This opposition has become much greater after the unpopular war of Viet Nam. The government is now considering the draft in peacetime because of the decreasing number of recruits for the armed services. There is considerable debate concerning the return to the system.

> reader from *any* emotional involvement in the material. Thus he can allow himself to write a sentence as callous as the last one in the second paragraph; or he can write the second sentence of the third paragraph (explaining why they were called "dumbell" tenements), a sentence that makes no sense until the reader realizes that the point of view M. D. has adopted is not the point of view of a person looking at the building from the street but of someone looking from above at a plan of the building drawn on a sheet of paper—only then do "top" and "bottom" make any sense. The development of the paper is about the most impersonal treatment of this subject that I can imagine from someone his age.

It is a plodding, mechanical paper; there are appalling oversights in what he writes. This boy's rigid approach to the assignment is clearly manifest in his writing.

Our critic has similar comments on where the text goes after the opening.

> In the body of the paper M. D. cannot help but become somewhat more personal—at least he has persons doing things. But there are still abundant verbal strategies to shift the point of view as far away from the reader and the writer as possible. Thus, the first mention of filth comes as a complete surprise in the third sentence of the fifth paragraph. In this and the next paragraph M. D. is blaming the filthy living conditions on the architecture of the buildings, especially on the airshafts, but fails either to prepare us for or to explain the "stench-filled hallways." Similarly, he blames the airshafts for lack of privacy just before he explains that many families lived in the same apartment. M. D. consistently seeks the most simplified and objectified explanation that he can find. Thus, when he finally comes around to the main point of the paper, the social problems and the immigrants' surprising ability to overcome them, the reader is totally unprepared. Not only do the social problems come out of the blue—M. D. must think that the reader, too, can see their inevitability—but M. D.'s admiration for the success of the immigrants is greatly blunted by his dogged refusal throughout the rest of the essay to bring the writer close to them.

In concluding, the critic describes it as a "very boring paper" and speculates that this quality reflects the author's "determined effort not to let the distastefulness of the topic affect him." One can take the psychoanalytic position that the boy adopted this rigid approach to protect himself from the materials; his description of his experience, however, provides no evidence for this interpretation. It indicates only that he was unmotivated. He had simply not learned that writing holds challenges; hence the option of becoming more personally involved was simply not there.

In the second case, that of D. V., there is a clear thesis that has captured the author's interest; the injustice of conscription. As one reads through the paper, however, it is apparent that there is no real development of the idea: He simply lists points pro and con, with no effort to weigh them. Our critic summarizes his reactions to the paper as follows:

> This paper is unremarkable in most respects. It begins well enough, announcing its topics and setting up its point, but it does so too quickly and gives away too much of the point. The development is logical and the flow of topics relatively consistent, but the transitions tend to be abrupt and sometimes crude. D. V. has enough control and distance from his material to manage the shift to his personal point of view in the last paragraph pretty well and to prepare it successfully in his first sentence. But otherwise this is a pedestrian work; one topic at a time, little attention to the reader's possible reactions, little effort to make the paper interesting.

His text mirrors his personal state. Just as he couldn't find any excitement while writing on the topic, he was unable to provide the reader with any challenge to make the work interesting.

While the anxious students suffered from overambitious expectations, these students were stymied because they had few expectations at all. They did not envision their papers as anything more than a compilation of their notes. They seemed unaware of possibilities for finding challenge in their writing. No wonder it was boring.

Order and Disorder in Emotional States

DISEASES OF THE MIND

An extreme example of emotional disturbance is provided by a college student I interviewed who was writing a paper on William James's *The Varieties of Religious Experience*. He was a religious person and was very excited and challenged by this opportunity to refute James's attempt to reduce religion to psychology. The paper was a "platform" for him to say things he had been wanting to say for a long time, and he envisioned himself as a "bellwether," a "spokesman for the future." These grandiose expectations created enormous anxiety that had his mind reeling. When I first interviewed him, he had torn up numerous drafts and felt that everything he had written was "bullshit." Several months later when I checked back with him, he was still in a state of prostration. He had succeeded in getting an extension from his teacher but was still ripping up new drafts and tearing out his hair. His work had lost all sense of ordered sequence or systematic method; he was going in circles and had lost all conviction of making intelligent headway.

Anxiety, boredom, and their related states do resemble diseases: They are associated with afflictions of thought and action. Students' involvement with materials becomes chaotic or rigid; ideas get put down on the page impulsively or mechanically, without proper development or sensitivity to audience.

Students beset by these emotions become victims of turbulent passions. Among high school students, we have found this condition of internal disruption to be extremely common. Nearly everyone in a sample of 90 students doing the junior theme reported emotional problems: encounters with boredom, worry, loss of motivation (Larson, Hecker, & Norem, in press). Young writers, it seems, wasted many hours floundering in unproductive, distressed states.

At the heart of the issue is the problem of attention: How can writers maintain concentration on their work? In addition to the internal fragmentation generated by the writing process itself, students had other turmoils in their lives that were sources of constant distraction. These youths were at a stage of life when they were falling in love, falling out of love, having fights with their parents, or enduring herpes scares. They were getting carried away by excitements, panics, and other overpowering emotions. The question is, Where within this avalanche of emotions could they find the peace of mind to organize their thoughts?

INTEGRATIVE EMOTIONS

To understand fully the role of emotions in writing, it is important to examine conditions when things go right, to study people who achieve control over their attention and who experience a more constructive state. To do this it will be useful to step away from writing for a few moments.

My colleague, Mihaly Csikszentmihalyi, attempted to understand optimal states by researching their occurrence in creative and challenging leisure activities. He studied rock climbers, dancers, composers, chess players, and others to understand the dynamics of inner experience when things go well (Csikszentmihalyi, 1975, 1978, 1979). In these activities people describe the optimal state as one of enjoyment or "flow," a state in which they are absorbed in their activities and when actions follow smoothly from their thoughts. It is an emotion yet not one as a result of which people lose control. Attention is fixed and people feel in command of the situation: Dancers describe experiencing heightened control of their bodies; composers describe feeling on top of the compositional options before them. People feel motivated to be doing what they are doing, and their attention is whole.

An important question is, what produces and sustains this state? The answer to this question partly involves cognition. Csikszentmihalyi discovered that people describe a common set of predisposing conditions in how they each perceive and interact with the particular activity. The state of flow seems to occur when people have clear goals and a defined sense of how they will reach those goals. They know what they want to accomplish and understand the rules governing how one gets there. In addition, feedback, either explicit or self-generated, appears to be important: One has to know when one is doing something right and something wrong. The most central element, however, seems to be the balance between the perceived challenges of the activity and a person's skills: One must experience the activity as presenting opportunities for action that are inviting to one's talents. The chess player must have an opponent of matched ability; the rock climber must find a climb that is challenging to his or her skills.

Only when this balance occurs does the opportunity exist for enjoyment and deep involvement. If the challenges of the activity are too great for a person's skills (if the rock face is too steep, or one's chess opponent far superior), anxiety takes over. And anxiety can occur even if the challenges are only *perceived* to be too great for a person's abilities. This is the scenario encountered by the first two students we considered. On the other hand, if the challenges of an activity are too few for a person's skills (if a climb is too easy, or an opponent too weak)—or if one sees no way to make an activity challenging—boredom takes over. This is what seems to have happened to the second two students. In both circumstances, attention was severely impaired.

Too often we think of cognition as separate from emotion, as if cognitive processes could be understood independently of affective ones, and vice versa. But this is clearly not the case. What people think is affected by what they feel, and what they feel is affected by what they think. The perception of goals, constraints, feedback, challenges, and skills shapes a person's engagement. The systemic relationship a person has with the ongoing activity determines his or her level of involvement.

The question now is, Do young people have the ability to control their involvement in the activity of writing? Can they engineer the kind of internal balance required to become deeply involved in their work? This is the question we consider next.

Optimal Arousal: The Experience of Enjoyment

CREATING FLOW WITHIN THE PROCESS OF WRITING

I discover that many students experienced deep, flow-like involvement in their writing. They reported all of the elements of enjoyment, from deep absorption ("All my brain was there") to intrinsic motivation ("I just loved it"). They reported losing track of time, a common element of flow ("I'd get there at 6 o'clock and, before I knew it, it's 10 o'clock and time to go home"); and they reported great control over the materials ("I felt really powerful, like I had the information in the palm of my hand and could mold it any way I wanted"). Several students even used the word "flow" to describe the experience of rapt attention to their work.

What is most interesting is that these students appeared to be using deliberate internal strategies to make their work enjoyable. The first example I will discuss is that of a boy, S. N., who did a paper on the development of the DC-3 prior to World War II. This aircraft had interested him because of his aspirations to be an aeronautical engineer. His ability level was no different from that of the other four high school students we have already considered, and he had no more prior experience with writing, but he seemed able to control his internal state. I interviewed him three days before he turned in his final paper.

Like the bored students, he worked fairly methodically. He worked at the same time every day and set up goals for each session. The difference was in his willingness to adjust his schedule and redirect his work according to where it led. He began with a curiosity about the DC-3's use during the war but gradually focused in on its development before the war, because he found this period—before the plane was even flown—to be the most interesting and important. Unlike the others, his interest did not stop with the reading. He recognized the challenge of trying to explain to his reader why this period was interesting and important.

Like the anxious students, S. N. experienced times when he was overwhelmed by the quantity of his materials and the difficult task of bringing them all together. But usually he could anticipate when his work was going to be overwhelming and would plan a shorter work session to avoid being consumed: "If I knew it was going to be rough, I wouldn't spend as much time on it, but I wouldn't avoid it either." There was grandiosity in his ambitions for the paper, but he was aware of the need to control this internal impulse: "I had to keep stopping myself and saying, 'Okay, I'm doing a project here.'"

This sensitivity to the project and to his internal states protected him from the kind of overexcitement and anxiety that paralyzed the students writing on Mies van der Rohe and on William James. He put in a lot of effort and closely monitored his energy level: "It's like you're pouring everything you've got right into it. It would be like not turning the car on but turning on everything electrical in the car at the same time. Sure they'll work for awhile, but all of a sudden—it'll be time for a recharge."

What is striking in his strategies is how closely they follow prescriptions for creating flow. He seems to have been deliberately adjusting the challenges to his abilities. By moving cautiously through hard parts, by stopping himself when overexcited, and by monitoring his energy, he regulated the balance of challenges and skills, creating conditions for enjoyable involvement.

He related one occasion of particularly intense involvement, which he described as a "big personal high." His concentration was very deep: "I was really shut off from everything that was happening. My phone rang, and it took me three rings to realize it; I mean I was really engrossed." This was not a session of library work or notecard shuffling; it was a session of writing. He had succeeded in finding challenges and enjoyment in the process of putting thoughts down on the page. For him writing was not just a mechanical process; it was an opportunity for discovery and further exploration of ideas. The challenge was to communicate his excitement about this airplane to readers; in fact, he said that he couldn't wait to read the paper himself.

The second example I will present is that of a girl, A. R., who did a paper on the American composer, Charles Ives. Her career goal was to become a graphic designer; however, she was also involved in music and had developed a special interest in this composer. The information on her experience comes from questionnaires filled out at multiple points during her work.

At the beginning she was considering several topics, and she reported confusion and irresolution. However, once she settled on Charles Ives, she reported becoming absorbed in reading and taking notes. Like S. N., she worked methodically, setting up a plan for what she would do and deliberately arranging situations where she would be free from distraction. At this point she indicated that there were numerous parts she could work on and enjoy; the project was challenging, and she found herself wanting to work on it.

While she was gathering notes, she began to get anxious about how she would order the wide range of materials she was collecting: "I'm having trouble putting things together in logical order." Rather than give way to panic, however, she had a solution: She said she would experiment with different outlines to see how each worked. She was also prepared to leave things out if need be, even though she had now become tremendously fond of everything about Charles Ives. Indeed, things came into place. Later she stated, "As I was writing the rough draft and converting it to final copy, I sensed a real flow in the materials and I felt as if everything was finally falling together." It is noteworthy that she used an image of "falling" to describe writing, as if she were not in command. The experience of enjoyment is one of personal control, but it is also one in which actions seem to be effortless. If a person is working at a level of challenge matched to his or her skills, the sensation of effort and strain will not be there.

A. R. said she experienced the assignment as if it were a musical piece. Her work was a sequence of discovery, joy, and experimentation, occurring within some disciplined emotional guidelines.

EFFECTS OF ENJOYMENT

Enjoyment is associated with optimal physiological arousal. Heart rate and oxygen consumption increase; at the same time, muscle tonus is heightened, and visual gaze is steadied. Cognitively, enjoyment is associated with clear attention and command over one's thoughts (Csikszentmihalyi, 1975). A person is more likely to feel strong and competent and to perceive fullness and beauty in the world (Izard, 1977).

The relationship of this state to students' writing is apparent in the final papers produced by the two students just presented. In Figure 2-3 you can see how invitingly S. N. sets up his topic in his opening paragraphs, establishing the interactions between the idea of this new plane, the changing historic conditions of the prewar period, and the

S.N.'s paper:

On December 17, 1939 at little Clover Field in Santa Monica, California, an aircraft was born. The first Douglas DC-3 took off with Carl Clover, the company's vice president, as chief pilot and flew for over 30 minutes. Something magical had happened. Along with an aircraft an era was born. An era of speed and efficiency that would turn a nation's sagging air industry into an ever expanding business and technological enterprise. Quite soon, and without warning, this young upstart would face an even greater responsibility. It would be pushed into the skies of World War II and be expected to perform many functions. It proved to be up to the challenge. The Dc-3 withstood virtually every form of punishment imaginable and gained the respect of every airman ever associated with it.

The Model T of the air, as she was soon aptly named, quickly grew to accommodate 90% of all commercial air transport in the United States alone. The DC-3 simply formed the backbone of vicil aviation both in the United States and abroad; in war and in peace. The entire venture stemmed from Donald W. Douglas' ambition to fill the order for an aircraft that would "provide for a crew of two, pilot and copilot, with a cabin capable of carrying at least 12 passengers in comfortable seats with ample room and fully equipped with the many fixtures and conveniences generally expected in a commercial passenger aircraft." The success of this modern concept of the all metal airplane rested solely on the shoulders of Mr. Douglas. His ambition was to change the course of modern air travel and he accomplished this with the DC-3.

A.R.'s paper:

Charles Ives was the first American composer to create symphonic music in the image of his country's ideas rather than in the codes of European tradition. Before Ives, most symphonic music followed a somewhat restrictive harmonic law and just had a pretty sound. Ives, however, "plunged into the abyss of tonal freedom" which enabled him to create music that wouldn't have been possible under conventional standards. By using innovative techniques and American ideas, Ives achieved a more meaningful and more American type of music.

Ives was born on October 20, 1874 in Danbury, a small town in Connecticut. This town was, before Ives' time, hidden away from the European beliefs, inventions, and traditions that were arriving at the east cost in the nineteenth century. But, as Ives was growing up, this town started rapid industrial and population growth. New ideas came pouring through Danbury. Even the traditional folk songs, hymns, and band marches were being performed and experimented with in new and different ways. Certainly a growing of new musical ideas. These ideas were being created in the home of Charles Ives.

Figure 2-3. Opening paragraphs of papers by students who experience enjoyment and deep involvement.

ambitions of the plane's creator, Donald Douglas. S. N. had enough command of his thoughts and feelings to bring these different elements together.

Our critic expresses admiration for S. N.'s skillful topic development in the rest of the paper, particularly for his capacity to hold back with his points while systematically building up to them.

> His point is the success of the DC-3. But he manages to delay that part of the paper until page 5, at which time we get two and a half pages describing its accomplishments. These pages are the heart of the paper, the reason it was written; but by saving that material for the end, S. N. is able to include the other information he has collected without making it seem mere filler. This is a very mature structure—a staple of high-toned, general-circulation journals like *New Yorker* and *Altantic Monthly*. It requires that the writer have a good command of all his material (so that he can see it whole), that he be self-conscious (so that he can make product-, reader-oriented decisions rather than process-, writer-oriented decisions), and that he have the discipline to be patient.

This boy had no more experience than the other four students had; his basic abilities were no greater; furthermore, he reported putting in time that was no greater than what the others reported. Yet somehow his paper comes out much stronger and more ordered. I would like to suggest that his internal self-regulation and his ability to create enjoyment allowed him the patience and command of thought to lay out his materials in such a deliberate and compelling fashion.

The girl writing about Charles Ives was only slightly above the other students in her basic ability level. Her paper, however, is a qualitative step above those of the first four we have considered. About this paper, our critic writes:

> The global organization of this essay is as complex and sophisticated as S. N.'s, and most of what I said there applies here as well. A. R. is a little more programmatic (and less subtle) than S. N. in executing her structure, but she does a good job of setting up the topic and the point. The shift to the background material is also well managed through manipulation of topics. The major difference between A. R. and S. N. is that A. R. is less adept at managing the development of the main section of the essay. I won't speculate about causes, but it is clear that S. N. had much easier material to work with at this level. S. N.'s subtopic falls into a story (a structure that is relatively easy to handle), while A. R.'s subtopic requires her to develop a more analytical organization.

She demonstrates remarkable discipline and control in the manipulation of her difficult topic. Rather than acting as impediments, her passions about Charles Ives are used to help organize her ideas. The paper becomes an opportunity for her to systematically explore her admiration for his work and justify this admiration to her audience. In sum, her internal discipline and enjoyment seemed to make her better able to get access to inner feelings and adapt them to the rhetorical opportunities.

Both of these papers reflect a higher level of organization than the four earlier ones. Whereas the others were composed of fragmented facts and ideas, these two both contain a progressively developed train of thought. The first four students had lost control of their attention, which resulted in the production of impulsive or unreflective prose. These latter two students, in contrast, were able to command their attention and build coherent and sophisticated papers.

In the larger study with 90 students, we found enjoyment to be a strong, independent predictor of the grades students received (Larson, Hecker, & Norem, in press). Irrespective of their ability levels, the experience of enjoyment appeared to make a substantial difference in the quality of each student's final paper. Curiously, we also found that students who had experienced enjoyment reported putting no more time into their work: They appeared to get more out of each hour they worked. In sum, the ability to create enjoyment seemed to be related to more creative and efficient writing.

It would be presumptuous to conclude from these findings that enjoyment per se *causes* good writing, but it would be equally presumptuous to dismiss enjoyment as merely a *result* of good writing. Rather, it is likely that enjoyment as both cause and effect contributes to creating and sustaining flow in writing, that the conditions that create enjoyment and that create good writing are closely related.

Of course 6 students, even the 90 in the larger study, cannot provide conclusive proof of a thesis. The information discussed here is only suggestive. Nonetheless, the cases we have looked at indicate that emotional aspects of writing should not be ignored. There appears to be more to success in writing than cognitive ability or writing skills, since ability and writing experience accounted for only part of the differences among these students. Furthermore, merely having interest does not insure that a student will avoid the pitfalls of anxiety or boredom—several of the students we have discussed got into trouble because they were *too* interested, becoming emotionally overexcited and losing control of their work.

Successful writing depends in part on the relationship a writer has with the ongoing work. There must be a system of interaction between the person and the evolving manuscript that engenders and sustains attention, that keeps a person motivated and involved in the task. The two students just discussed provide examples of writers able to maintain a positive relationship with their writing. They deliberately monitored their internal states and regulated the challenges they were facing; they actively cultivated their relationship with their topics and skillfully avoided situations that might create debilitating emotions. Hence they enjoyed their work, and this enjoyment helped keep them engaged and thus ultimately helped them to produce better papers.

Conclusion

Having started this essay quoting Kant, it may be indecorous to conclude by quoting Tom Wolfe from *The Right Stuff*. However, in his popular book on the astronauts, Wolfe describes the experience of test pilots in a way that is applicable. Each new flying machine, we are told, has glorious new performance capabilities. It can roll and twist and climb in ways that previous planes could not. But each new plane also has specific limits: It can turn just so sharply and climb just so steeply without tumbling out of control. The range within which a plane maintains aerodynamic stability is called its performance envelope, and this envelope defines the potential and magnificence of each machine. If the pilot exceeds this range, if he pushes it too far, the plane may shatter or careen to the earth.

Young writers, unfortunately, spend a lot of time outside of their performance envelopes. They put themselves in situations they cannot handle and cannot escape. Debilitating emotions result; their thinking becomes fragmented and directionless; and their work tumbles out of control. Often these situations result from challenges they have set that are beyond their abilities, tasks that are too large or undefined for them to deal with. In these cases their experience takes the form of anxiety. Other times it is absence of genuine challenge that creates the problem. They are unable or unwilling to find anything engaging within their writing, and boredom ensues.

I have suggested that optimal conditions occur when a person feels challenged at a level appropriately matched to his or her talents. As Csikszentmihalyi has found in performance of music, sports, and art, these are conditions that facilitate the experience of enjoyment, a state that combines positive motivation with command of attention. Maintaining these conditions, sustaining this internal balance is by no means simple. Ultimately it is as complex as the person involved and the multifaceted topic with which he or she struggles.

ACKNOWLEDGMENTS

This research was carried out in collaboration with the English Department of Oak Park and River Forest High School with support from the Spencer Foundation. The author wishes to express special thanks to Gregory Colomb for his assistance with the research and to Mike Rose for helpful editing.

An earlier version of this chapter was presented at the Institute on Writing and Thinking at the University of Chicago on May 21, 1983.

REFERENCES

Averill, J. R. (1980). Emotion and anxiety: Sociocultural, biological, and psychological determinants. In A. O. Rorty (Ed.), *Explaining emotions* (pp. 37–72). Berkeley: University of California Press.

Csikszentmihalyi, M. (1975). *Beyond boredom and anxiety*. San Francisco: Jossey-Bass.

Csikszentmihalyi, M. (1978). Attention and the wholist approach to behavior. In K. Pope & J. Singer (Eds.), *The stream of consciousness*. New York: Plenum.

Csikszentmihalyi, M. (1979). The concept of flow. In B. Sutton-Smith (Ed.), *Play and learn* (pp. 335–358). New York: Wiley.

Daly, J. A., & Miller, M. D. (1975). The empirical development of an instrument to measure writing apprehension. *Research in the Teaching of English*, *9*, 242–49.

Easterbrook, J. (1959). The effect of emotion on cue utilization and the organization of behavior. *Psychological Review*, *66*, 183–201.

Fenichel, O. (1951). On the psychology of boredom. In D. Rapaport (Ed.), *Organization and pathology of thought* (pp. 349–361). New York: Columbia University Press.

Getzels, J., & Csikszentmihalyi, M. (1976). *The creative vision*. New York: Wiley-Interscience.

Hogan, T. (1980). Students' interests in writing activities. *Research in the Teaching of English*, *14*, 119–126.

Hunt, J. (1965). Intrinsic motivation and its role in psychological development. In D. Levine (Ed.), *Nebraska Symposium on Motivation* (Vol. 12, pp. 189–282). Lincoln, NE: University of Nebraska Press.

Izard, C. E. (1977). *Human emotions*. New York: Plenum.

Kant, I. (1978). *Anthropology* (V. L. Dowdell, Trans.). Carbondale, IL: Southern Illinois University Press. (Original work published 1798)

Larson, R., & Csikszentmihalyi, M. (1982). *The praxis of autonomous learning*. Unpublished manuscript, University of Chicago.

Larson, R., Csikszentmihalyi, M., & Graef, R. (1980). Mood variability and the psychosocial adjustment of adolescents. *Journal of Youth and Adolescence*, *9*, 469–490.

Larson, R., Hecker, B., & Norem, J. (in press). High school research projects: A cognitive, emotional, and motivational task. *The High School Journal.*

Nietzsche, F. (1964). *Thus spoke Zarathustra* (R. J. Hollingdale, Trans.). New York: Penguin. (Original work published 1885)

Smith, R. (1981). Boredom: A review. *Human Factors, 23*, 239–340.

Thackray, R. I. (1981). The stress of boredom and monotony: A consideration of the evidence. *Psychosomatic Medicine, 43*, 165–176.

Writing Apprehension 3

JOHN A. DALY

Some people enjoy, even savor, the experience of putting pen to paper. Others find it a troublesome, uncomfortable, and even fearful experience. The idea that people differ in their enjoyment of and propensity to writing is an old one. Allusions often have been made to these differences. Descriptions of writer's block, procrastination, and hesitancy dot popular literature in the form both of stories (e.g., Updike, 1982) and of authors' perspectives on the writing process (e.g., Durell, 1976; Hemingway, 1976; Isherwood, 1976; Rosen, 1981). In addition, there are psychoanalytic interpretations of writers' anxieties (Federn, 1930/1957); investigations of psychosomatic writer's cramp (Callewaert, 1927a, 1927b, 1930; Crisp & Moldofsky, 1965); descriptions in any number of textbooks about procedures for gaining confidence in writing (e.g., Mack & Skjei, 1979); and even cynically humorous advice on techniques for procrastinating and avoiding writing (Upper, 1974; Walker, 1978). Only recently, however, have there been systematic investigations of people's feelings about writing. This chapter summarizes the research on one class of these feelings referred to as "writing apprehension." It also explicates recent work completed by the author on a broader conceptualization of people's attitudes and beliefs about writing.

One impetus for the research described in this chapter has been the observation that many people seem abnormally hesitant about and fearful of writing. Teachers of compositions, journalism, communication, and related fields can recount stories of students, often descriptively called anxious or apprehensive, who find writing unrewarding

John A. Daly. College of Communication, University of Texas, Austin, Texas.

and even punishing. Their apprehension often is reflected in their performance on writing-related tasks. Outside of classes, the propensity of individuals to write, as well as to actively seek out experiences that include writing, also varies. Some people find the idea of writing an intolerable one; others find it an engaging and relaxing pursuit.

Writing-apprehension research reflects a belief that a multidimensional view of writing is essential to understanding and assessing writing. How one writes—indeed, whether one writes—is dependent on more than just skill or competence. The individual must also want to write or, at the very least, must also find some value in the activity. An individual's attitude about writing is just as basic to successful writing as are his or her writing skills. For no matter how skillful the individual may be as a writer, without a willingness to engage in writing one can expect little more than the atrophying of composing skills. A positive attitude about writing is associated with, and may even be a critical precursor of, the successful development and maintenance of writing skills.

The primary concern of this chapter is with people's "dispositional feelings" about composing. These feelings are conceived to be relatively enduring tendencies to like or dislike, approach or avoid, enjoy or fear writing. People are assumed to behave in a more or less consistent manner when it comes to writing: Some people are typically more apprehensive or anxious about writing than others.[1] This chapter summarizes research on the construct of writing apprehension by examining its measurement, correlates, development, and modification. The chapter emphasizes dispositional apprehension because there has been little work on and no systematic study of situationally bound writing anxiety. In the final portions of this chapter, however, the reader will find a conceptual framework that broadens and deepens our understanding of both the dispositional and situational dimensions of writing attitudes and beliefs.

Measuring Writing Apprehension

When assessing any dispositional characteristic, a number of measurement procedures are available. However, in the case of writing apprehension, a self-report procedure is the predominant assessment mode, where respondents indicate their apprehension by responding to a series of statements about writing. Other techniques sometimes encountered in the assessment of individual differences, such as observational indices, projective techniques, and physiological procedures, have not been extensively used in writing-apprehension research.

The first systematic attempt to assess writing apprehension was completed by Daly and M. D. Miller (1975b). They entered the field with a background in research on oral communication apprehension (i.e., reticence, shyness; see Daly & McCroskey, 1984), interested in exploring their observation that people differ in the amount of writing they produce as they compose.[2] They devised 63 statements about writing that focused on respondents' perceptions of their anxiety about the act of writing; their likes and dislikes about writing; the responses they had to peer, teacher, and professional evaluations of their writing; and their self-evaluations of writing. Respondents were asked to read each statement and indicate their reaction to the statement by circling one of 5 responses ranging from "strongly agree" to "strongly disagree."

A group of undergraduate students ($n = 164$) completed the initial 63-item measure. The respondents represented a diverse sample of students drawn from a variety of academic majors, backgrounds, and locations. Their responses to the items were correlated. Generally, the correlations among items were of moderate to high magnitude. A factor analysis suggested a predominant single factor.[3] The 26 items having the strongest loadings (i.e., weights) on the first factor were selected for inclusion in the apprehension measure. The instrument is presented in Figure 3-1. A shorter, 20-item instrument was also created for use outside of the writing class by deleting 6 items that dealt specifically with composition classes.[4] The shorter measure correlates well with the longer measure and can be used to assess the apprehension construct both within and outside the classroom.

An important characteristic of any measure is its reliability, which indicates the degree to which people respond consistently to the items in the instrument. The Daly–Miller Writing-Apprehension Scale, whether it be the 20- or 26-item version of the measure, is highly reliable. In the first group of studies, the internal consistency of the measure was quite high (.94). Later research with the instrument has always found values close to that figure. Test–retest reliability is also high: In one investigation over a one-week period, the correlation was .92 (Daly & M. D. Miller, 1975b). Later studies that extended over more than three months found test–retest coefficients greater than

Directions: Below are a series of statements about writing. There are no right or wrong answers to these statements. Please indicate the degree to which each statement applies to you by circling whether you (1) strongly agree, (2) agree, (3) are uncertain, (4) disagree, or (5) strongly disagree with the statement. While some of the statements may seem repetitious, take your time and try to be as honest as possible.

	SA	A	U	D	SD
1. I avoid writing.	1	2	3	4	5
2. I have no fear of my writing being evaluated.	1	2	3	4	5
3. I look forward to writing down my ideas.	1	2	3	4	5
4. I am afraid of writing essays when I know they will be evaluated.	1	2	3	4	5
5. Taking a composition course is a very frightening experience.	1	2	3	4	5
6. Handing in a composition makes me feel good.	1	2	3	4	5
7. My mind seems to go blank when I start to work on a compositon.	1	2	3	4	5
8. Expressing ideas through writing seems to be a waste of time.	1	2	3	4	5
9. I would enjoy submitting my writing to magazines for evaluation and publication.	1	2	3	4	5
10. I like to write my ideas down.	1	2	3	4	5
11. I feel confident in my ability to clearly express my ideas in writing.	1	2	3	4	5
12. I like to have my friends read what I have written.	1	2	3	4	5
13. I'm nervous about writing.	1	2	3	4	5
14. People seem to enjoy what I write.	1	2	3	4	5
15. I enjoy writing.	1	2	3	4	5
16. I never seem to be able to clearly write down my ideas.	1	2	3	4	5
17. Writing is a lot of fun.	1	2	3	4	5
18. I expect to do poorly in composition classes even before I enter them.	1	2	3	4	5
19. I like seeing my thoughts on paper.	1	2	3	4	5
20. Discussing my writing with others is an enjoyable experience.	1	2	3	4	5
21. I have a terrible time organizing my ideas in a composition course.	1	2	3	4	5
22. When I hand in a composition I know I'm going to do poorly.	1	2	3	4	5
23. It's easy for me to write good compositions.	1	2	3	4	5
24. I don't think I write as well as most other people.	1	2	3	4	5
25. I don't like my compositions to be evaluated.	1	2	3	4	5
26. I'm no good at writing.	1	2	3	4	5

Figure 3-1. The 26-item version of the Daly–Miller Writing-Apprehension Scale.

.80. The Daly–Miller measure has been used with college students (e.g., Daly, 1977, 1978; Daly & M. D. Miller, 1975b), high school pupils (Harvley-Felder, 1978; National Assessment of Educational Progress, 1980), grade schoolers (National Assessment of Educational Progress, 1980; Zimmerman & Silverman, 1982), and adults (Claypool, 1980; Daly & Witte, 1982; Gere, Schuessler, & Abbott, 1984).

There are some other, more recent measures of writing apprehension reported in the literature. They include the Jeroski and Conry (1981) Attitude Toward Writing Scale; questionnaire devised by Kroll (1979), King (1979), Thompson (1978, 1979b), and Blake (1976); as well as multidimensional measures reported by Stacks, Boozer, and Lally (1983), and Daly and T. Miller (1983a). The conceptual base for the last measure is discussed at the conclusion of this chapter. While all appear to have good internal consistency, none have validity checks such as those available for the earlier Daly–Miller measure. All correlate highly with the Daly–Miller measure (Daly & Wilson, 1983).

Correlates of Writing Apprehension

INDIVIDUAL-DIFFERENCE CORRELATES OF WRITING APPREHENSION

Since writing apprehension is conceived of as a relatively enduring disposition, it's important to specify its relationship with other dispositions or trait-like constructs. By framing the apprehension construct within a broader map of general personality characteristics, researchers have refined its description. Research has related writing apprehension to sex difference, trait and test anxiety, various subject-specific attitudes, self-esteem, and other personality variables.

Sex Difference. A number of investigations have discovered a modest sex difference in measurements of writing apprehension: Women are often found to be slightly less anxious about writing than men. The first study exploring this difference was by Daly and M. D. Miller (1975c). Reasoning from research that indicates that females receive more positive teacher reactions to their writing than do males, Daly and Miller hypothesized that, to the extent that writing apprehension is a function of a history of negative responses to one's writing, males would be more apprehensive because they generally are rewarded less than females for their writing. They found such a difference among undergraduates. Jeroski and Conry (1981), using their Attitude Toward Writing Scale, found a significant relationship between sex and attitudes about writing. The correlation (.32) suggested that female students (grades 8 and 9) had a more positive attitude toward writing than male students had. It is interesting that they also found that after sex and grade level had been controlled, the relationship between their writing-attitude scale and a number of performance measures was relatively small (see below under "Performance Correlates of Apprehension": "Writing Behavior Correlates"). Dickson (1978) found a similar difference in a large (n = 754) correlational study of writing apprehension, although she quite accurately pointed out that the magnitude of the effect was quite small. In fact, some studies have failed to find a statistically significant sex difference in apprehension, perhaps because the magnitude of difference is so small (e.g., Reed, Vandett, & Burton, 1983; Schultz & Meyers, 1981). And there is one study that found the opposite effect: Of a group of returning college students over the age of 22, the females were significantly more anxious about writing than the males were (Thompson, 1981). Thompson attributed this finding to the likelihood of greater writing experiences held by the males in her sample.

Traits and Test Anxiety. M. D. Miller and Daly (1975) correlated the apprehension questionnaire to Spielberger's trait-anxiety measure, (Spielberger, Gorsuch, & Lushene, 1970) and found a nonsignificant correlation. On the other hand, Thompson (1981) and Salovey and Haar (1983) found positive and significant correlations between writing anxiety and general anxiety. Dickson (1978) related the writing-apprehension instrument to a test-anxiety measure and found a positive and significant relationship, although it was of low magnitude.

Subject-Specific Attitudes. In an extensive study of personality correlates of writing apprehension, Daly and Wilson (1983) related the writing-apprehension questionnaire to measures of attitudes toward reading, math anxiety, oral communication anxiety, and attitudes toward science. They found consistently inverse and significant relationships between apprehension and math anxiety (average $r = -.30$), no significant association with attitudes toward science, positive and significant correlations with attitudes toward reading (average $r = .32$), and positive and significant correlations with oral communication apprehension (average $r = .39$). M. D. Miller and Daly (1975) also related the writing-apprehension instrument to a measure of oral communication apprehension. In that study, the correlation between the two was .28. Burgoon and Hale (1983a, 1983b) found that the three factors they derived from the writing-apprehension measure were positively correlated with public speaking anxiety and interpersonal communication anxiety.

Self-Esteem. Daly and Wilson (1983) conducted a series of studies exploring the relationship between writing apprehension and self-esteem. The results of these studies suggest that general self-esteem is only moderately associated with writing apprehension while esteem specific to writing is more strongly associated. In terms of general self-esteem, writing apprehension was significantly and inversely related to Rosenberg's (1965) measure of esteem ($r = -.31$ in one study, and $r = -.11$ in another); to Pervin and Lilly's (1967) self-esteem questionnaire ($r = -.23$); to Berger's (1952) self-acceptance measure ($r = -.14$); and to questionnaires tapping self-perceptions of competence (average $r = -.31$), composure ($r = -.14$), and extroversion ($r = -.36$). Daly and Wilson also related writing apprehension to a multidimensional measure of esteem specific to writing, a measure that tapped 14 dimensions of esteem tied directly to writing. The multiple correlation between the apprehension measure and the 14 dimensions was $-.73$. These studies suggest that writing apprehension is modestly related to general self-esteem and more strongly related to writing-specific self-esteem.

Other Personality Variables. Daly and Wilson (1983) also describe a series of studies where writing apprehension was related to a number of other personality measures. By and large, the correlations were small and mostly nonsignificant. In these investigations, writing apprehension was related to locus of control ($r = .03$), dogmatism ($r = .12$), machiavellianism ($r = .05$), achievement need ($r = .08$), social approval seeking ($r = -.04$), receiver anxiety ($r = .19$), tolerance for ambiguity ($r = -.21$), powerlessness ($r = -.10$), normlessness ($r = .10$), isolation ($r = -.11$), alienation ($r = -.12$), and anomie ($r = -.04$). Burgoon and Hale (1983a, 1983b) found that "ease of writing" and "rewards in writing" (both drawn from the Daly–Miller writing-apprehension measure and scored so that a high value represented anxiety) were positively related ($r = .31$ and $r = .26$, respectively) to judgments that communication was an untrustworthy, unproductive activity. Stafford and Daly (1984) found writing apprehension was modestly associated with public self-consciousness ($r = .13$), private self-consciousness ($r = -.15$), and social anxiety ($r = .17$). Daly, Bell, and Korinek (1983) related writing apprehension to social approval seeking, a general trait emphasizing the tendency of people to respond in socially desirable ways, and found no significant relationship ($r = -.03$). Pfeifer (1982) found positive correlations between writing apprehension and two of the dimensions of the Myers–Briggs Type Indicator (Myers, 1962), those of tendencies toward introversion ($r = .17$) and toward perceptions ($r = .23$). The former relationship matches well with other research that suggests a positive correlation between writing apprehension and various measures of communication anxiety. The latter association suggests that as writing apprehension increases so does an individual's tendency to await and adapt to events.

The general conclusion to be drawn from studies linking writing apprehension to other individual differences is that the apprehension construct is relatively independent of other personality dimensions. There appears to be a slight sex difference, and small but reliable relationships of writing apprehension with attitudes toward (inverse), oral communication anxiety (positive), attitudes toward reading (positive), and self-esteem (inverse).

WRITING APPREHENSION CORRELATED WITH ATTITUDES, EXPECTATIONS, AND CHOICES ABOUT SCHOOL AND WRITING

A second focus of research on the correlates of writing-apprehension has been the relationship between apprehension and various attitudes, expectations, and choices about school and writing. The general hypothesis has been that these attitudes, expectations, and choices should relate to writing apprehension.

In an early investigation, Daly and M. D. Miller (1975c) probed the relationship between apprehension and student attitudes about and expectations of courses requiring writing. Highly apprehensive students reported significantly lower expectations of success in such courses than less anxious pupils. Not surprisingly, when contrasted with less apprehensive students, highly apprehensive students expressed less willingness to enroll in writing-oriented courses. In addition, and perhaps providing a partial explanation for their lower expectations of success, highly apprehensive students felt they had not performed well in previous classes where writing was demanded in comparison to how the less apprehensive students reported feeling. And in such courses highly anxious students were less satisfied than their less anxious counterparts. Jeroski and Conry (1981) found that responses by young adolescents to their Attitude Toward Writing Scale were significantly correlated with responses to three questions assessing their satisfaction with curriculum, estimation of improvement in their writing, and interest in their writing activities. In each case, the relationship was in the expected direction: The more positive the students' attitudes about writing, the more they reported satisfaction, perceived improvement, and interest. Selfe (1981a, 1981b), using interviews with a small sample of writers with high- and low-apprehension, found that highly apprehensive writers disliked composing, had little confidence in their writing abilities, and feared evaluation of their written products.

These attitudes, expectations, and choices can be tied to at least four general effects. First, highly apprehensive students are seldom found in advanced writing courses. In one study, Daly and M. D. Miller (1975c) found that the average apprehension score of students enrolled in advanced composition classes was significantly lower than that of the general student population. Second, the desirability of various academic majors and careers is tied to writing apprehension. In three studies (Daly & M. D. Miller, 1975b; Daly & Shamo, 1976, 1978) writing apprehension was found to have interacted with the perceived writing requirements of jobs or majors so as to affect the desirability of those jobs or majors. Highly apprehensive individuals preferred occupations and majors that they perceived as demanding comparatively little writing. Low-apprehensives liked jobs and majors that in their eyes required more writing. Third, this effect on the desirability of jobs and majors is reflected in actual choices. In a number of investigations, writing apprehension has been linked to the amount of writing perceived to be required in chosen occupations or majors (e.g., Daly & M. D. Miller, 1975b; Schultz & Meyers, 1981). Consistently, highly apprehensive writers felt that their jobs and majors had lower writing demands than those of jobs and majors selected by less apprehensive writers. Fourth, teachers have different expectancies for highly apprehensive and less apprehensive students. Daly (1979a, 1979b) had both elementary and secondary school teachers read descriptions of hypothetical students who were described identically except for two manipulations. The first manipulation had to do with each student's level of writing apprehension. One student had prototypically high apprehension; the other had prototypically low apprehension. The second manipulation had to do with the hypothetical student's sex. Teachers, after reading one of the four descriptions, made a series of predictive judgments about the student. There was a large and statistically significant main effect for apprehension. Teachers offered significantly better expectancies for the low-apprehension student than for the high-apprehension one. This effect must be couched within the finding of a significant interaction between student sex and student apprehension. Teachers regarded the high-apprehension female and the low-apprehension male least positively; they regarded the high-apprehension male and the low-apprehension female most positively. The interaction was interpreted by Daly as potentially reflecting a general sex bias: People expect that females will like to write and that males won't. A violation of the expectation in either direction (i.e., a male who likes to write or a female who doesn't) yielded a negative judgment of the person.

Another focus of research in attitudinal correlates of writing apprehension involves teachers' own writing apprehension and its relationship to what teachers consider important, what they judge relevant, and how they teach students by using different kinds of writing assignments. Claypool (1980) assessed how often high school instructors assigned tasks that required writing. She found a significant difference between highly and less apprehensive teachers in the number of assignments they made. Highly apprehensive teachers on the average reported making only 7 assignments yearly compared to the annual average of 19.9 by low-apprehensives. Claypool found a significant correlation (−.28) between apprehension and the number of assignments made by her sample of teachers. She also divided the teachers into four subject groups: language arts, social studies, math and science, and applied arts and sciences. Language arts teachers had the lowest apprehension level while math and science teachers had the highest. This last finding indirectly buttresses the Daly and Wilson (1983) report of a positive relationship between writing apprehension and anxious attitudes toward reading (or, in this case, toward language arts) and an inverse association between writing apprehension and math anxiety.

Daly and Witte (1982) also probed the relationship between apprehension and teachers' attitudes. Using responses of 185 elementary and secondary school teachers, they found that writing apprehension was inversely and significantly related ($r = -.25$) with the teachers' perceptions of the relevance of writing in their chosen subject areas as well as with their emphasis on writing in their classrooms ($r = -.26$). Teachers also indicated on a series of scales how much they required various sorts of writing from students. The types of required writing include essay exams, classroom as well as at-home compositions, journal writing, letter-writing exercises, written book-reports, and diary writing. Daly and Witte found a significant and inverse relationship between the frequency of a composite of these writing assignments and the level of teachers' apprehension. However, after the perceived writing requirements of the teachers' subject areas were partialed out, the correlation between assignments and apprehension became nonsignificant. Apprehension was also related to teachers' reports of their own writing behavior. Teachers indicated how often they wrote personal letters, business letters, memos, notes to parents, newsletters, diary notes, and creative prose and poetry. The correlation between a composite index of these writing behaviors and apprehension was significant ($r = -.37$). In a secondary analysis, Daly and Witte subdivided their sample of teachers into grade levels. They found that the correlations between apprehension and the four teacher indices (their perceptions of the relevance of writing in their subjects, their emphasis on writing in their classrooms, their teaching methods, and their own writing behavior), were strongest for teachers in the third through fifth grades. These grades, interestingly enough, are where many important writing skills are taught.

Gere, Schuessler, and Abbott (1984) found that teachers' writing apprehension was positively related to their concerns that students use standard English (especially among female teachers and teachers in higher education) and inversely related to their judgment of the importance of linguistic maturity or the use of a wide variety of instructional techniques in the teaching of composition.

There have been a number of other allusions to the characteristic beliefs and behaviors of highly apprehensive individuals. For example, Boice (1982b) proposed that "blocked" academicians tend to avoid actual writing by engaging in alternative activities, intellectualizing about other demands on their time, setting unrealistic goals, engaging in "binge" writing, and falling into poor work habits for writing. Jones (1975) argues that avoidance of writing results primarily from grandiose and unrealistic expectations L. Z. Bloom (undated) suggests that apprehensive writers adhere too strictly to rules about writing; hold unrealistic, mythical beliefs about the characteristics of writers; suffer from problems of self-esteem; and have an excessive concern about evaluation. Rose (1980) offers an extensive, more cognitive orientation on some of the beliefs highly apprehensive writers may have about writing. He suggests that blocked writers suffer from a case of rule rigidity: They take useful rules about writing and try to stick to them rigidly. In some cases, they overuse rules; in others, they approach a particular writing experience with rules irrelevant to that event; and, in still other cases, they use an overabundance of rules, an approach that leads to seemingly unsolvable conflicts.

PERFORMANCE CORRELATES OF APPREHENSION

Standardized Correlates. A series of investigations have linked writing apprehension to performance on standardized tests of writing ability. The general relationship is small but significant and consistently an inverse one. It's important to note that one should expect *no more* than a modest relationship between apprehension and performance. One underlying assumption of the apprehension construct is that it focuses on a characteristic different from but related to actual writing behavior or competence.[5]

Daly and M. D. Miller (1975c) found a small but statistically significant correlation (−.19) between writing apprehension and self-reported scores on the Scholastic Aptitude Test (SAT). This study was limited by the fact that self-reports are open to various inaccuracies. Later investigations have not suffered from this problem. Dickson (1978) replicated the effect using scores on the American College Testing (ACT) instrument obtained from school sources. In a population of 754 undergraduates, she found a small, inverse, but statistically significant correlation (−.16) between apprehension and performance on the composite ACT. More important, she observed a larger, inverse, and significant relationship (−.29) between apprehension and scores on the English subtest of the ACT. Dickson was concerned that the writing apprehension she measured might have been confounded with test anxiety; but when she partialed out test anxiety, a significant inverse relationship between writing apprehension and performance remained. Correlations between writing apprehension and other subtests of the ACT (e.g., math, social studies, science) were minimal.

A number of other studies have obtained similar findings using a variety of standardized measures. For example, Daly (1978) used a 68-item measure tapping 12 dimensions of writing competency. He found significant differences between highly and less apprehensive writers in regard to their competence in dimensions such as spelling, punctuation, case, adjectives and adverbs, recognition of sentence fragments, agreement, recognition of faulty references and pronouns, diction, and parallelism. In every case, the difference favored the low-apprehension group. Glynn, Muth, Matthews, and Garrido (1982) found inverse correlations between writing apprehension and verbal SAT scores in two studies. Although in neither study were the correlations statistically significant, they were of a magnitude to suggest a reliable relationship had samples been larger. Fowler and Kroll (1980), using a large sample of undergraduates, found a statistically significant and inverse correlation between apprehension and composite scores on the ACT. Faigley, Daly, and Witte (1981) examined the differences between high- and low-apprehensives on a number of standardized measures of writing competency. They found significant differences between high- and low-apprehensives in the performances on the Test of Standard Written English, the English Composition Test, the SAT verbal measure as well as the SAT vocabulary subtest, and the language mechanics and paragraph comprehension portions of the McGraw-Hill Reading Test. Reed, Vandett, and Burton (1983) found a significant relationship between apprehension and writing skills as assessed by the Missouri College English Test.

Other studies have noted a relationship between writing apprehension and performance in writing classes by using course grades as an indicator of classroom performance. Powell (1980), for example, found that highly apprehensive students were more likely than less apprehensive students to receive low grades in composition courses. Fowler and Ross (1982) found a significant and inverse correlation between apprehension and college students' grades in composition courses. Apprehension scores also significantly discriminated between the top and bottom third of the grade distribution. Fowler and Kroll (1980), on the other hand, found no significant relationship between apprehension and grades in a large composition course. Grades are probably at best a very coarse index of the performance factors that might be correlated with apprehension: A student's final grade in a composition course typically represents an aggregation of a large number of factors, only a few of which may be directly linked to apprehension.

The results of studies exploring the relationship between writing apprehension and performance by individuals on standardized tests of writing-related competencies consistently indicate the expected relationship. The higher the writing apprehension, the lower the performance on these measures. Two caveats are important here. First, the magnitude of the relationship is typically small to moderate, as would be expected. Second, there is no causal relationship imputed between apprehension and performance in any of these findings. It would be incorrect to draw any conclusion that rests either on the claim that writing apprehension causes performance deficits or on the claim that performance deficits lead to apprehension. Both claims are plausible as is one that posits a bidirectional relationship.

Writing Behavior Correlates. There have been a number of studies linking writing apprehension to actual writing. Two major approaches have been taken. The first identifies quantitative indices of writing behavior (such as number of words written or the number of T-units present) and relates them to a measure of writing apprehension. The second has readers evaluate a piece of writing, and those evaluations are then related to a measure of writing apprehension.

Daly and M. D. Miller (1975c) examined the relationship between writing apprehension and language intensity. "Language intensity" refers to the degree to which the words chosen by a writer deviate from neutrality: More intense language is more extreme. The underlying rationale for the Daly and Miller study lay in research on cognitive stress. Highly apprehensive writers versus low-apprehensives were expected to experience greater cognitive stress when placed in a writing situation, and their increased stress was hypothesized to result in the use of less intense language. College students were given a passage with a number of blanks in it, and they were to fill in the blanks with words listed at the bottom of the passage. The words had previously been scored for intensity. Results of the study supported the hypothesis: The messages encoded by high apprehensives were significantly less intense than those written by low apprehensives (cf. Burgoon & Hale, 1983a, 1983b).

Daly (1977) asked individuals previously classified as high or low in writing apprehension to write a short composition on an essay they had just read. No specifications other than time limit (10 minutes) were made about the nature, approach, or style of the composition. A number of quantitative indices were derived from these extemporaneous passages. To begin with, high-apprehensives' essays had significantly fewer words and statements than those written by low-apprehensives. Then, after adjusting for the differences in the amount of language produced, significant effects were found for apprehension on three measures of verbal qualification: High-apprehensives, when compared to low-apprehensives, wrote essays that included significantly fewer words ending in "ly," fewer commas, and a smaller number of delimiting punctuation marks. No effects were found for apprehension on measures of diversity, reading ease, or other assessments of verbal production. The readability issue was also probed by Burgoon and Hale (1983a). They found positive and significant correlations between apprehension and essay readability. An obvious concern here is the definition of "readability." The index used both by Daly and by Burgoon and Hale was a quantitative one that calculates reading ease as a function of complexity and sentence length. That sort of measure taps only a very limited aspect of readability.

Book (1976) found results similar to those reported by Daly. In her study, low-apprehension writers produced three times more words than did high-apprehensives. Additionally, the messages written by low-apprehensives had significantly more paragraphs; more words per paragraph; more sentences; more nouns, pronouns, adjectives, and prepositional phrases. Her high-apprehension writers made more spelling errors than did low-apprehensives. Finally, using an index she created to measure the amount of information conveyed by the written messages, Book noted that essays written by high-apprehensive conveyed significantly less information than did those written by low-apprehensives. Burgoon and Hale (1983a) found that the enjoyment-of-writing dimension of the Daly–Miller writing apprehension instrument was inversely associated with the complexity (−.26) and lexical diversity (−.23) of essays written by student writers. ("Complexity" was defined as the ratio of the number of syllables to the number of words in the essay. "Lexical diversity" was operationalized as the type-token ratio—that is, as the division of the total number of words into the total number of different words.) When Burgoon and Hale correlated the entire apprehension instrument to these two variables, they found that apprehension was significantly related to complexity but not to lexical diversity. In a study of writers composing business letters, Stacks, Boozer, and Lally (1983) found writing apprehension was positively related to the use of the passive voice, less conditionality, and negative audience perceptions by the writers.

Garcia (1977) examined the syntactic characteristics of essays written by high- and low-apprehension students. He found differences between high- and low-apprehensives on seven grammatical variables (infinitives; participles; gerunds; prepositional phrases; adjectival, adverbial, and nominal clauses) but no differences on five other indicators of syntactic development (words per T-unit, words per clause, clauses per T-unit, total T-units, and total words). His analysis was limited by a comparatively small sample ($n = 32$). Using a larger sample and a more complicated design, Faigley, Daly, and Witte (1981) examined writing samples composed by undergraduates who were either high or low in writing apprehension. They selected from a larger sample 110 students who fell at the extremes of the Daly–Miller writing-apprehension measure. Each student wrote two essays. The first essay was meant to elicit narrative and descriptive writing that drew heavily on personal experience, while the second was designed to elicit argumentative discourse. High apprehensive writers versus low apprehensives wrote essays with significantly fewer words per T-unit; fewer words per clause; fewer T-units with final nonrestrictive modifiers; and fewer words in what final nonrestrictive modifiers there were. Furthermore, the essays written by high apprehensives were shorter overall than those written by low apprehensives. However, the main effects due to apprehension need to be considered in light of a secondary analysis that revealed that the effects occurred only in the narrative–descriptive essays. Between high- and low-apprehension writing samples on the argumentative topic, there was only the one difference of overall length. Further, a multiple correlation between apprehension and the different writing measures yielded a much larger correlation between apprehension and performance on the descriptive–narrative assignments than on the argumentative ones. Faigley, Daly, and Witte interpreted their findings in terms of the self-expressive nature of the narrative–descriptive tasks. High-apprehension writers performed differently from low apprehensives only on assignments that elicited elements of self. In argumentative assignments where students did not use personal experiences, there was no effect for apprehension. This was the first writing-apprehension study to systematically vary modes of writing assignments. It highlights the critical importance of carefully selecting writing tasks.

The relationship between apprehension and the quality of writing has also been a focus of research. Daly (1977) found a significant relationship between apprehension and quality evaluations: Essays written by low-apprehensives were evaluated as significantly better than those composed by highly apprehensive writers. Richmond and Dickson (1980) had 135 undergraduate students complete the writing-apprehension instrument and a measure of test anxiety as well as compose a brief essay. Dividing the students into three groups on the basis of their writing apprehension, Richmond and Dickson found a significant relationship between apprehension and writing quality. Highly apprehensive writers wrote essays that were rated significantly lower in quality than those written by writers in the middle range of apprehension. In turn, low-apprehension writers wrote essays that were significantly higher in quality than those written by moderate-apprehensives. An analysis of covariance controlling for test anxiety yielded the same results. Garcia (1977) also found an effect for apprehension on writing quality. The difference was in favor of the essays written by low-apprehensives.

Faigley, Daly, and Witte (1981) found that on narrative-descriptive essay topics high-apprehensives wrote essays that were judged significantly lower in quality than those written by low-apprehensives. On argumentative topics, however, there was no difference in quality between essays written by high- and low-apprehensives. In line with Faigley, Daly, and Witte's finding, Richardson (1980) failed to find any significant difference in quality ratings of essays composed by high- and low-apprehensives on a topic that could be construed as argumentative (writing to a television station to explain why a particular program should be taken off or kept on the air). Salovey and Haar (1983) also found a pattern of nonsignificant relationships between ratings of writing quality and measures of writing anxiety, but they fail to describe the nature of the assignments used in their study.

Jeroski and Conry (1981), using the instrument for their Attitude Toward Writing Scale, found significant relationships between the responses by eighth- and ninth-grade students to the attitude measure and holistic judgments of the students' ability to organize details and produce narrative writing. In an unpublished study, Daly (1976) asked graduate teaching assistants who regularly taught composition courses to read essays written by undergraduate students. The students, unknown to the readers, had previously been classified as high or low in writing apprehension. Essays written by highly apprehensive individuals were rated significantly lower in insight, organization, style, logic, and overall quality than those written by low-apprehension students.

Overall, studies tying writing apprehension to writing behaviors consistently demonstrate a reliable, if small, relationship: Highly apprehensive individuals appear to write in ways different from those of their less apprehensive counterparts.

COGNITIVE CORRELATES OF APPREHENSION

There have been a few studies probing correlates of writing apprehension that are more cognitive in nature. The first was completed by Toth (1975). She investigated the relationship between writing apprehension and the amount of attitude change obtained when people performed a counterattitudinal writing task. The typical manipulation in studies of counterattitudinal persuasion requires people to write a message at variance with their present attitude about a personal or social issue. For example, if a person were opposed to busing, he or she might be asked to write an essay arguing for busing. After writing such a message, the individual's attitude is assessed. Research in this form of persuasion generally finds that people modify their attitudes in the direction of the counterattitudinal essay. Toth extended this manipulation to measures of writing apprehension. She found that low-apprehensives experienced significantly greater attitude change than either moderate- or high-apprehensives after such a task. She surmised that the low-apprehensives may engage in more effort while composing, effort that as a consequence may yield greater attitude change.

Selfe's study (1981a, 1981b) of the composing processes of high- and low-apprehensives represents a second strand of cognitive research related to writing apprehension. She identified undergraduates who were either high or low in apprehension and had them compose essays. As they were composing, they talked about the process. The composing-aloud sessions were coded behaviorally using a scheme drawn from work by Flower and Hayes (1979), Perl (1979), and Sommers (1978). Selfe found that during prewriting highly apprehensive individuals drew less from the composition assignment (in terms of extracting and inferring information about such matters as audience), engaged in less planning, and did less written "prefiguring" than did their low-apprehension counterparts. During the writing phase, high-apprehensives spent less time composing individual sentences than did low apprehensives. Finally, after completing the writing task, highly apprehensive writers spent less time editing and reworking their manuscripts than did low-apprehensives. While the study suffered by depending on very small samples (four students in each group), it did highlight some potential cognitive and process-related differences between high- and low-apprehensives (see Selfe's contribution, Chapter 4 of this volume).

L. Z. Bloom (1980) observed similar differences in her study of the writing processes of apprehensive and nonapprehensive writers. As opposed to Selfe, Bloom spent time in classroom settings attempting to modify the writing behaviors and attitudes of individuals as she constructed images of their writing processes. She found a number of notable differences between high- and low-apprehensives. Hayes (1981) also completed a process analysis of high- and low-apprehension writers. In his study he identified two students, one of whom was highly apprehensive and the other a low-apprehensive. Using a method different from Selfe's, Hayes waited until his writers completed their compositions and then had them comment on their writing while watching videotapes of their activity (this method may have introduced significant problems; see Kail & Bisanz, 1982). From analysis of transcripts as well as from a questionnaire completed by the two writers, Hayes found that the anxious writer (versus the nonanxious writer) took longer to complete writing assignments, produced fewer words per minute, spent less time on the actual writing, paused more while writing, and completed fewer drafts of an assignment.

In another vein is work by Stafford and Daly (1984) who conducted a study of conversational memory. College students interacted for a short period of time in dyads and then were asked to recall their interactions. One member of each dyad recalled the interaction orally, while the other recollected by writing down what he or she recalled from the conversation. Stafford and Daly found that apprehension was significantly related ($r = -.37$) to the amount individuals recalled when they wrote their recollections.[6]

Development of Writing Apprehension

The importance of writing apprehension as a construct should be clear by this point. It has a number of relationships with other variables that are directly or indirectly related to actual writing. The next, crucial question is, How does writing apprehension develop? What causes it in the first place? And how is it maintained? There has been surprisingly little research on these topics.

In a very early explication of the idea of writing apprehension, Weil and Lane (1956) described something they labeled "stagefright in writers." This psychological barrier to writing was hypothesized to be caused by (a) overestimation on the part of the writer of his or her deficiencies as writer; (b) inadequate time to complete writing assignments; (c) an inability in the writer to see the purpose of his or her reports, an inability that leads to a belief that writing is a waste of time; and (d) excessive criticism and repeated, arbitrary revision of the writer's work by editors and supervisors. Aldrich (1979, 1982) surveyed adults in the Washington, D.C., area and suggested that writing anxiety arose because of a lack of knowledge about the value of preparation and a lack of methods to adequately cope with one's occupational writing demands. Duke (1980) has devised an exercise that asks students to describe the origins of their poor attitudes about writing. His explication of some of what basic writers relate as causes of their anxiety closely fits those described above.

There have been few systematic investigations of potential causes of apprehension or related constructs. In studies focusing on the development of writing apprehension, causal agents and those conditions that might maintain anxiety have been confounded. The nature of the construct really precludes any clear separation of the two variables. The only method that could completely isolate causal agents would be one that systematically attempts to create writing apprehension. That procedure would be subject to considerable ethical problems.

In her dissertation, Harvley-Felder (1978) had tenth-graders complete a slightly revised version of the Daly–Miller writing apprehension measure and a questionnaire assessing potential contributory causes for the anxiety. A factor analysis of the responses to this questionnaire yielded three factors. The first dimension was labeled "punishment." The common characteristic of the items concerning this factor was their emphasis on negative teacher reactions to a student's writing (e.g., "My papers have come back with a lot of red marks"; "My elementary school teacher said my papers were messy and my handwriting sloppy"). The second factor was called "positive reinforcement"; its major items stressed the amount and degree of encouragement and praise received by students for writing from teachers, peers, relatives, and parents. In addition, a few of the items considered the role of models (e.g., "Relatives encouraged me to practice my writing"; "My elementary school teachers said I would make a good writer"; "A friend of mine practices writing outside of school"). The third dimension represented "communication seeking behaviors"; its items involved students' requests for help with their writing (e.g., "When I don't understand a paper assignment the first time, I ask my teachers to explain it"; "When I am given a dull topic to write about, I ask my teachers to let me change it"). Harvley-Felder found that each dimension significantly discriminated between levels of apprehension in the expected direction. High-apprehensives reported more punishment, less positive reinforcement, and less communication seeking behavior than low-apprehensives.

In an unpublished, informal survey of elementary and secondary school teachers discussing their students, Daly (1979a) derived nine interrelated explanations for writing apprehension: (a) lack of appropriate skills, (b) teachers' reactions to mechanical problems, (c) the nature of writing assignments, (d) the tendency to associate writing with aversive consequences, (e) perceptions by the apprehensive writer that teachers are a source of punishment, (f) public comparisons of students' work that lead to ridicule and cause the writer embarrassment, (g) negative reactions by teachers to the content of compositions, (h) poor self-perceptions on the part of writers, and (i) inadequate role models.

Previous research has suggested a number of explanations for the development and maintenance of writing apprehension.[7] But there is an additional explanation that has not, to date, been suggested in the literature. I call it the "comparison deficiency" explanation. As writers compose and review what they have written, they go through a process of comparing their intentions with their actual products. Apprehension in part arises and is maintained when writers consistently believe that what they have written inadequately matches what they had in mind as they composed. This comparison between what was intended and what appears on the paper takes at least two forms: In one case, a comparison with a cognitive intention, writers feel they "know" what they want to write but somehow what finally appears on paper fails to match, in any satisfying way, what was intended. In the other case, a comparison with an "oral" version of an intention, writers feel that what they've composed inadequately matches what they had, or could have spoken either before or during the writing session—people sometimes report that when they "talk through" an idea it "sounds better" than when it is written. In either of these two cases, a deficiency in the written product is perceived. A consistent sense of this deficiency, over time, is punishing. The writer learns to avoid writing in order to avoid the resulting sense of inadequacy. The logic here is simple: The apprehensive writer has found, and continues to find, his or her writing deficient when compared to what he or she wants it to be. The nonapprehensive individual has probably (a) discovered that writing requires a good deal of effort before it even somewhat matches what is intended or uttered, (b) recognized that the written word may be different from what is conceived or spoken, or (c) failed to find the comparison deficiency salient.

Changing Writing Apprehension

There has also been some interest in the modification of writing apprehension. This interest in remediation takes two major forms. The first examines the impact of educational programs on writing apprehension. In this sort of research, an investigator typically assesses the writing apprehension of a group of students before and after they complete a particular kind of composition course. The second approach identifies and tests various therapeutic strategies aimed at alleviating writing apprehension. This approach emerges from, and takes, a clinical orientation. It's important to note that both approaches assume that a positive attitude about writing is a desirable characteristic and that individuals who are unusually anxious about writing should at the very least have the opportunity to reduce their apprehension. The set of values underlying these assumptions has not been clearly elucidated or discussed. There may well be arguments for the inappropriateness of attempting to modify writing apprehension. The conceptual—indeed, philosophical—justification for modifying writing attitudes is an important issue, but to date it remains unexamined.

Therapeutic interventions for alleviating writing apprehension are covered by Boice in Chapter 9.[8] Following is a brief survey of studies of the impact of educational programs on writing apprehension. Kroll (1979) had students in four freshman writing courses complete his writing-attitude measure at the start and at the end of the semester. He found that, overall, students had significantly more positive attitudes toward writing at the end of the semester than they had at the beginning. Basile (1982), Schultz and Meyers (1981), and Fox (1980) found a similar effect of writing courses: Over a semester of composition instruction, writing apprehension decreased significantly. Fox further found that a particular approach to composition instruction—one emphasizing student-centered, sequential workshops—reduced apprehension significantly more than a more traditional, instructor-centered approach did. Walters, Weiss, and Maggitti (1980) found that the use of learning-centered writing in a variety of academic courses reduced, although not significantly, the apprehension of students. Thompson (1979a) contrasted five different approaches to composition instruction for their effect on writing anxiety. She found that only a language-study approach (Thompson, 1978, 1979b) that included discussions of procrastination, inability to concentrate, and the development of a "personal writing rhythm" led to a statistically significant change in writing anxiety. Zimmerman and Silverman (1982) found that the writing apprehension of fifth-grade students could be changed through instructional emphasis on prewriting activities, expressive writing, and positive evaluation.

In a nonempirical study, Craven (1980) found that by modifying the way an evening composition course was taught he could successfully reduce something akin to writing apprehension. Craven's procedures included having students read materials they had themselves selected, inviting professional writers into the class, devising assignments that fit with student interests, publishing the better pieces produced by the students, and ensuring public awareness of the fact that students had composed the published essays. Bartholomae (1979) describes the development of a six-credit course for "basic" writers that significantly reduced students' writing apprehension. The primary focus of the course appeared to be the improvement of students' reading skills and their ability to respond in writing to the readings. L. Z. Bloom (undated, 1980, in press) has developed a workshop to reduce writing anxiety. In her program she emphasizes peer assistance, daily writing that increases over time, daily record-keeping of the amount composed, belief modification through discussion and example, and skill enhancement in a nonthreatening fashion. Other studies conducted in classroom settings have examined the impact on students' writing attitudes of journal writing (Reece, 1980), grades (e.g., Bell & Price, 1980; Dreussi, 1976; Veit, 1980; Wagner, 1975), structure of instruction (e.g., Adams, 1971; Gorrell, 1980), and increased special attention (Auman, 1970). Further, Diamond, Haugen, and Kean (1980) have devised a large number of classroom exercises for working with the anxious or reluctant writer. Each activity is tied to a particular grade level ranging from first grade through high school.[9]

Reconceptualizing Writing Attitudes and Beliefs

The concept of writing apprehension has proved useful for study and application. However, a close examination of the construct suggests that it taps in only a very limited way attitudes or beliefs about writing. There are a variety of other attitudes and beliefs writers hold about the act of composing. This section will offer a short description of these different attitudes and beliefs. Daly and T. Miller (1983a, 1983b) and Daly, T. Miller, and Meyer (1984) have developed questionnaires that reliably assess each dimension.

A useful distinction can be made between dispositional and situational attitudes and beliefs. "Dispositional" attitudes and beliefs are those generalized feelings and perceptions that endure in a relatively consistent fashion over time and across situations. The preceding review of writing-apprehension research focuses on one such disposition, writing apprehension. "Situational" attitudes and beliefs are transitiory feelings closely tied to a particular situation or event. For instance, a student may experience a feeling that arises in a particular classroom on a certain day while working on a single assignment for one teacher. Situationally based attitudes and beliefs have to date received far less attention than have dispositional responses in research on writing-related attitudes and beliefs. Only Daly and Hailey (1984) report specific empirical research on writers' situational anxiety. They devised a measure of situational writing anxiety and then independently manipulated five situational variables in a simulated manner to observe their impact on situational anxiety. The five variables—evaluation, conspicuousness, novelty, ambiguity, and prior experience—each affected self-reported situational anxiety about writing.[10] In the remainder of this chapter, writers' dispositional attitudes and beliefs will be described first, followed by situationally based ones. The purpose of this bifurcation is not to make any hard and fast categorization but rather to allow for clear exposition.[11]

DISPOSITIONAL ATTITUDES AND BELIEFS

The dispositional attitudes and beliefs held by people about writing are grouped into three broad categories: cognitive, affective, and behavioral. While these groupings of dispositions are interrelated, each category allows a different kind of approach to writers' attitudes and beliefs.

Cognitive Dispositions. People hold a number of beliefs about writing. In the present conceptualization, five are considered. They are (a) writers' attributions of their successes and failures in writing, (b) their level of consciousness or awareness about writing, (c) their perceptions about the utility of writing, (d) their rules about the process of writing, and (3) their beliefs about the writing process.

The first cognitive dimension concerns the attributions writers offer when explaining their writing performances to themselves and others. In line with work on attributional processes in other disciplines (Weiner, 1974), four potential attributions of writers' performances on writing tasks are considered. They are attributions to luck or chance, ability, task difficulty, and effort. Writers might say they were successful or unsuccessful because of luck ("I just happened to hit on a topic the teacher liked"), ability ("Yeah, I knew all along I was going to do well—I'm a good writer"), task difficulty ("The reason I did well on the assignment was because it was so easy"), or effort ("Boy, did I work hard on that assignment!"). The four dimensions can be collapsed into some interesting composites. For example, an individual can explain his or her success or failure in a writing activity in terms of internal (self) variables such as ability and effort or in terms of external (non-self) variables such as task difficulty and luck. Alternatively, the individual may explain his or her performance in terms of stable causes (ability and task difficulty) or variable causes (effort and luck).[12]

It is very important to understand writers' attributions. For instance, in classroom settings pupils' attributions of their performances can profoundly affect how they react to teacher evaluations. Poor writers often attribute their failures to a lack of ability and their successes to luck. When they do well, they don't believe they had anything to do with the performance—luck or an easy task deserve the credit. But when they don't do well, they're responsible—their lack of effort or more often their perception of the ability deficit is what, in their minds, accounts for the poor performance. As long as they believe that their success is due primarily to luck, it's difficult to focus them on developing their own sense of ability or on recognizing that they may in fact have certain talents for writing. On the other hand, there are some writers who overestimate their writing proficiency. When these individuals succeed in a task, they tend to assign responsibility—that is, attribute causality— to their supposed ability. When they don't do well and teachers try to suggest some weaknesses in their writing, they tend to interpret the hint of failure as poor luck or attribute the failure to an unusually difficult task. As a result, they may not take helpful criticism seriously, believing themselves not responsible for problems in their compositions. The issue, in any case, is that attributions can affect both how much and what people learn from their performances.

The second cognitive dimension is the individual's consciousness or awareness of writing. Individuals vary in how aware and conscious they are of the written word. Some individuals savor words, play with them, find them a challenge to understand; appreciate slight verbal nuances; and generally are highly conscious of and sensitive to the written word. Others are far less conscious of writing. They recognize its uses, may indeed regularly engage in writing, but seldom expend much effort considering writing in terms other than its functional value. For example, one person may read a paragraph and think about why the author wrote that paragraph in one way rather than another, why one word was chosen over another, why some phrase was turned in a particular manner. Another individual, less conscious of writing, might read the paragraph and simply take away the broad meaning that the message communicates. Individuals highly conscious of writing may differ in a number of ways from individuals less conscious about writing. One difference may involve the degree to which they can profit from literature-based composition courses. Highly conscious individuals may learn much from reading exemplars of good writing. Others, less conscious of writing, might garner more from other approaches that emphasize, more directly, actual composing activity.

The third cognitive dimension is the individual's beliefs about the utility of writing. People differ in how valuable they find writing. Some think it serves them every day no matter what their profession or situation may be. Others find little use in writing; it just isn't that important to them. This dimension is, like all writing attitudes and beliefs, of potential importance in the composition classroom. The belief that writing is a useful activity may be essential for the acquisition and maintenance of writing competencies. If students think writing is not useful, effective instruction in the composition class is difficult. Recent moves to emphasize writing instruction in disciplines outside its traditional boundaries highlight the utility issue. Operating under a variety of names and models, a core belief of this movement is that if individuals learn to write within the context of professionally and personally salient subject matters, they will come to understand the importance of writing to their lives. Further, the move for more cross-disciplinary writing instruction assumes that if writing is taught within people's chosen fields, then they, seeing its utility, will attend more to writing instruction.

The fourth cognitive dimension is the group of beliefs or rules individuals hold about composing. This concept is drawn from work by Rose (1980) and others that emphasizes the tendency of many writers to experience difficulty in composing because of the rules about writing they bring with them. They are blocked by too many rules applied too rigidly to the task at hand. Individuals may differ in how many rules they hold about writing, how rigidly they apply them, and how much they let the rules block or impede their writing progress. Some rules are, of course, both important and advantageous in writing. They offer heuristic methods or simplifications that help writers to complete a text. Other rules, however, are detrimental to writers. By clinging to them, writers fail to broaden their repertoire of composing strategies and sacrifice exploration in favor of following rules that, while perhaps once useful to them, are now applied too prescriptively.

The final cognitive dimension is "process knowledge." The concept of process knowledge involves people's individual awareness of and attitudes toward the writing process. In recent years, considerable emphasis has been placed on specifying the differences between skilled and unskilled writers. A major finding has been that the groups differ in how they go about writing. Skilled writers engage in composing processes that differ substantially from those used by more unskilled writers (see, e.g., Flower & Hayes, 1979; Perl, 1979; and Sommers, 1978). To date, process research has primarily used observational techniques. My colleagues and I wonder if it is also possible to assess composing processes by asking people through questionnaires what they do when they write. We attempt to assess beliefs about the writing process, proposing that people vary in their beliefs about that process. Some people conceive of writing as a pattern of behaviors that, according to current researchers' thinking, represent more or less optimal writing-process behaviors. Other individuals don't conceive of writing in terms of the many behaviors that typically are considered optimal for effective composing. This dimension represents our initial attempt to systematically define and integrate some of the critical components that are representative of the writing processes of expert writers. Clearly this dimension, more than any other cognitive disposition, has an ideological, indeed almost prescriptive flavor to it—one that demands caution and careful application.

Affective Dispositions. The second major category of dispositional beliefs and attitudes is the affective one. Broadly defined, this category is represented by the writing-apprehension construct and by a group of variables referred to as "attitudes toward written products." In earlier research, various measures of affect were created. Questionnaires were devised that measured how anxious an individual was about writing, how much he or she enjoyed writing, how much he or she feared writing, and so on. In analyses, the responses to the different measures were highly correlated. They were in fact empirically virtually identical. Consequently, they were collapsed into a single dimension represented by the writing-apprehension construct. Individuals vary in the degree to which they find the act of writing pleasant, comfortable, and nonproductive of anxiety. At one extreme, people enjoy writing and seek it out because they find it pleasurable. At the other extreme, people have just the opposite reaction: Writing for them is a painful, fearful, and anxiety-producing experience. Earlier portions of this chapter have thoroughly examined the conceptual nature of and empirical findings associated with the construct.

The construct of "attitudes toward written products" is composed of a group of variables that center on how people feel about their written products. The variables composing the construct are: evaluation, organization, tempo, accuracy, competence, meaningfulness, timeliness, interest, readability, clarity, mechanics, support, honesty, and forcefulness. Daly and Wilson (1983) summarize the scales used to assess each of these dimensions. The construct attempts to frame peoples' feelings about their writing by focusing on their feelings about the products they produce. While correlated, the different dimensions clearly tap various aspects of their reactions.

Behavioral Dispositions. The third major dispositional category is the behavioral dimension. This category is divided into four constructs: (a) the frequency that a person composes, (b) his or her tenacity once writing, (c) the blocking the individual experiences while writing, and (d) his or her tendencies to procrastinate when writing is expected.

Individuals vary in how frequently they write. Some people write each and every day; others write only when it is required. This construct represents the general, self-reported tendencies of a person to write frequently or seldom. The second construct is "tenacity." Individuals differ in how tenacious they are in completing writing tasks. When writing is required, some people sit down and work on the task until it is completed; others have a difficult time concentrating on the task—any distraction serves as a ready excuse for abandoning the writing. The third construct is "writer's block." Writer's block occurs when individuals who are willing to write find that, as they try to write, nothing comes. Blocking occurs during the composing activity. In distinction from blocking is the fourth and final construct of the behavioral dimension, "procrastination." Procrastination refers to people's avoidance of writing activity. Procrastinators postpone writing tasks, seek other activities to avoid writing, and generally put off assignments until, perhaps, it is too late to complete them well.

There are some important distinctions here that are often blurred and confounded in the literature. One distinction is that blocking, procrastination, frequency, and tenacity are conceived of as very different constructs. An individual can be blocked yet at the same time have no problem with frequency, tenacity, or procrastination. It is conceptually inappropriate in most cases to view the four constructs as similar.

Another reason for distinguishing between these four constructs concerns the choice of therapies for the modification of unprofitable habits associated with each. Remediation programs are best determined by a clear understanding of the specific characteristics of the writing problem. Consider as an example the difference between procrastinating and blocking. One potentially appropriate therapy for procrastination lies in teaching something akin to time management. The writer learns to go to a specific location each day at a certain time and do nothing but write: No distractions are permitted. While this behavioral management technique may work with procrastinating writers, it may have little impact on blocked writers. What may be appropriate for them is "forced" writing, where something must be put down on paper whether it is meaningful or not (e.g., writing whatever comes to mind; free-flowing brainstorming). Misdiagnosis of or confusion about the nature of a writing problem will lead to inappropriate therapies of limited effectiveness.

SITUATIONAL ATTITUDES AND BELIEFS

Situational beliefs and attitudes about writing have three major components. They are perceptions of writing contexts, responses to the writing situation, and perceived outcomes. Each will be briefly discussed. In many cases, the constructs are similar to those already elaborated under the dispositional label. In those cases, no special explication will be required.

The nature of the context within which writing takes place is of vital importance in understanding writers' attitudes, beliefs, and behaviors. Writing contexts can be examined in two ways. First, contexts may be considered as they vary between themselves. Investigators can contrast situation A with situation B, seeking differences between the two. This approach is common in writing research that compares how people write in two different contexts, for example on a job or in a classroom. An obvious limitation of this approach is that an infinite number of contexts are potentially available for comparison. There are innumerable situations, and the curious investigator who starts out to examine how different contexts affect writing could easily spend the remainder of his or her career simply comparing one context with another, and another, and another. An alternative approach is to specify a limited number of dimensions that account for virtually every context. Core characteristics are identified that are present, in varying degrees, in many contexts. Individual situations can then be placed within the matrix of general dimensions. The value of the latter approach is that it parsimoniously identifies relatively few though very general dimensions of writing contexts.

In our reconceptualization we opted for the latter technique (Daly, T. Miller, & Meyer, 1984). There are at least eight dimensions of writing situations. They are (a) the degree of evaluation perceived present in the setting, (b) the amount of perceived task ambiguity, (c) the degree of conspicuousness felt by writers, (d) the perceived level of task difficulty, (e) the amount of prior experience writers feel they have for a task, (f) the personal salience or centrality of the task to writers, (g) the degree of novelty attached to both setting and task, and (h) the perception by writers of their audiences' likely reactions to and interests in the topic. Two points about these eight dimensions are critical. First, they are all perceived variables. It is impossible for anyone other than the writer to adequately or accurately judge a situation by its contextual characteristics. Attempts by others to judge the contextual nature of a situation, where it falls along the various continua, only approximate at best the writer's perceptions. Second, the role of these variables (along with other potential contextual dimensions) cannot be underestimated. People respond to the situations they work within. By knowing the nature of those situations, the understanding of a writer's performance is clearly aided. It is amazing that to date so little work in writing has focused directly on the contextual characteristics of setting where writing occurs.

The second major category of situational attitudes and beliefs is labeled "responses to the writing situation." These constructs, in some cases, may be seen as intervening between the various contextual dimensions and the "outcome" variables discussed below. The first construct is "situational writing apprehension." This is the fear and anxiety experienced by writers as they engage in a particular writing activity. The anxiety has two interrelated components: anxiety about the task and anxiety about the writing situation. Daly and Hailey (1984) provide further discussion of the construct. The second construct included among responses is "process knowledge." Considerable theory and research suggests that the way in which individuals approach writing tasks affects their products. Certain process behaviors are expected to contribute to more effective composing. To date, process behaviors have been conceived of in terms of dispositions or knowledge—that is, writers are conceived as varying in the degree to which they are predisposed or able to engage in the behaviors. One example of this dispositional orientation is research contrasting the composing of expert and novice writers. While the dispositional approach is important, it's just as important to recognize that situational characteristics can influence whether and how in the various processes. Since writers vary their enactment of different process strategies in different contexts, a situationally based construct is a useful addition to our understanding of writers' process behaviors.

The third major category of situational attitudes and beliefs is "outcomes." Writing outcomes are classed into three groups: cognitive, behavioral, and affective. The cognitive group is composed of attributions, judgments of consciousness arousal, and perceived situational utility. All of these are similar to the cognitive constructs discussed in the section on dispositional attitudes and beliefs. Here, however, they are framed as cognitive responses to varying situational characteristics. Writers may explain their performance on specific tasks with attributions to luck, effort, task difficulty, or ability. Situations may arouse varying levels of consciousness about writing. And some settings and tasks may elicit the perception of the utility of writing more than others. The second cluster of outcomes is the behavioral group composed of blocking, procrastination, tenacity, and frequency. While each has a dispositional meaning, each also can be conceptualized in a situational sense. That is, each can be affected in significant ways by the particular contextual characteristics of a writing task. The final cluster of outcomes is composed of four affective variables and a composite attitude toward the written product. The four affective variables are judgment of how successful writers feel they were in completing the task, how much they enjoyed the task, their perceptions of the audience reaction to their writing, and their certainty of the outcome. The construct of attitudes toward the written product is identical to the one described for the affective dimension of dispositional attitudes, with the exception that its various components are tied directly to the immediate writing task. The various components represent some of the feelings writers may have when they finish composing.

Conclusion

This chapter has summarized recent research on writing apprehension and related constructs as well as introduced a broad conceptualization of attitudes and beliefs people have about writing. For the past eight to ten years, serious and intensive scholarship has attempted to measure and validate the apprehension construct. The many studies reviewed in this chapter indicate that the construct is both measurable and valid. Future investigations must be conducted to broaden the construct, exploring the entire subjective world of the writer. An initial attempt at such investigation has been made in this chapter by explicating a theoretical typology of writers' attitudes and beliefs. This typology opens up a wealth of opportunities for future research.

ACKNOWLEDGMENTS

The author would like to acknowledge the aid of Thomas Miller and Stephen Witte in the writing of this chapter.

NOTES

1. While writing apprehension is conceived of as a continuous variable, it is descriptively easier to talk of prototypically high and low apprehension. Throughout this chapter, reference will be made to highs and lows. Implicit in these descriptions should be the understanding that underlying the dichotomy is a continuum, anywhere along which an individual may lie. Further, no perfect, one-to-one match between behaviors and apprehension is suggested (Jaccard & Daly, 1980). Nor is there an assumption that a person's writing is solely affected by apprehension. The impact of the disposition is obviously affected by various other characteristics, including different situational parameters (Daly & Hailey, 1984).

2. Daly and M. D. Miller chose the term "apprehension" over the more familiar terms "fear" or "anxiety" because of the historical definitional ambiguity of the latter two labels. Freudian psychology and contemporary psychology are at odds over the meanings of both. Rather than immerse themselves in a potentially distracting and unprofitable definitional morass, Daly and Miller opted for the more neutral term "apprehension." For expository purposes in this chapter, "apprehension," "anxiety," and "attitude" are often used interchangeably.

3. The dimensionality of the Daly–Miller measure has not been carefully examined since the first study. Burgoon and Hale (1983a, 1983b) suggest the instrument has three factors which they label ease in writing, enjoyment of writing, and rewards in writing. The three dimensions have strong intercorrelations but, at least in their studies, yield distinctly different correlations with writing behaviors. Stacks, Boozer, and Lally (1983) also argue for the multidimensionality of the construct, although they devise new items to assess many of their proposed dimensions. A useful avenue for future research would be an exploration of the dimensionality of the measure. At the same time, a strong argument, based on both parsimony and the high average intercorrelation among factors, can be proffered for the value of a unidimensional measure for purposes of assessment.

4. In the original article presenting the scales (Daly & M. D. Miller, 1975b), there was an error in the presentation of the formula used to score the writing-apprehension measure: The plus and minus signs were inadvertently interchanged in the formula.

5. A conceptual issue needs mentioning. Research attempting to link a very general personality disposition such as writing apprehension to very specific behaviors has often been indicted because of the low magnitude of relationship that is typically

observed. Two considerations should moderate this critique. First, attitudes and personality are not, per se, expected to be linked in a one-to-one way with behavior. If they were, either the attitude and personality construct or the behavior index would be unnecessary. Second, and more important, general measures should not be expected to strongly relate to specific indices. Jaccard and Daly (1980) have made this point explicit. A very general measure such as an attitude or personality questionnaire should be strongly linked to a very general measure of behavior, not to a measure of a specific behavior.

6. There is another topic that should be added to the list of kinds of correlates of writing apprehension. This is the case of "writer's cramp." The topic of writer's cramp has for a long time evoked some interest among psychiatrists and behavioral psychologists (for short histories, see Arora & Murthy, 1976; Beech, 1960; Crisp & Moldofsky, 1965; Gibson, 1972; Pai, 1947; Sylvester & Liversedge, 1960). The cramp typically manifests itself in tremors and spasms of the muscle of the hand, forearm, and sometimes upper arm and in excessive pressure exerted by the writer's thumb against the pen (Liversedge & Sylvester, 1955). Writer's cramp rarely occurs before age 20 (Gibson, 1972), its origins are unclear, and its direct relationship with writing apprehension has not been empirically established. However, most of the theoretical work on the topic relates it to some sort of anxiety that is tied in some way to writing. The typical patient is able to use his or her hands in all situations other than ones that demand writing (Sylvester & Liversedge, 1955). This is not to say that anyone suffering from high apprehension necessarily experiences cramp. Rather, it seems likely that many of those who have extreme cases of writer's cramp are also highly apprehensive (Slyvester & Liversedge, 1955).

7. In a different vein of research on development of apprehension, Sanavio (1982) proposed a four-stage model of the development and maintenance of writer's cramp. The first stage is a temporary disruption in writing by neuromuscular tensions that arise with increased arousal under stress. In the second stage, the cramping becomes conditioned as the subject focuses on the disruptions while he or she writes. The cramp, in essence, becomes a classically conditioned response to the stress. Escape and avoidance behaviors are learned by the individual during the third stage as ways of reducing the conditioned tension. Some of the more common escape behaviors described by Sanavio include turning the wrist inward, tightly gripping the pen, rubbing hands, and a variety of other behaviors akin to behavioral tics. The fourth phase is the development of a group of cognitive behaviors that tend to maintain the cramping response.

8. Representative research in this area includes Beech (1960); Boice (1982a, 1982b, 1983); Cornelio, Levine, and Wolpe (1980); Davis (1983); Harris (1971); Jones (1975); Liversedge and Sylvester (1955); Menks (1979); Minninger (1977); Passman (1976); and Sanavio (1982).

9. Powers, Cook, and Meyer (1979) have demonstrated that there are classroom settings where writing apprehension can be *increased* over the term of an eight-week basic composition course. They found that, overall, apprehension increased significantly for the basic writers enrolled in the course. Another finding was that individuals who were initially classified as low-apprehensives tended to increase their apprehension during the course (although regression effects and impression management concerns need to be considered here). This research seems to suggest that there are cases where composition instruction may have an undesirable effect, that of making the student more apprehensive about writing. This idea was first introduced by Daly and M. D. Miller (1975b), who suggested that required writing may do little more than raise the level of anxiety of already anxious students.

10. Daly and Hailey (1984) devised two measures of situational anxiety. The first measured situational anxiety about a writing assignment; the second assessed anxiety

about the situation. The two were strongly related to one another. Both measures had only moderate relationships with trait or dispositional writing apprehension, suggesting the importance of considering both situational and dispositional issues.

11. Before specifying each of these dimensions, it is important to raise two issues. First, as is the case throughout this chapter, the exposition of the constructs makes use of extreme descriptions, even though in reality each construct is perceived to have an underlying continuity. Thus, for example, when high evaluative situations are contrasted with low evaluative situations, the implication should not be that there are only two levels of evaluation but rather that there is a continuum ranging from high to low evaluation along which different situations fall. Or when a writer is described as perceiving much utility in writing or as thinking of writing as comparatively useless, the continuum from high utility to low utility should be understood. Second, dispositions and situational reactions are inherently intertwined. Dispositions affect situational reactions and the particular situation may make a particular disposition more salient than other dispositions.

12. Obviously, the person can utilize all four of the attributions to varying degrees at the same time. For instance, he or she might suggest that luck and task difficulty played major roles in his or her performance while effort and ability made only minor contributions. Further, the individual may offer attributions of his or her performance other than those described. The four explicated here were selected because they have played such a predominant role in attributional research in fields such as social psychology.

REFERENCES

Adams, V. A. (1971). Study of the effects of two methods of teaching composition to twelfth-graders. (Doctoral dissertation, University of Illinois). *Dissertation Abstracts International, 32*, 5526.

Aldrich, P. G. (1979). *Adult writers: Some factors that interfere with effective writing*. Washington, D.C. Educational Resources Information Center. (ERIC Document Reproduction Service No. ED 209 675)

Aldrich, P. G. (1982). Adult writers: Some factors that interfere with effective writing. *Research in the Teaching of English, 16*, 298–300.

Arora, M., & Murthy, R. S. (1976). Treatment of writer's cramp by progression from paintbrush in supinated hand. *Journal of Behavioral Therapy and Experimental Psychiatry, 7*, 345–347.

Auman, W. W. (1970). *The effects of process intervention on the attitudes and learning in a college freshman composition class*. Unpublished doctoral dissertation, University Michigan.

Bartholomae, D. (1979). Teaching basic writing: An alternative to basic skills. *Journal of Basic Writing, 2*, 85–109.

Basile, D. D. (1982). Do attitudes about writing change as composition skills improve? *Community College Review, 9*, 22–27.

Beech, H. R. (1960). The symptomatic treatment of writer's cramp. In H. J. Eysenck (Ed.), *Behavior therapy and neuroses* (pp. 349–376). New York: Pergamon.

Bell, E., & Price, A. (1980). *Some effects of induced grade anxiety on motivation and performance in composition sections*. Paper presented at the annual meeting of the Pennsylvania Council of Teachers of English, Allentown. Washington, D.C. Educational Resources Information Center. (ERIC Document Reproduction Service No. ED 197 379)

Berger, E. M. (1952). The relation between expressed acceptance of self and expressed acceptance of others. *Journal of Abnormal and Social Psychology, 47*, 778–782.

Blake, R. W. (1976). Assessing English and language arts teachers' attitudes towards writers and writing. *The English Record, 27*, 87–97.

Bloom, L. Z. *Myths and mastery. Teaching anxious writers: Implications and applications of research.* Undated manuscript.

Bloom, L. Z. *The composing processes of anxious and non-anxious writers: A naturalistic study.* Paper presented at the annual Conference of College Composition and Communication, Washington, D.C.

Bloom, L. Z. (in press). Identifying and reducing writing anxiety: Writing anxiety workshops. In D. Butturff (Ed.), *The psychology of composition.* Conway, AR: Language and Style Books.

Boice, R. (1982a, August). *Does imposing contingency management on writing impede or facilitate the appearance of creative ideas?* Paper presented at the annual conference of the American Psychological Association, Washington, D.C.

Boice, R. (1982b). Increasing the writing productivity of "blocked" academicians. *Behaviour Research and Therapy, 20*, 197–207.

Boice, R. (1983). Experimental vs. clinical treatments of writing blocks. *Journal of Consulting and Clinical Psychology, 51*, 183–191.

Book, V. (1976, November). *Some effects of apprehension on writing performance.* Paper presented at the annual conference of the Western Speech Communication Association, San Francisco.

Burgoon, J., & Hale, J. L. (1983a). Dimensions of communication reticence and their impact on verbal encoding. *Communication Quarterly, 31*, 302–311.

Burgoon, J., & Hale, J. L. (1983b). A research note on the dimensions of communication reticence. *Communication Quarterly, 31*, 238–248.

Callewaert, H. (1927a). Pathogénie de la crampe des écrivains. Epreuve de la rééducation: 1. Présentation des maladies. *Journal of Neurology and Psychiatry, 6*, 371–377

Callewaert, H. (1927b). Pathogénie de la crampe des écrivains: Epreuve de la rééducation: 2. Discussion. *Journal of Neurology and Psychiatry, 6*, 419–426.

Callewaert, H. (1930). Pathogénie de la crampe des écrivains: Influence des techniques professionales défecteuses. *Journal of Neurology and Psychiatry, 30*, 814–822.

Claypool, S. H. (1980). *Teacher writing apprehension: Does it affect writing assignments across the curriculum?* Washington, D.C.: Educational Research Information Center. (ERIC Document Reproduction Service No. ED 216 387)

Cornelio, R., Levine, B. A., & Wolpe, J. (1980) The treatment of handwriting anxiety by an *in vivo* desensitization procedure. *Journal of Behavioral Therapy and Experimental Psychiatry, 11*, 49–51.

Craven, J. (1980). *Motivating reluctant students to write.* Paper presented at the annual meeting of the Rocky Mountain Language Association, Denver, CO. Washington, D.C.: Educational Research Information Center. (ERIC Document Reproduction Service No. ED 198 547)

Crisp, A. H., & Moldofsky, H. (1965). A psychosomatic study of writer's cramp. *British Journal of Psychiatry, 111*, 841–858.

Daly, J. A. (1976). *Quarterly judgements and writing apprehension in a composition course.* Unpublished manuscript.

Daly, J. A. (1977). The effects of writing apprehension on message encoding. *Journalism Quarterly, 54*, 566–572.

Daly, J. A. (1978). Writing apprehension and writing competency. *Journal of Educational Research, 72*, 10–14.

Daly, J. A. (1979a). *Teacher explanations for writing apprehension.* Unpublished manuscript.

Daly, J. A. (1979b). Writing apprehension in the classroom: Teacher role expectancies of the apprehensive writer. *Research in the Teaching of English, 13*, 37–44.

Daly, J. A., Bell, R. A., & Korinek, J. (1983). *Interrelationships of subject specific attitudes.* Unpublished manuscript, University of Texas, Department of Speech Communication, Austin, TX.

Daly, J. A., & Hailey, J. L. (1984). Putting the situation into writing research: State and disposition as parameters of writing apprehension. In R. Beach & L. S. Bridwell (Eds.), *New directions in composition research* (pp. 259–273). New York: Guilford.

Daly, J. A., & McCroskey, J. C. (Eds.). (1984). *Avoiding communications: Shyness, reticence, and communication apprehension.* Beverly Hills, CA: Sage.

Daly, J. A., & Miller, M. D. (1975a). Apprehension of writing as a predictor of message intensity. *Journal of Psychology, 89,* 175–177.

Daly, J. A., & Miller, M. D. (1975b). The empirical development of an instrument of writing apprehension. *Research in the Teaching of English, 9,* 242–249.

Daly, J. A., & Miller, M. D. (1975c). Further studies in writing apprehension: SAT scores, success expectations, willingness to take advanced courses, and sex differences. *Research in the Teaching of English, 9,* 250–256.

Daly, J. A., & Miller, T. (1983a). *Writers' dispositional attitudes and beliefs: Conceptualization, measurement, and interrelationships.* Paper presented at the annual conference of the American Educational Research Association, Montreal, Quebec, Canada.

Daly, J. A., & Miller, T. (1983b). *Writers' situational attitudes and beliefs: Conceptualization, measurement, and interrelationships.* Paper presented at the annual conference of the American Educational Reseach Association, Montreal, Quebec, Canada.

Daly, J. A., Miller, T., & Meyer, P. (1984). *Empirical structure of writers' attitudes and beliefs.* Paper presented at the annual conference of the American Educational Research Association, New Orleans, LA.

Daly, J. A., & Shamo, W. (1976). Writing apprehension and occupational choice. *Journal of Occupational Psychology, 49,* 55–56.

Daly, J. A., & Shamo, W. (1978). Academic decisions as a function of writing apprehension. *Research in the Teaching of English, 12,* 119–126.

Daly, J. A., & Wilson, D. (1983). Writing apprehension, self-esteem, and personality. *Research in the Teaching of English, 17,* 327–341.

Daly, J. A., & Witte, S. P. (1982). *Relationship of writing apprehension to teachers' classroom behaviors and emphasis on writing activities.* Paper presented at the annual conference of the American Educational Research Association, New York.

Davis, D. M. (1983). *Using systematic desensitization as a treatment procedure for writing apprehension.* Paper presented at the annual conference of the International Communication Association, Dallas, TX.

Diamond, I. M., Haugen, N. S., & Kean, J. M. (Eds.). (1980). *A guide to helping the reluctant writer.* Washington, DC: Educational Resources Information Center. (ERIC Document Reproduction Service No. ED 193 654)

Dickson, F. (1978). *Writing apprehension and test anxiety as predictors of ACT scores.* Unpublished master's thesis, West Virginia University, Morgantown, WV.

Dreussi, R. M. E. (1976). A study of the effects of expressive writing on study attitudes (Doctoral dissertation, University of Texas). *Dissertation Abtracts International, 37,* 2806.

Duke, C. R. (1980, Winter). Writing apprehension: 2. Where does fear of writing come from? *Illinois English Bulletin,* pp. 16–23.

Durrell, L. (1976). [Interview]. In G. Plimpton (Ed.), *Writers at work* (2d Series, pp. 257–282). New York: Penguin.

Faigley, L., Daly, J. A., & Witte, S. P. (1981). The role of writing apprehension in writing performance and writing competence. *Journal of Educational Research, 75,* 16–21.

Federn, P. (1957). The neurotic style (W. Federn, Trans.). *Psychiatric Quarterly, 31,* 681–

689. (Originally published in *Abhandlungen aus der neurologie, psychiatrie, psychologie und ihren grenzgebieten* [Vienna], 1930, *61*, 194–201)

Flower, L., & Hayes, J. (1979). *A process model of composition* (Tech. Rep. No. 3). Pittsburgh, PA: Carnegie-Mellon University, Document Design Project.

Fowler, B., & Kroll, B. M. (1980). Relationship of apprehension about writing to performance as measured by grades in a college course on composition. *Psychological Reports, 46*, 583–586.

Fowler, B., & Ross, D. (1982). The comparative validities of differential placement measures for college composition courses. *Educational and Psychological Measurement, 42*, 1107–1115.

Fox, R. F. (1980). Treatment of writing apprehension and its effects on composition. *Research in the Teaching of English, 14*, 39–49.

Garcia, R. J. (1977). An investigation of relationships: Writing apprehension, syntactic performance, and writing quality (Doctoral dissertation, Arizona State University). *Dissertation Abstracts International, 77*, 4211.

Gere, A. R., Schuessler, B. R., & Abbott, R. D. (1984). Measuring teachers' attitudes toward writing instruction. In R. Beach & L. S. Bridwell (Eds.), *New directions in composition research* (pp. 348–361). New York: Guilford.

Gibson, H. B. (1972). Writer's cramp: A behavioral approach. *Behavioral Research and Therapy, 10*, 371–380.

Glynn, S. M., Muth, K. D., Matthews, J. L., & Garrido, M. (1982). *Influence of verbal SAT and anxiety on persuasive writing.* Paper presented at the annual conference of the American Educational Research Association, New York.

Gorrell, D. K. (1980, Winter). Writing apprehension: 1. Combating fear of failure. *Illinois English Bulletin*, pp. 9–15.

Harris, M. B. (1974). Accelerating dissertation writing: Case study. *Psychological Reports, 34*, 984–986.

Harvley-Felder, Z. C. (1978). Some factors relating to writing apprehension: An exploratory study (Doctoral dissertation, University of North Carolina). *Dissertation Abstracts International, 39*, 6503.

Hayes, C. G. (1981, March). *Exploring apprehension: Composing processes of apprehsensive and non-apprehensive intermediate freshman writers.* Paper presented at the annual Conference on College Freshman Composition and Communication.

Hemingway, E. (1976). [Interview]. In G. Plimpton (Ed.), *Writers at work* (2d Series, pp. 215–210). New York: Penguin.

Isherwood, C. (1976). [Interview]. In G. Plimpton (Ed.), *Writers at work* (4th Series, pp. 209–242). New York: Penguin.

Jaccard, J., & Daly, J. A. (1980). Personality traits and multiple act criteria. *Human Communication Research, 6*, 367–377.

Jeroski, S. F., & Conry, R. F. (1981). *Development and field application of the Attitude Toward Writing Scale.* Paper presented at the annual conference of the American Educational Research Association, Los Angeles.

Jones, A. C. (1975). Grandiosity blocks writing projects. *Transactional Analysis Journal, 5*, 415.

Kail, R. V., & Bisanz, J. (1982). Cognitive strategies. In C. R. Puff (Ed.), *Handbook of research methods in human memory and cognition* (pp. 229–257). New York: Academic Press.

King, B. (1979). *Measuring attitudes toward writing: The King Construct Scale.* Paper presented at the annual Conference on College Composition and Communication, Minneapolis, MN. Washington, DC: Educational Resources Information Center. (ERIC Document Reproduction Service No. ED 172 258)

Kroll, B. M. (1979). Assessing students' attitudes toward writing. *The English Record, 30,* 6–9.

Liversedge, L. A., & Sylvester, J. D. (1955). Conditioning techniques in the treatment of writer's cramp. *Lancet, 7,* 1147–1149.

Mack, K., & Skjei, E. (1979). *Overcoming writing blocks.* Los Angeles: J. P. Tarcher.

Menks, F. (1979). Behavioral techniques in the treatment of a writing phobia. *The American Journal of Occupational Therapy, 33,* 102–107.

Miller, M. D., & Daly, J. A. (1975, April). *The development of a measure of writing apprehension.* Paper presented at the annual conference of the International Communication Association, Chicago.

Minninger, J. (1977). Reteachering—Unlearning writing blocks. *Transactional Analysis Journal, 7,* 1.

Myers, I. B. (1962). *The Myers–Briggs Type Indicator Manual.* Palo Alto, CA: Consulting Psychologists Press.

National Assessment of Educational Progress. (1980). *Writing achievement, 1969–79*: Results from the Third National Writing Assessment (Vols. 1-3). Denver, CO: Education Commission of the States. Washington, DC: Educational Resources Information Center. (ERIC Document Reproduction Service No. ED 196 042, 043, 044)

Pai, M. N. (1947). The nature and treatment of "writer's cramp." *The Journal of Mental Science* (now *The British Journal of Psychiatry*), *93,* 68–81.

Passman, R. (1976). A procedure for eliminating writer's block in a college student. *Journal of Behavior Therapy and Experimental Psychiatry, 7,* 297–298.

Perl, S. (1979). The composing processes of unskilled college writers. *Research in the Teaching of English, 13,* 317–336.

Pervin, L., & Lilly, R. (1967). Social desirability and self-ideal self ratings on the semantic differential. *Educational and Psychological Measurement, 27,* 845.

Pfeifer, J. (1982). *The relationship of personality trait characteristics to writing apprehension.* Unpublished manuscript, Abilene Christian University, Abilene, TX.

Powell, B. J. (1980). *The importance students place on writing and their desire to succeed academically influence the degree to which their level of writing proficiency is raised: A comparison of students' attitudes and success in writing.* Unpublished manuscript, Virginia State University, Petersburg, VA.

Powers, W. G., Cook, J. A., & Meyer, R. (1979). The effect of compulsory writing on writing apprehension. *Research in the Teaching of English, 13,* 225–230.

Reece, S. C. (1980, March). *The journal keeps the person in the process.* Paper presented at the annual Conference on College Composition and Communication, Washington, DC.

Reed, W. M., Vandett, N., & Burton, J. K. (1983). *The effects of writing skills, sex, preparation and knowledge of the composing process on writing apprehension.* Washington, DC: Educational Resources Information Center (ERIC Document Reproduction Service No. ED 228657)

Richardson, E. M. (1980). The quality of essays written for distant and intimate audiences by high and low apprehensive two-year college freshmen (Doctoral dissertation, University of Cincinnati). *Dissertation Abstracts International, 41,* 971.

Richmond, V. P., & Dickson, F. (1980, April). *Two studies of the validity of the writing apprehension test.* Paper presented at the annual conference of the Eastern Communication Association, Ocean City, MD.

Rose, M. (1980). Rigid rules, inflexible plans, and the stifling of language: A cognitivist analysis of writer's block. *College Composition and Communication, 31,* 389–401.

Rosen, R. D. (1981, April 12). The pen is a heavy oar. *New York Times Book Review,* pp. 3, 32–34.

Rosenberg, M. (1965). *Society and the adolescent self-image.* Princeton, NJ: Princeton University Press.

Salovey, P., & Haar, M. (1983, April). *Treating writing anxiety: Cognitive restructuring and writing process training.* Paper presented at the annual conference of the American Educational Research Association, Montreal, Quebec, Canada.

Sanavio, E. (1982). An operant approach to the treatment of writer's cramp. *Journal of Behavioral Therapy and Experimental Psychiatry, 13,* 69–72.

Schultz, L. M., & Meyers, G. D. (1981). *Measuring writing apprehension in required freshman composition and upper-level writing courses.* Paper presented at the annual conference on College Composition and Communication, Dallas, TX. Washington, DC: Educational Resources Information Center. (ERIC Document Reproduction Service No. ED 203 326)

Selfe, C. L. (1981a). *The composing process of four high and four low writing apprehensives: A modified case-study.* Unpublished doctoral dissertation, University of Texas.

Selfe, C. L. (1981b). *The composing processes of high and low writing apprehensives: A modified case-study.* Washington, DC: Educational Resources Information Center. (ERIC Document Reproduction Service No. ED 216 354).

Sommers, N. (1978). Revision in the composing process: A case study of college freshmen and experienced writers (Doctoral dissertation, University of Oklahoma). *Dissertation Abstracts International, 39,* 5374.

Spielberger, C., Gorsuch, R., & Lushene, R. (1970). *Manual for the state–trait Anxiety Inventory.* Palo Alto, CA: Consulting Psychologists Press.

Stack, D. W., Boozer, R. W., & Lally, T. (1983). *Syntactic language correlates of written communication apprehension.* Paper presented at the annual conference of the Southwest Division of the American Business Communication Association, Houston, TX.

Stafford, L., & Daly, J. A. (1984). Conversational memory: The effects of instructional set and recall mode on memory for natural conversations. *Human Communication Research, 10,* 379–902.

Sylvester, J. D., & Liversedge, L. A. (1960). Conditioning and the occupational cramps: In H. Eysenck (Ed.), *Behaviour therapy and the neuroses* (pp. 334–347). Oxford: Pergamon.

Thompson, M. O. (1978). The development and evaluation of a language study approach to a college course in freshman composition. Unpublished doctoral dissertation, The American University.

Thompson, M. O. (1979a). *A study of writing anxiety. The effects of several classroom strategies.* Washington, DC: Educational Resources Information Center. (ERIC Document Reproduction Service No. ED 206 339)

Thompson, M. O. (1979b). *Writing anxiety and freshman composition.* Paper presented at the annual conference of the Northeastern Conference on English in the Two-Year College, Pittsburgh, PA. Washington, DC: Educational Resources Information Center. (ERIC Document Reproduction Service No. ED 183 235)

Thompson, M. O. (1981). *The returning student: Writing anxiety and general anxiety.* Paper presented at the annual conference of the Northeast Regional Conference on English in the Two-Year College, Baltimore, MD. Washington, DC: Educational Resources Information Center. (ERIC Document Reproduction Service No. ED 214 558)

Toth, D. (1975). *The effects of writing apprehension on attitude change in the counterattitudinal paradigm.* Paper presented at the annual conference of the Speech Communication Association, Houston, TX.

Updike, J. (1982). *Bech is back.* New York: Knopf.

Upper, D. (1974). The unsuccessful self-treatment of a case of "writer's block." *Journal of Applied Behavior Analysis, 7,* 497.

Veit, R. (1980). *Reducing anxiety in writing instruction*. Paper presented at the annual meeting of the National Council of Teachers of English, Cincinnati, OH.

Wagner, E. N. (1975). The impact of composition grading on the attitudes and writing performance of freshman English students (Doctoral dissertation, University of Virginia). *Dissertation Abstracts, International, 36*, 5232.

Walker, J. R. (1978). Writing avoidance: A professional approach. *Personal and Guidance Journal, 57*, 218–219.

Walters, S. A., Weiss, R. H., & Maggitti, P. (1980). *Writing apprehension: Implications for teaching, writing, and concept clarity*. Paper presented at the annual conference on College Composition and Communication, Washington, DC.

Weil, B. H., & Lane, J. C. (1956, December 17). Psychological barrier to writing. *Chemical and Engineering News*, pp. 6244–6248.

Weiner, B. (1974). *Achievement motivation and attribution theory*. Morristown, NJ: Silver Burdett.

Zimmerman, J., & Silverman, R. (1982). The effects of selected variables on writing anxiety. *Diagnostique, 8*, 62–70.

An Apprehensive Writer Composes 4

CYNTHIA L. SELFE

The term "writing apprehension," originally coined in 1975 by Miller and Daly, refers to a generalized tendency to experience "some form of anxiety" when faced with a writing task (Miller & Daly, 1975, p. 2). To most teachers of composition, this construct is an intuitively credible one. They know that a class seldom goes by, either at the elementary, secondary, or college level, without yielding one or more students who seem to allow their dread of composing to come between them and effective written expression. And yet our progress in learning how to cope with highly apprehensive writers in the composition classroom has been limited by the absence of research on this concept since Miller and Daly introduced the term a decade ago.

Although Daly has continued to refine the theoretical construct of writing apprehension and to explore the statistical correlations and predictive functions of the construct with regard to personality measures and measures of group performance, only in depth, single-subject studies can begin to tell us exactly how writing apprehension affects the composing process. Few studies of this kind have been completed. This chapter describes a case study of one highly apprehensive writer named Bev and takes a detailed look at how her apprehension affected her composing activities.

Procedures

The investigation reported here took place at The University of Texas in the fall semester of 1979. Bev, after scoring 93 out of 130 possible

Cynthia L. Selfe. Humanities Department, Michigan Technological University, Houghton, Michigan.

points on the Daly-Miller Writing-Apprehension Scale (Miller & Daly, 1975), was selected as a case study subject and scheduled for three different observation sessions within a period of two weeks. During the first of these sessions, Bev described her regular composing processes, making a detailed report of how she would go about writing a theme for a freshman English class. During the second session, Bev was asked to think aloud while composing in response to the following freshman theme assignment.

> Pretend that you have been asked to come back to your old high school to give an assembly for college-bound seniors on "Those Things I Wish I had Known before I Went to College." . . . When you sit down to write this speech, you realize that the most effective way to get your point across to these skeptical seniors would be to tell them a story about something that has happened to you in college.[1]

Bev was encouraged to respond as she would normally to a composition assignment and to take as much time as she needed to complete the task. During the third and final session, Bev was asked to review a videotape of her composing-aloud session and to discuss the differences between those processes she felt she used normally and those she felt she exhibited only in the investigative setting. All of Bev's comments during these sessions were audiotaped and later transcribed for analysis.

Background: Bev's Composing Attitudes

Bev, an 18-year-old freshman music major with a Scholastic Aptitude Test score of 480 and a 2.54 grade point average, called her fear of writing "realistic." She maintained that she had never been taught "how to really write" and remembered doing very little writing during her elementary school years. Even in high school, Bev recalled, she wrote "very few papers . . . a book report or something in a science class . . . on an experiment." Bev linked what she saw as her limited writing practice and instruction in elementary and high school to the writing problems she was experiencing in her classes the The University of Texas. She blamed her status as a "straight C student" in part on her past English teachers.

Because Bev lacked confidence in her past writing instruction, she had become increasingly apprehensive about having to write in an academic setting and had come to have little faith in her own composing skills: "I will never understand . . . writing. It just doesn't . . . I could sit there all day, but I just don't grasp it. You know every year I get, 'Write it this way; write it this way,' or 'This time do it this way." But you know I just don't know how." Feeling that she lacked the skills necessary to produce a successful composition, Bev found the process of academic writing far more punishing than rewarding and repeatedly used the words "hate" and "fear" in connection with her writing. Much of Bev's fear of writing stemmed from her belief that teachers expected "letter-perfect" papers from their students—papers she felt she could not deliver.

One result of this uncertainty and apprehension was that Bev had ritualized procrastination to the point where it had become a necessary part of her composing process: "I have this procrastination problem about writing papers because I'm so scared about having them graded . . . pressure is definitely a big factor in my writing. I get an assignment, stick it away, and mark the [due] date on my calendar." It was only on the day before an assignment was to be collected that the pressure of a due-date would begin to outweigh her apprehension about writing. Only then could Bev force herself to retreat to her favorite library cubicle to "write furiously" until she had an acceptable draft. To Bev as a highly apprehensive writer, this avoidance behavior had its own strange logic. If no part of a paper had been written, nothing could be criticized. And when compositions *had* to be done, if they were written and typed at the last possible moment, then Bev could always attribute failure to the harried circumstances under which the paper was composed.

Bev's apprehension about her past writing instruction, her limited repertoire of writing skills, and her inability to attack academic writing problems successfully affected her composing activities during the composing-aloud session of the investigation.

Bev's Composing Session

BEV'S ESSAY

College begins a totally different lifestyle within a time period of just a few short months. College is perhaps the biggest step one takes in life. It seems as though a student is expected to mature drastically from a giggly, immature high school student to a mature responsible adult in three months when it took them eighteen years to become a giggly, immature senior. College is a time to accept responsibility for oneself and one's activities. But along with this adjustment in one's personality, one must also concentrate on studying—the main reason for making the grade in college. College has always been a symbol of freedom. All at once there is nobody making suggestions as to how you spend your time.

When I began to college, I had decided to make college the most worthwhile thing that I could do. I decided that my purpose was to study and practise music from early morning until late at night. There was no use wasting money on college if I was going to spend time partying. After about two weeks, my sister finally confronted me with the fact that I had turned into one of the biggest bores on campus. She explained that by studying constantly I was losing opportunityes to learn other things than just facts from books. I had also discouraged friendships with people because I was always on my way to the library.

After my sister's talk, I began to see how I had shut myself off from the real object behind college. After my realization; classes, tests, and early morning practise sessions became more bearable because I could always count on a friend to cheer me up or just listen to a few moments of heavy self-pity. And I could help my friends in the same way.

Granted, you must regulate and restrict you extra caricular activities but without them college is merely facts on a page and has no relationship to real life. College is a time to learn from books but it is also a time to learn about human behavior through friendships and dealings with other people. If you only practise one aspect of college, you will be wasting more than just money, you will be wasting several informative years of your life.

AN OVERVIEW OF THE SESSION

When Bev began to compose in response to the assignment, her initial apprehension encouraged her to abbreviate her composing efforts, to write quickly and "get it over with" as soon as possible. Thus Bev allowed herself only 40 seconds of prewriting "panic" before she began to compose a broad statement she called the "topic sentence" of her composition. Beyond this 40-second period, she engaged in no other prewriting activities. Using this statement as a starting point and a general stimulus, Bev began to free write—exploring one idea in connection with her topic sentence, pausing briefly when she came to a dead end or when she lost her tenuous train of thought, and then taking off in a new direction: "I just started writing and that led to something else. And then, every now and again . . . I'd stop and start on something else." After 21 minutes of composing in this fashion, Bev had explored five or six very different ideas in connection with her topic sentence and was no closer to identifying a focus for her theme than she had been when she began her draft. Although Bev admitted that she had often had to search for a topic through half of a paper before deciding "exactly where . . . to go with it for sure," she was nonetheless frustrated by her lack of direction in this theme: "I think I'm off the track here, I really do. I know what I'm trying to get at, but it's just not coming out that way." At this point Bev's composing was hurried and yet, because she had no concept of where her essay was leading her, often hesitant: "It seems as though a student is expected to—expected to *what* for Pete's sake?"

Bev did not find a focus for her essay until 23 minutes into the composing-aloud session, when she remembered a story involving her older sister that she could use to illustrate one of the ideas she had touched on in her free writing. At this point it became clear that the writing Bev had done in the first half of the session had served primarily as a method of generating ideas and searching out a topic on which she could expand. But Bev's problems with her paper were far from over. Although she no longer had to worry about where her paper was going, she became concerned that the rather rambling introduction "didn't flow" into the more focused narrative that followed and that the entire effect was one of a "disorganized" composition.

As she continued to write the second half of her essay, Bev translated this apprehension that she was not writing a more structured theme into a concern for correctness at the sentence and word level; she began attending to mechanical correctness rather than to organizational and logical soundness. As a result of this concern, Bev devoted a full quarter of the time she spent on the initial draft of her paper to revising what she had just written.

By the time Bev reached the end of her first draft, she was able to conclude her paper with a fairly focused statement of her topic in the last sentence. She remained dissatisfied, however, with the structure and the coherence of her theme: "I think that's my problem. I don't think I do organize my writing, or I'd have a better idea of where I was going to go with this paper." The thrust of Bev's revision, which did not involve a major rewriting of the initial draft, was to tie the rambling introduction to the more focused narrative that followed. This process seemed a familiar one to Bev who explained that she often had to "go back . . . and fill in the gaps" in the papers she wrote. She eschewed major revisions that might have necessitated prolonged involvement in the writing process and instead primarily reworked phrases and single sentences, "adding something or exchanging something" with the aim of making the various parts of the paper adhere.

During the final moments of the session, Bev reread the entire paper ("Let's see how bad it is"), hoping to find that her later modifications had "done some good." She found, however, only a loosely connected pastiche of ideas that she evaluated negatively, rereading her own words in a mocking tone or making comments on her lack of verbal facility: "Jeez, that sounds so corny! I can't believe I wrote some of this stuff."

To a great extent, Bev's composing activities during this session were determined by her fear of academic writing. The speed at which she hurried through the composing process, her choice of writing strategies, her concern with mechanical correctness rather than with underlying structural soundness, and her truncated revising efforts resulted from her paucity of composing skills, her lack of confidence in the skills she did have, and her anxiety about engaging in a task for which she felt unprepared.

RACING THROUGH THE COMPOSING PROCESS

One of Bev's primary methods of reducing her apprehension about academic tasks in this session involved completing a first draft in what she described as a "mad, frantic, get-everything-you-can-down-on-paper rush." At this rapid pace, Bev wrote approximately 3 pages of material, 457 words, and 24 sentences in a session lasting 51 minutes and 15 seconds. Bev used this technique of writing "furiously until you run out of ideas" to produce a draft of a paper in a minimal amount of time and with a minimal amount of prewriting or revising.

From previous experience, Bev knew that this initial headlong rush would ensure her a quick, if not high quality, draft of her composition. This method was acceptable and even desirable to Bev as an apprehensive writer because she was less concerned with *what* she wrote than she was with "getting something down" and "finishing" the writing task in which she had been forced to engage.

COMPROMISING BETWEEN STRUCTURED AND UNSTRUCTURED WRITING

Before Bev even began to compose her essay about adpating to life in college, it became evident that her apprehension was heightened by the disparity she perceived between the processes she felt or suspected she should use to compose and those she actually did habitually use. On one hand, Bev believed in the efficacy of her normal free writing technique; it made a quick job of what was for her a very unpleasant task. On the other, she realized that writing successful compositions required "something else"—a "topic sentence," paragraphs that "relate to one specific thing . . . in the topic sentence," and a "conclusion" that reiterated the points made in the body of the essay. Because she suspected that such a structured essay required more careful and deliberate composing methods than those she generally employed and a set of writing skills that she suspected she lacked, the prospect of writing such a theme only made the task seem more formidable to the anxious freshman. Of course, Bev could have combined these two methods quite successfully by free writing a first draft and more carefully focusing and structuring subsequent drafts. However, she saw her free writing technique not as an exploratory tool that could lead to further drafts, but rather as a method that allowed her to abbreviate the writing process into "one, mad, frantic . . . rush."

To reconcile two conflicting approaches—one arising from her desire to complete the theme in one rapid burst of free writing and the other from her belief that a successful theme had to be carefully constructed according to a specific format—Bev settled on a compromise, taking a minute and a half to formulate a general topic sentence and then proceeding to "write furiously" in search of a real focus for her essay.

As she herself suspected, the extent to which Bev was able to employ a more structured approach duing this writing session was limited not only by her apprehension, which encouraged her to rush through the draft, but also by her limited repertoire of composing skills and strategies, a limitation that made her so anxious about writing in the first place. Bev commanded, for example, very few invention heuristics, outlining skills, or diagramming strategies that could help her give a coherent, global structure to her essay at the prewriting stage; and she knew few rewriting, reorganizing, or rethinking skills that could help her create a more structured essay during the drafting and postdrafting movements. Bev was in fact caught in an all too familiar bind. Her apprehension about writing had been sparked by an accurate perception of her limited composing skills, and yet that very apprehension kept her from involving herself in composing activities and thus exercising, perhaps improving, the skills she did have.

MISTAKING MECHANICAL CORRECTNESS FOR STRUCTURAL SOUNDNESS

During the remainder of her first draft, Bev translated her apprehension that she was not writing a more structured theme into a concern for accuracy at the sentence and word level, mistaking mechanical correctness for organizational and logical soundness. As a result of this concern, she spent 24.6 percent of her total drafting time editing or revising what she had just written.

This continual editing had several effects on Bev's composing processes. First, it forced her to establish a hesitant composing rhythm, at least once every sentence distracting her attention from matters of content and focusing it on matters of style and mechanics. For example, she began one sentence in her fourth paragraph with enthusiasm, trying to recall the lesson she learned from her sister: "After my sister's talk, I began to see for myself how I had shut myself off from the real meanen . . ." Realizing that "meanen" was a misspelling, Bev stopped writing, crossed out the first version, and substituted "meaning." She acknowledged, however, that she had forgotten what she was trying to say and went back to reread the sentence. As she did, she noted the repetition of "myself" and reread the sentence again before deciding to delete the first occurrence of that word. After effecting the deletion, Bev read the edited sentence again only to come to the conclusion that "meaning" should be changed to another word. In searching for a word to replace "meaning," Bev had to read the sentence two more times before she could retrieve and substitute the alternative word, "object." She then had to read the entire passage one last time before she could finish with the phrase "behind going to college." This particular sentence, which consisted of 23 words in its final version, took Bev 5 minutes and 51 seconds to compose.

This attention to matters of mechanical correctness at an early stage of her composition not only caused Bev to lose her train of thought but also served to distract her attention from larger, more important concerns such as how best to relate the ideas she had generated and which details to choose that would be most effective in presenting her narrative to the target audience. When her essay required carefully considered rhetorical changes, Bev was too busy effecting minor surface repairs.

Moreover, even the surface repairs that Bev made in her draft were ineffective because she found her limited editing skills unequal to the complex problems she encountered. Bev spent much of her editing time writing *around* problems—avoiding words she suspected she misspelled by using alternatives she was more "sure of," and resolving difficulties with lengthy clauses that did not "sound right" by constructing two separate sentences. Because she often could not identify specific problems, Bev's edited passages frequently turned out to be as troublesome as the originals. At one point during the session, for example, Bev stopped writing to change "Students must regulate they're own activities" to "A student must regulate their own time," thus exchanging one surface error for another. Bev also relied heavily on the aural appeal of her sentences to alert her to needed editing and revision. Unfortunately, the sound of a passage, which was helpful in revealing information about syntax and grammar, told Bev nothing about logic, content, or even spelling and proved to be a less than adequate technique of evaluation, an inadequacy demonstrated by the first sentence of her draft: "College begins a totally different lifestyle within the period of just a few short months."

SUBSTITUTING EDITING FOR REVISING

After she concluded the first draft of her paper 45 minutes into the composing session, Bev became highly anxious about the remainder of the writing process. Convinced that her essay was not successful and worried that she did not have the skills necessary to make it so, Bev flipped distractedly through the pages of her initial draft, shaking her head and remarking with weary disgust that it needed "tons of work." Faced with what seemed to be a Herculean task of rewriting, Bev chose to concentrate her efforts only on the most obvious of the essay's flaws by bringing the first part of the composition in line with the narrative that followed. "It all went back to the opening . . . and having to talk about everything I was going to talk about in the paper . . . I had to get it all in there." Unwilling, however, to commit herself to rewriting major portions of the text and uncertain about what she could do to improve them if she did, Bev again chose to ignore major rhetorical considerations, making only minor sentence level changes in the introduction in an effort to connect it more closely with the narrative. It is important to note here that Bev's efforts to produce her ideal essay through revision were plagued by the same problems that had sabotaged her initial draft: the limited repertoire of skills and strategies she had available for successful revision and the ever present apprehension that encouraged her to rush toward the conclusion of a writing task as quickly as possible. "I really don't like that introduction, but I'll go ahead with it."

Discussion

To date, our study of apprehensive writers is embryonic. Even the close examination of Bev's composing processes provides only a superficial understanding of how apprehension functions in connection with writing. To expand our knowledge of writing apprehension we may find it helpful to turn to other disciplines. One fertile area for future research is the striking similarity that exists between the phenomenon of "apprehension" we have observed in writers like Bev and the phenomenon of "anxiety" that is so widely discussed in the literature of psychology. It seems reasonable to assume, for example, that when Bev must write for school she is experiencing what Freud describes as "the sensation of unpleasure" (1926/1961, p. 25) or what Rollo May calls "painful" feelings of "uncertainty and helplessness" (1950, p. 190) and that she is, moreover, quite consciously aware of these feelings (Basowitz, Persky, Korchin, & Grinker, 1955). Further connections between what psychologists have discovered about anxiety and what we as composition specialists have observed about writing apprehension may help us better understand students like Bev.

Psychological studies may, for example, offer credible explanations for the specific composing behaviors we observe in apprehensive writers. We may learn that when Bev procrastinates she is doing two things: avoiding a task she is very anxious about (Lazarus & Averill, 1972) and, perhaps paradoxically, waiting until her anxiety is strong enough to act as a "special kind" of motivating device (Cattell, 1972, pp. 176–177). When Bev gets anxious enough about the prospect of getting a paper done, she may compose if only to reduce her anxiety. We may also learn more about the distinctive composing behaviors of highly apprehensive writers—for instance, Bev's refusal to spend time engaged in prewriting activities, her fondness for "speedwriting," and her insistence on minimal revision—if we study them as "coping behaviors," activities that individuals employ to reduce their anxiety to acceptable levels (Lazarus & Averill, 1972).

In the last analysis, however, it is Bev's actions and comments that speak most eloquently and that inspire us to ask the clearest questions about the effects of writing apprehension. We are forced to wonder how individuals develop such intense apprehension. Do they, as some psychologists suggest, have a general tendency toward anxiety that, in turn, intensifies their reaction to specific situations? Or does their apprehension arise from a successive series of failures that initiates a spiraling cycle of anxiety (see Spielberger, 1972)?

We may also wonder what role education plays in the development of writing apprehension. What specifically, for example, do we as English teachers do to encourage or dampen anxiety in the students who attend our composition classes? Do we, as the teachers in Daly's study (1978b) suggest, encourage high writing apprehension by evaluating highly apprehensive students less positively than we do less apprehensive students, by "overemphasizing mechanical issues," by "responding less than favorably to disagreeable content regardless of the quality of writing," or by generally "leading students to associate writing attempts with punishment" (p. 23)?

Closely connected to questions about possible causes of high writing apprehension is the question of how closely such apprehension is related to writing skill. Bev's profile, for example, matches in many ways the profiles of "basic" or "unskilled" writers that have been reported in recent studies of composing processes. "Unskilled" writers (as opposed to "skilled" writers) have been reported to avoid situations in which they are forced to write (Warters, 1980), to deal less effectively with rhetorical considerations such as audience (Atlas, 1979), to be less effective in producing "reader-based prose" (Flower, 1979), to spend less time involved in prewriting activities (Pianko, 1979), and to be more worried about mechanics and less concerned with content (Bechtel, 1980). These comparisons suggest an interesting possibility: High writing apprehension and lack of writing skills may be related, and the investigations mentioned above may well be exploring different manifestations of the same complex problem. Certainly Daly's findings (1977, 1978a), which link lower scores on tests of "writing competency" and lower evaluations of "writing quality" with high writing apprehension, suggest that possibility.

It seems logical to assume that subjects who lack a repertoire of skills or strategies for successfully completing composing tasks will be apprehensive about writing. What we do not know is how, when, and why these conditions develop; whether their development is sequentially and/or causally related to each other; and under what circumstances development of apprehension might be reversible.

Finally, Bev's example inspires us to define more precisely the effects apprehension has on the composing processes of all our students. We have not, for example, thought about what beneficial effects moderate levels of apprehension may have on learning how to write and how to approach a writing problem, and we have done little work to compare the composing processes of high- and low-apprehension writers.

The term "writing apprehension" touches a tender chord in those of us who are forced to produce relatively large quantities of written material as a part of our daily routines. Many of us admit to being mildly anxious about a piece of writing we have committed ourselves to completing, an article we have neglected to produce, or a report we have failed to work up. However, as teachers of writing we can also recognize a much more intense, more pronounced writing apprehension in certain of our students whose loathing of the composing process is exceeded only by their fear of failing grades. What this case study of Bev has shown us is that apprehension can be tied to a whole array of composing-process problems. But much work remains to be done if we hope to identify and explain the difficulties these students experience as they struggle through academic writing situations in our classes.

NOTE

1. The theme assignment was adapted from Hairston (1974).

REFERENCES

Atlas, M. (1979). *Addressing an audience: A Study of expert–novice differences in writing* (Tech. Rep. No. 3). Pittsburgh, PA.: Carnegie-Mellon University, Document Design Project.

Basowitz, H., Persky, H., Korchin, S. J., & Grinker, R. R. (1955). *Anxiety and stress.* New York: McGraw-Hill.

Bechtel, J. (1980, May). *Videotape analysis of the composing processes of six male college freshmen.* Paper presented to the annual conference of the Canadian Council of Teachers of English, Ottawa, Ontario, Canada.

Cattell, R. B. (1972). The nature and genesis of mood states; A theoretical model with experimental measurements concerning anxiety, depression, arousal, and other mood states. In C. D. Spielberger (Ed.), *Anxiety: Current trends in theory and research* (Vol. 2, pp. 115–183). New York: Academic Press.

Daly, J. A. (1977). The effects of writing apprehension on message encoding. *Journalism Quarterly, 54,* 566–572.

Daly, J. A. (1978a). Writing apprehension and writing competency. *Journal of Education Research, 72,* 10–14.

Daly, J. A. (1978b, April). *Writing apprehension in the classroom: Teacher role expectancies of the apprehensive writer.* Paper presented at the annual convention of the International Communication Association, Chicago.

Flower, L. (1979). Writer-based prose: A cognitive basis for problems in writing. *College English, 41,* 19–37.

Freud, S. (1961). *Inhibitions, symptoms, and anxiety* (J. Strachey, Trans. and Ed.). London: Hogarth Press. (Original work published 1926)

Hairston, M. (1974). *A contemporary rhetoric.* Boston: Houghton Mifflin.

Lazarus, R. S., & Averill, J. R. (1972). Emotion and cognition: With special reference to anxiety. In C. D. Spielberger (Ed.), *Anxiety: Current trends in theory and research* (Vol. 2, pp. 241–283). New York: Academic Press.

May, R. (1950). *The meaning of anxiety.* New York: Ronald.

Miller, M. D., & Daly, J. A. (1975, April). *The development of a measure of writing apprehension.* Paper presented at the annual conference of the International Communication Association, Chicago.

Pianko, S. (1979). A description of the composing processes of college freshmen writers. *Research in the Teaching of English, 13,* 5–22.

Spielberger, C. D. (1972). Anxiety as an emotional state. In C. D. Spielberger (Ed.), *Anxiety: Current trends in theory and research* (Vol. 1, pp. 23–49). New York: Academic Press.

Warters, S. (1980, May). *The writing processes of college basic writers.* Paper presented at the annual conference of the Canadian Council of Teachers of English, Ottawa, Ontario, Canada.

Problems with Monitor Use in Second Language Composing 5

STAN JONES

Commonly, problems faced by writers working in a second language are thought to be linguistic ones, problems that can be overcome simply by becoming more proficient in the linguistic code of the new language—by learning more vocabulary and more about the syntactic patterns.[1] However, work by my colleague, Jacqueline Tetroe, and myself (Jones, 1982; Jones & Tetroe, 1983) has shown that other factors may be of equal or greater importance in limiting second-language writing. In particular, we have shown that the planning strategies that characterize the first language composing of a writer may be carried over to the second language task. If these strategies are not effective, then an increase in second language linguistic skill is not in itself enough to improve overall holistic evaluations of the writer's work (though it obviously improves the ratings of grammaticality).

In this chapter I want to explore another nonlinguistic source of difficulty in second language composing, a difficulty that can result either from the instructional setting or from the cognitive style of the writer, though the former is more frequently the source. The problem, which I will refer to as overuse of the monitor, is similar to the writer's block problem described by Rose (1980, 1984) though, in the cases I will examine, the writer does not report the usual sort of difficulties we associated with blocking—the inability to start or to continue a piece of writing. Rather, the problem I am discussing renders the composing process less efficient so that the compositions that the writer produces

Stan Jones. Department of Linguistics, Carleton University, Ottawa, Ontario, Canada.

do not reflect her full competence. The problem is that the writer relies on conscious knowledge to evaluate the grammaticality of the sentences she produces, and this conscious "monitoring" of syntactic form takes precedence over other parts of the process (such as generating ideas and connecting them, and organizing them for the audience). Underuse of this monitor may also affect composing, and I will briefly explore this problem as well. I will attempt to relate the analysis to a general theory of second language acquisition, the Monitor Theory.

I will try here not to prove the Monitor Theory's elegance or to refine it (though see footnote 3 for some defense of the theory), but to demonstrate that some of the concepts developed in the theory are useful in the analysis of second-language composing problems. The general plan of the chapter will be first to outline the theory and to review several studies which use the theory and which are relevant to the analysis of composition. In this I will be particularly concerned to identify several different ways in which second language competence may be employed in performance and to set up several classifications of second language users. The central part of the chapter is a report of a descriptive case study of two second language learners who represent two extreme types. While the principal goal of this central section will be to discuss these two cases, an intended side effect will be to demonstrate the utility of the Monitor Theory. I will conclude with a few notes on how the two subjects may have developed their composing strategies.

The Monitor Theory

Stephen Krashen has developed a theory of second language acquisition which poses two different ways that second language competence is developed.[2] The first, which he calls "acquisition," is a largely nonconscious process.

> . . . language acquirers are not usually aware of the fact that they are acquiring language, but are only aware of the fact that they are using the language for communication. The result of language acquisition, acquired competence, is also subconscious. We are generally not consciously aware of the rules of the languages we have acquired. Instead, we have a "feel" for correctness. Grammatical sentences "sound" right, or "feel" right, and errors feel wrong, even if we do not consciously know what rule was violated. (Krashen, 1982, p. 10)

The other process, "learning," is the more familiar of the two, the one most of us experienced in the classrooms where we were taught second languages. It is a conscious process:

> We will use the term "learning" henceforth to refer to conscious knowledge of the second language, knowing the rules, being aware of them and being able to talk about them. (Krashen, 1982, p. 10)

While most of Krashen's own work has been concerned with the acquisition process, in particular with how to create classroom settings which encourage acquisition rather than learning, my interest is in how these different kinds of competence result in different kinds of second language performance, in particular in how learning and the associated monitor affect the composing process. Krashen has argued that learned competence is available only as a "monitor," as a device which functions as a filter on the output of the acquired competence system.[3] This monitor can only scan the output of the generative system and "patch it up." Only the acquired system can initiate utterances. Figure 5-1 provides a graphic representation of the performance relationship between acquired and learned competence.

As Figure 5-1 indicates, use of the monitor is not an essential part of performance; the linguistic material generated by acquired competence need not be checked by the monitor before it becomes speech or writing. Indeed, research suggests that monitor use is affected by two factors, factors that can put its use out of the question: generous time boundaries, and focus on grammatical form.[4] Because use of learned competence is a highly conscious process, it requires some amount of time and some considerable use of short-term memory. This condition is generally not met in normal face-to-face conversation; turns in such conversations require quick responses. Any teacher of English as a second language can recount stories of students whose learned knowledge of English was high (as determined from scores on grammar tests) but who could not carry on a conversation because they relied on the

Figure 5-1. Performance relation between acquired and learned competence (adapted from Krashen, 1982, Figure 2-1).

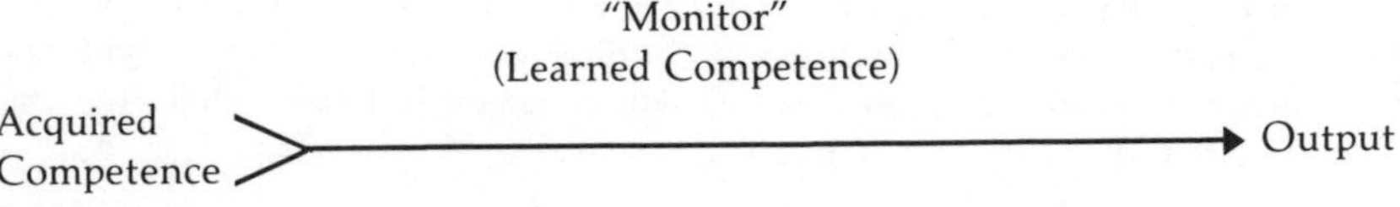

monitor at all times. On the other hand, writing does seem to provide the time to use the monitor, though, as I will argue, overreliance on the monitor can have unfortunate consequences here as well. The second condition necessary for monitor use—focus on form, on correctness—is also more likely met in writing than in conversation. Sociolinguistic factors make it more likely that the monitor will be used in writing than in conversation because the social consequences of producing obviously ungrammatical utterances in conversation are much less severe than those of making similar errors in writing. The second language acquisition literature contains a number of studies of individuals whose conversation contains errors that they are able to avoid in writing or on tests (see particularly Cohen & Robbins, 1976; Krashen & Pon, 1975).

There have been only a few detailed studies of how the monitor is actually used. Stafford and Covitt (1978) attempted to identify monitor use in composing through a post hoc technique. They asked their four subjects, who were selected to represent a range of monitor use,[5] to locate and correct grammatical errors in essays each had written. When a subject made a change in the text, Stafford and Covitt asked for a reason for the change; reasons based explicitly on a grammar rule were considered to represent reliance on the monitor. They concluded that the two students who, by this criterion, used acquisition strategies (and thus, theoretically, did not rely as much on the monitor) produced compositions that were not inferior to those of a monitor user. Because they found no benefit for monitor use, for explicitly taught grammatical knowledge, the Stafford and Covitt study has pedagogical implications. But Stafford and Covitt have no direct evidence that the students who seemed to rely on acquisition strategies truly were nonusers because they did not look directly at the composing process; they could only infer what went on during composing from their discussions about the editing with the subjects. While this might tell us something about monitor use during directed editing, it does not provide much information on how these subjects might have employed or not employed the monitor during composing.

Other evidence for the existence of the difference between learned and acquired linguistic competence comes from several studies by Krashen. In these studies (summarized in Krashen, 1982), Krashen attempted to identify monitor use through the types of errors made in performance. He argues that acquisition follows a natural sequence and so the errors in unmonitored performance should conform to this sequence. If a second language learner has late-acquired items correct, then he or she should also have early-acquired items correct if the performance is unmonitored. For example, it has been found in studies with children (Dulay & Burt, 1974) and adults (Bailey, Madden, and Krashen, 1974) who were learning English as a second language that, in general, control of the present progressive form of the verb (-ing) is attained early while control of the third person singular form of verbs and the possessive form of nouns comes late. Thus, second language users in an unmonitored setting would be expected to make more errors with the latter two forms than with the former. On the other hand, learning need not follow a natural sequence since it is determined by the teacher's idiosyncratic syllabus. In such a syllabus the teacher may provide instruction on the third person singular early in the course but postpone the progressive. When monitoring, using this learned competence, a learner may have some typically late-acquired items correct (because they had been taught) while missing early-acquired ones that had not yet been covered in the course.[6] This too is only an indirect indicator of monitor use. Krashen concludes that the monitor is little used in composing because, in his analysis of compositions (not of composing, note), he has found the acquisition order. While this evidence from products may tell us whether the monitor was in fact used, it does not tell us how it was used, how the learned competence was employed.

A Monitor Overuser and an Underuser

Such studies of second language learners provide some evidence that individuals differ in their reliance on the monitor. Some appear to rely heavily on the monitor even when it interferes with fluent performance (Krashen, 1978); I will refer to these as monitor overusers. The overuser I will be discussing in this case study, Lianna, a native speaker of South American Spanish, received most of her instruction in English as a second language (ESL) in traditional foreign language classes, classes in which the principal instructional technique was translation between first and second language with accuracy in the second language as the goal. At the time she participated in the study, she scored 88 percent on an exam that focused on grammatical knowledge and vocabulary; a score of 85 percent on this exam would allow a student to enter full-time university studies with no further instruction in

English. She had received 88 percent (in a university system in which 85–89 percent represents an A) on the final examination of her advanced general ESL course. She reported that she felt accuracy was very important in composition, although she accepted fluency as a more important goal in speaking. In fact, she was not a fully typical overuser in that she did not always monitor heavily while speaking. She was interested in grammatical rules and asked questions about them in class and often compared English rules to Spanish ones.

At the other extreme are underusers, second language acquirers who seldom monitor, even when it would be appropriate to do so. In many cases, they may not even consciously know many rules. Catrina, a native speaker of Brazilian Portuguese, the underuser on whom I will report, scored 75 percent on the same grammar/vocabulary exam on which Lianna scored 80 percent; the difference of 5 percent between their scores is statistically significant, but it does not represent a large difference in knowledge of English. Catrina's compositions, for example, do not have a noticeably greater number of errors. On a 9-point scale such as Carroll's band system (1980), both would rate in Band 6, the fourth from the top—that is, as competent users who cope well in most situations but occasionally misunderstand or make significant errors—though Lianna would rank slightly higher than Catrina. Still, Catrina had little difficulty communicating with native speakers of English and had many friends who were monolingual English speakers, unlike Lianna whose friends nearly all spoke Spanish as their principal language. In discussion, Catrina expressed little interest in learning or using rules as long as she could be understood. She identified limited vocabulary as her major difficulty.

Prior to the analysis of their composing behaviors, these two subjects were identified respectively as a monitor overuser and underuser through interviews, observation, and discussions with teachers who had taught both students. The goal of the study was not to develop a method to identify different types of users but to describe the language behavior of individuals who seemed to fit the categories.

METHOD

If we are to study how the different second language competencies are used, we need some record of that use. Of the two methods for obtaining on-line records in composing research, one, the use of think-aloud protocols, may invite unwelcome intrusions in studies of monitor overusers.[7] Overusers usually monitor their spoken as well as their written language. If we ask them to talk while composing, we may well introduce distortions in their composing by unwittingly encouraging further use of the monitor, both as they speak and as they write. A second approach is to videotape the writer as he or she composes. Such a videotape of the composing session provides a record without imposing on the oral or written fluency of the subjects. This technique has been employed by Matsuhashi (1981) and Pianko (1979), among others, in their studies of composing, and by Rose (1981, 1984) in his study of writer's block.

In this study we used a single camera pointed at the writer's developing text and used the videotape to study her composing process.[8] After each session we discussed the composition with each subject; but we did not review the tapes in stimulated recall, nor did we go over the compositions line by line as did Rose (1981, 1984). I had sessions with each of the subjects to discuss composing, including a session on what differences each perceived between first and second language composing.

The study included nine subjects in all, though only two are included in this report. All were enrolled in an advanced ESL composition class at the time of the study; all had completed the most advanced general ESL class at a Canadian university the previous term. All indicated they intended to study at an English-speaking university. Each of the subjects wrote three essays, in three consecutive weeks, while being videotaped. They were given as much time as they needed to complete each paper, but all except Lianna finished within one hour. The topics were selected from those used by Pianko (1979) in her study of college freshman writers and were chosen in order to produce three different types of discourse: personal experience (tell about an experience where something went wrong), description (describe how a national holiday or birthday is celebrated in your country), and generalization (discuss a case of the abuse of freedom). The subjects did not always produce the type of discourse expected. Lianna was the most compliant; all her essays fit the intended type. Catrina also produced all three types (although she wrote a personal experience essay for the description topic and a description for the personal experience one). So we have similar types of essays for both subjects.

There are two kinds of evidence available from the videotapes that are relevant to an analysis of monitor use: pauses and revisions. A videotape provides a complete record of the location and extent of pauses in the composing process, periods when the writer was not putting text on the page. During these pauses the writer may have been doing any number of things—planning the next section of text, reviewing the text for editing and revision, rereading the text to re-orient herself, or even just daydreaming.

Clark and Clark (1977) present a general scheme of sentence production that is useful for thinking about the relation of pausing and monitor use. They propose three levels of plans in the production of any utterance: discourse, sentence, and constituent. The first is the kind most familiar in writing-process studies, but the latter two are the ones central to monitoring. Clark and Clark present evidence that the general syntactic plan of the sentence is worked out before lexical items and phrases are chosen. It appears that the opposite occurs when the monitor is used: The general semantics of the sentence are worked out, then lexical items are chosen, and then a syntactic structure is imposed on the lexical material. If this is a correct description, then the selected lexical items must be kept in short-term memory (STM) while the grammatical rules are being used to construct the syntactic form. Because the monitor requires conscious use of rules, the monitor itself also uses some space in STM, reducing the capacity for text. Further, in order that the rules can be applied to it, the text must be in STM in sentential rather than in gist form because the actual lexical items and the choice of phrases must be available for the output constraints that constitute the monitor to review; this, too, reduces STM capacity. As we will see, a syntactic phrase is the usual working unit for the overuser. Writers who monitor heavily are likely to work with very short chunks of text since only a limited amount of information can be held in STM. Thus we would expect heavy monitor users to pause more frequently than other writers and for longer periods: since they must not only generate the text; they must consciously formulate, evaluate, and revise it before they can put it on the page. In comparing the two writers we will want to compare the frequency and length of pauses as well as the syntactic location of the pauses.

The second kind of videotaped evidence, revising, is relevant because monitor overusers are likely to polish up one piece of text before moving on to work on the next. Because their primary concern is accuracy, they must ensure correctness before they can proceed; and once they have done all they can to be accurate the first time, there is little incentive to review the paper. Optimal users and, to the extent that they monitor at all, underusers are more likely to generate longer stretches of text and to return later to revise and edit.

In order to investigate differences in pausing behavior, each pause of 0.1 second or longer was recorded and its connection to the text noted. As well, each revision was identified and its location in the composing process recorded. Matsuhashi (1981) found that discourse type influenced pause times; in her study, subjects required less time to plan and organize for reporting than they did for generalizing or persuading. In the same way, discourse type influenced pause times of this study's second language students. As Table 5-1 indicates, the personal experience essays (Lianna 1, Catrina 2) required less planning time than the others. We also found that the patterns of pause length in our subjects' protocols were the same as those in Matsuhashi's study. As can be seen from Table 5-2, the pauses at T-unit boundaries were significantly longer than those within T-units, and those at paragraphs were longer still. Further, the pauses at T-units of different levels of abstraction (Nold & Davis, 1980) followed the same pattern that Matsuhashi found: As Table 5-3 shows, pauses before T-units which are superordinate to the ones preceding them were longer than pauses before T-units at coordinate levels, and, in turn, the pauses before T-units at coordinate levels were longer than those before T-units subordinate in their predecessors. These results suggest that no

Table 5-1. Composing and Writing Units, with Averages, for Each Essay by Each Subject

Essay	Total words	Total pauses	Average number words between pauses	Total pause time (sec)	Mean pause length (sec)	% total time in pausing
Catrina 1 (description)	260	32	8.13	478.5	15.0	43
Catrina 2 (personal experience)	165	17	9.71	98.5	5.8	20
Catrina 3 (generalization)	276	33	8.36	314.5	9.5	34
Catrina total	701	82	8.55			32
Lianna 1 (personal experience)	259	67	3.87	1605.5	24.0	70
Lianna 2 (description)	224	50	4.48	1950.5	39.0	74
Lianna 3 (generalization)	282	81	3.48	2697.5	33.3	68
Lianna total	765	198	3.86			70

Table 5-2. Average Length (in Min and Sec) of Pauses at Various Text Boundaries of Each Essay by Each Subject

Essay	All pauses	Pauses at T-units	Pauses at paragraphs	Pauses at T-units not at paragraph	Pauses within T-units
Catrina 1	0:15.0	0:20.5	0:35.4	0:13.0	0:12.3
Catrina 2	0:05.8	0:05.4	0:06.0	0:05.3	0:06.4
Catrina 3	0:09.5	0:11.2	0:12.5	0:10.5	0:07.1
Lianna 1	0:24.0	0:38.8	1:12.2	0:29.9	0:15.2
Lianna 2	0:39.0	1:19.6	2:03.3	1:00.3	0:22.6
Lianna 3	0:33.3	1:27.5	1:59.0	1:13.3	0:22.4

unusual disturbances in the composing process occurred in our study. They also demonstrate that second language composing is organized in much the same way as first language composing, a result discussed in detail in Jones and Tetroe (1983).

However, the two writers differed dramatically from each other in just the ways predicted by monitor theory. The overuser, Lianna, paused for much longer times and paused more frequently than Catrina, regardless of discourse type. Over the three essays, Catrina wrote an average of 8.55 words between each pause; while Lianna, the overuser, wrote on the average only 3.86 words between each pause (Table 5-1). As expected, the overuser wrote much shorter chunks of text at a time. In fact, the chunks were very small, considering that her average T-unit length was 15.6 words and her average for clauses was 7.6 words, which as Table 5-4 shows was similar to Catrina's. The size of Lianna's writing chunks suggests that for her the composing unit was no more than a phrase. The result is that her writing is full of

Table 5-3. Pause Time (in Min and Sec) before T-Units of Different Levels of Abstraction (All Essays Combined)

Level of abstraction	Essay type		
	Personal experience	Description	Generalization
Superordinate	0:55.2	1:22.2	1:30.2
Coordinate	0:18.3	0:27.3	0:35.0
Subordinate	0:08.8	0:24.5	0:18.5

Table 5-4. Total Words, T-Units, and Words per T-Unit for Each Essay, with Means for Each Subject

Essay	Words	T-units	Words per T-unit
Catrina 1	260	15	17.3
Catrina 2	165	12	13.8
Catrina 3	276	19	14.5
Catrina mean	233.7	15.3	15.2
Lianna 1	259	20	13.0
Lianna 2	224	13	17.2
Lianna 3	282	17	16.6
Lianna mean	255.0	16.7	15.6

starts and stops; it develops no apparent flow. Her text seems more disconnected than Catrina's as well. Lianna reported that she was, in fact, doing what I have described as monitoring during these pauses. Catrina, on the other hand, did not report monitoring behavior; when asked about pauses that were not at T-unit boundaries, she reported that she was searching for the appropriate lexical item rather than formulating the syntactic form of the text. Thus one difference the theory would predict between overusers and underusers did in fact occur.

Lianna also paused longer than Catrina did. Of course, since she paused more frequently, her total pause item was greater (70% of total composing for Lianna versus 32% for Catrina, Table 5-1); but, as well, the individual pauses were longer. As Table 5-1 indicates, the average pause length in every essay was at least twice as long for Lianna as for Catrina. When we consider only pauses at similar syntactic boundaries, T-units and paragraphs (Table 5-2), we find even greater differences: Catrina averaged 12.4 seconds at T-units, while Lianna averaged just over 1 minute at these boundaries. Again, the overuser performed consistently with the predictions of monitor theory.

I have suggested that heavy reliance on the monitor taxes the short-term memory of the composer and that that is why the production of the text by an overuser occurs in such small chunks. This effect on STM is apparent in the following episode from the protocol of the third essay by Lianna. In the very long pause (over 2 minutes) before sentence one, Lianna looked up "subtle" in the dictionary (pause times are in parentheses): (2:22.3) "But we never speak about the lack of freedom (1:41) which can be very sub(0:10.6)tle." When she got to the beginning of the relative clause, she apparently forgot something about the word, because she looked it up again. By the time she was ready actually to write "subtle," she had forgotten it again and had to turn to the dictionary a third time. No such episode occurred in the composing by Catrina. (This I take as evidence, also, that lexical items are selected early in the sentence-planning process of overusers.)

Since Lianna paused longer at T-unit and paragraph boundaries than within T-units, we must assume that an overuser does some planning at a level higher than the chunk-by-chunk level. The planning for "subtle" is direct evidence for this higher level planning. This too is consistent with monitor theory; we can assume that some sort of gist for the following T-unit (or paragraph) is arrived at during this pause, but its transformation into text must be organized phrase by phrase. Catrina, the underuser, must plan gist at T-unit boundaries as well; but its formulation as text can occur as it is being written, since it need not be passed through the monitor.

Of course, from these pause times alone we do not know whether Lianna was really doing something different from Catrina or simply doing more of the same thing. But the post hoc interviews, together with the analysis of the texts and the videotapes, provide some evidence that Lianna and Catrina were not doing the same thing during the pauses. Additional evidence is available from observing what behaviors occurred during the pauses, particularly the occurrence of revisions: For Lianna, the text was complete when it was written down; for Catrina, the text was always subject to change.

Lianna seldom made changes in the text once it was written down. There are only 3 changes to the first essay she wrote, 6 in the second, and 8 in the third. All but 3 of these 17 changes were to add or change a lexical item, changes that did not alter the grammatical structure of the sentence. The other 3 were to correct spelling (or, more accurately, handwriting) flaws, and each of these occurred immediately without a pause. Lianna never reviewed her text after she reached the final word. In fact, she extensively reread only one of her three texts while it was in progress: In the second essay, when she had completed the first page, she reread it, but she made no changes to her text. This behavior, too, is consistent with what we would expect from someone who relies heavily on the monitor. If the monitor works over each phrase as it is formulated to ensure its fit with correct syntactic form, there is nothing more it could do if the text were reviewed. Because the monitor is primarily a filter on syntactic form, it may not solve all lexical problems—a better word may come to mind at any time.

Catrina, on the other hand, made many editing changes in her text: 28 in the first paper alone, more than Lianna made in all three of her papers. There are 7 changes in the short (165 words) second essay, and 12 in the third. Not all her revisions are improvements (for example, she changed "there were no free doctors at the hospital" to "there had no free doctors at the hospital"). Many were not made immediately but were made while Catrina reviewed the text. In fact, only those related to lexical items occurred while she was actually composing. It is interesting to note that at several points Catrina started a word that she did not finish; she paused after having written a few letters, crossed them out, and then went on to produce a different lexical item.[9] This behavior suggests that Catrina did not monitor during formulation of text but checked text only after it started to appear on the page. This is consistent with the use of the acquired system; once the text becomes noticeable, it may not "feel" right. Indeed, the "no free doctors" sentence doesn't sound right (I think it should be "there were no doctors who were free"), but Catrina's lack of full proficiency didn't allow her to find the right correction.

THE COMPOSING PROCESS IN DETAIL

By observing each of these writers making choices during their composing activity we can further illustrate the difference between the underuser and the overuser. Figures 5-2 and 5-3 provide the first compositions by Catrina and Lianna, respectively. The topic was "Tell about an experience where something went wrong." Pause times and locations are indicated in parentheses, sections of the text that the writer produced and then crossed out are enclosed in braces, and later additions to the text are enclosed in square brackets. As the reader should note, there are few of these latter two in Lianna's protocol. Now let us closely look at each of the students' composing pauses.

Catrina spent nearly 1 minute from the time she was given the topic to when she began writing. Her first pause occurred after writing "an," but before "accident." That she wrote "an" suggests that she had already decided on "accident," but the pause after "an" suggests that she began to change her mind; "medical" was immediately inserted and "an" changed to "a." There are many instances in this protocol (and her other two as well) where Catrina appears to have been trying out lexical items. In sentence two she pauses after "world," then writes

(0:57.2) Prewriting

I will describe a{n} (0:04) [medical] accident that happened in my city in Brazil. (0:05)
There is many kinds of doctors in the world (0:05) {ones} those who are very dedicated to the profession and others worried about their own finan{c}cial situation. (0:04.8)
One day, (0:11.2) a child was crossing a {ro} (0:08.8) highway (0:04.4) {xx} when a car (0:06.2) passed over him. (0:02.4)
Scared the driver stopped the car, carried the 12 years old boy into the car and took him to the nearest hospital in th{e}(0:03.5)at area. (0:06.9)
As soon as they got the small hospital {the} nurse told the man there (0:05.4) {were} [had] no free doctors at the hospital. (0:01.9)
So they must [have to] wait for at least half an hour. (0:02.2)
However, the child was bl{i}eeding so badly th{e}at the man decided to call any doctor from the neighbor{s}hood town. (0:26.8)
{I} Unfortunately, there was only one (0:06.8) Doctor living in that town. (0:18.4)
Whithout choise the man (0:09.6) dialed (0:47.1) his number, (0:06) but the Doctor stupidly answered/responded him that it was Sunday, he was not oblied to work and {the} (0:13.2) that (0:08.4) the small hospital had its own doctors (0:28.8) to attend the pacients. (0:05) {xx} (0:16.2)
the poor man didn't know what to do. (0:25.6)
1/2 hour later so the {little boy} (0:09.2) hemophiliac boy died for careless. (0:35)
that night the Doctor's son didn't come home. (0:01.3)
Calling for police help he learned his son had died in the neighborhood town that afternoon. (0:02.4)
{because}
What that unresponsible Doctor didn't know was that when he refused to {attend} save a life he was killing his own child. (0:04.8)
{That's the result of} (2:21.8)
That's shows how a lazy doctor can be dangerous. (0:30.8)

Figure 5-2. Catrina's first essay. ( ) = Pause times; { } = sections crossed out; [ ] = sections added. The topic was "Tell about an experience where something went wrong."

"ones," immediately crosses it out, and replaces it with "those." In the third sentence, she pauses several times, apparently to solve two lexical problems: the choice between "road" and "highway," and an attempt to decide what the car did (unfortunately, "passed over" is not quite right). Many of the pauses in Catrina's protocols are to solve these local lexical problems. She also has several false starts that suggest she did not monitor before she wrote. Before the second from the last sentence,

(1:14) Prewriting

Maybe I should describe (0:44.2) the experience (0:04.2) of this morning. (0:37)
I am surprised how difficult is to get visas from southamerican countries (0:04.4), even (0:28) being yourself a southamerican [citizen]. (0:26)
I come from Chile (0:02), but I live in Switzerland since 1973. (0:22.4)
I am in Canada only for one year; (0:23) so, (0:06.2) before (0:03.7) coming back to Switzerland (0:29.5) we wanted (0:49.6) to {visit} visit (0:28.7) some {countries} (0:24.8) latinoamerican countries (0:23.3)
Someone told us (0:05.5) it took (0:08.8) very long to get the visas (0:15.2) for these (0:03.3) countries; (0:12.3) therefore, (0:05.3) we decided (0:03.4) to begin (1:21.7) several months before leaving. (3:38.2)
This morning we went to (0:08.2) several embassies (0:05.3); Colombia, Peru (0:11.3), Venezuela, Bolivia (0:03.4) and Ecuador (0:07.6).
We couldn't get any visa. (0:22.7)
In most of the ambassies you have to fill out (0:17.7) a special (0:25.4) paper asking for the visa. (0:36.2)
This paper must go to the respective country; (0:04) as the post service is not really good (0:04.7) either in Canada or in the southamerican country they suggested (0:11.4) us to send it (0:18.8) by special delivery (0:11.1) at our (0:15.2) {payment} (0:08.2) cost (1:30.4)
The answer might take several days or months. (0:50)
At another embassy (0:07.9) the person who (0:23.2) is charged of visas was not there (0:16) at that moment; so, (0:03.2) nobody could (0:16.2) tell us (0:05.7) what (0:08.2) was necessary to do (0:19.3) to get the visa (3:21.4)
At (0:12.9) the (0:05.3) Ecuador's ambassy we were received by the ambassador himself (0:25.9)
After a long (0:03.4) speech about the friend(0:03.8)ship between Chile and Ecuador (0:03.8) he told (0:10.9) us he was very sorry (0:29.3) but he only gave special diplomatic visas, current visas should be asked in Montreal (:09.4)
After that we decided (0:18.9) to make a trip to Montreal tomorrow (0:27.8).
Maybe we are (0:26.3) are going to (0:08.6) come ba(0:06.1)ck (0:05.1) right to Switzerland (0:09) without visiting latinoamerica. (0:11.6)

Figure 5-3. Lianna's first essay. ( ) = Pause times; { } = sections crossed out; [ ] = sections added. The topic was "Tell about an experience where something went wrong."

she starts writing "because" but immediately changes her mind. In the second-from-last sentence itself, she starts with "attend" and changes to "save." She begins to end the paper with "That's the result of" but stops and pauses for over 2 minutes. In the postwriting interview she reported having difficulty knowing how to end; she wanted to give a moral to her story, but wasn't certain how to do it. That she tried out semantically related lexical items of the appropriate syntactic form suggests that she had the gist and syntactic form in mind but not the specific textual realization. We can tell she had not planned the text in detail at the T-unit boundary because these lexical problems remain, but she had determined the general direction of her discourse.

Lianna has very few of these lexical tryouts. Only two occur in the protocol of essay one, and one of these is of a different character. In the fourth sentence, she is unhappy with "countries" by itself. In discussion after completing the essay, she reported that her difficulty was that she did not want to repeat "southamerican," which she had used twice in the second sentence, but did not know how else to refer to South America in English. She first tried to avoid referring to it, then saw that that wouldn't work; she thought again about it and resorted to an attempt to anglicize the Spanish form she did know.

There is, in fact, very little to comment on in Lianna's process. She worked out short chunks of text in her mind and then wrote them down. While she did work out the gist of each sentence during the pause at its boundary, she also reported planning its surface form in detail before starting to write. Lianna had some idea of how the sentence would end before she started it (though she frequently lost track in the middle). In contrast, Catrina said she did not always know how a sentence would come out as she started it; the number of false starts in her protocol are evidence for this as well. There are no false starts in Lianna's protocols.

Conclusions

The difference in composing behavior between Catrina and Lianna seems consistent with the assumption that Lianna relied heavily on the monitor, on her learned competence, while Catrina relied on acquired competence. It is important to note that, while Lianna had somewhat higher scores on grammatical tests and obviously paid more attention to grammaticality during composing than did Catrina, her texts are not substantially freer of error. By my count, there are only three sentences in Lianna's first essay that are free of some grammatical error (one of these she has not punctuated as a sentence, however). If we ignore spelling, Catrina was also able to produce three grammatical sentences. In both cases these were among the least complex sentences in the essays. So monitoring is not necessarily an effective second language strategy. In fact, it can often be an impediment.

There are, if this analysis is accepted, significant differences between the composing behavior of a second language writer who can be identified as a monitor overuser and the behavior of one who can be identified as an underuser. The overuser pauses more frequently and for longer periods. She writes in shorter chunks. Her composing is interrupted by her monitoring. The differences that can be found by directly observing the behaviors, however, do not lead to significant differences in the actual compositions. While Lianna obviously attended more closely to grammatical form than did Catrina, her compositions do not reflect the additional effort. Rose (1984) argues that writers who block do not necessarily produce poor papers. As in the case of monitor overusers, the problem is not the product but the process.

The discovery that monitoring does not lead to improved writing is important. Monitoring did not make Lianna a more grammatical writer than Catrina, even though Lianna "knows" more grammar than Catrina (80% versus 75% correct on the grammar test). It may be that the proficiency level these two writers were working at learned competence was simply not sufficient for dealing with their problems. Output filters may not be capable of dealing with fundamentals of grammatical form. While Krashen and Pon (1975) claim that monitoring during composing improved the grammaticality of their subject's products, it is clear from their description that she was at a higher level of proficiency than Lianna and Catrina. Learned competence may only be effective in dealing with idiosyncratic syntactic forms or with forms that differ markedly in informal and formal discourse (but see Pringle, 1983, for some cautions in this regard). Whatever we may speculate about its effective use, it is clear that it was not effective for Lianna; it did not allow her to do better than Catrina, who did not monitor.

It was not only ineffective for Lianna; it also caused her problems. She was dissatisified with her English compositions; she did not feel that she was able to convey what she wanted to say in them. She remarked that she did not think they were as effective as they should have been. Because she is intelligent, she also recognized that additional knowledge of English is not the only important step toward improving her composing behavior (although she also knew that she wrote ungrammatically). Her reliance on the monitor prevented her from keeping track of her developing gist, because it drew her attention away from content to form and because it left little processing capacity for evaluating her text against her content plan.

Perhaps paradoxically, her reliance on the monitor may also be one of the reasons she wrote so ungrammatically. She certainly did not know all the rules of English; there were at least 28 percent of the rules she was tested on that she did not know or, more likely, knew incorrectly. She may have been like the student of French who reportedly defined the feminine gender as being used for "everything that was good and beautiful" (quoted in Hatch, 1978). Because we do not know exactly what rules Lianna was applying (we have only her report that she was applying rules), we cannot be certain that her rules were correct ones. I have already noted that some of Catrina's "corrections" actually turned grammatical sentences into ungrammatical ones; Lianna may, during her pauses to formulate text, have been doing the same.

Krashen's study (1982) contains an important discussion of rules. In essence, he argues that the rules that linguists know are only a subset of all the rules of English; experienced teachers do not know, formally, all the rules linguists have formulated and are able to teach only part of the rules they do know; students learn only some of the rules that they are taught; and, finally, students can actively use only some of the rules they have managed to learn. Reliance on the monitor is not even an effective means to achieve the goal of grammaticality, because the second language learner simply cannot learn enough rules. Acquisition is a more effective strategy. In both my study here and Stafford and Covitt's (1978), students who we believe did not monitor were able to produce compositions with no greater number of errors than those produced by students we believe did rely heavily on monitoring. Further, in this study the learner who did not monitor knew (in the testing sense of) fewer rules than did the learner who monitored; yet she was able to write as grammatically as the monitor user, despite her lower proficiency. In short, monitoring does not give Lianna an advantage even though she knows more to monitor with.

Monitoring also takes time, a lot of time. It always took Lianna over twice as long as Catrina to produce the same number of words. Lianna reported that she was usually rushed to finish her regular academic writing even when she had started well ahead of time (she was a conscientious student) and that she never had time to review her work. She also felt that her time was not well spent, that the product was not as good as the time spent on it would merit. Catrina regarded her compositions as being far from perfect; but they satisfied what she wanted to achieve, and she felt they properly reflected the time spent on them.

Catrina also had problems with composing, though they bothered her less than Lianna's did her. Some monitoring is undoubtedly required. There are some idiosyncratic syntactic rules that probably do need to be consciously learned; these may well be rules that native speakers also must consciously learn. The learners studied by Krashen and Pon (1975) and Cohen and Robbins (1976) were effective monitorers; their written compositions were more grammatical than their oral productions.

There are obvious parallels betwen the cognitive strategies that characterize the blocking writer (Rose, 1980, 1984) and those typical of the monitor overuser. The composing takes far more time than it should; the writing itself detracts from the composing; the rules the writers follow do not do what they are supposed to do. There is an important difference, however. Monitor overuse, for some second language writers at least, occurs because the learner has no other means for using his or her knowledge of the second language. Learned competence can be used only as an output filter, as a monitor. It is not so much the learner's strategy for using his or her second language linguistic competence that is directly at fault, but the nature of that competence.

This characteristic of second language competence may help us explain why Lianna was an overuser of the monitor and Catrina an underuser. Although Krashen (1978) proposes a personality factor—overusers tend to be self-conscious while underusers are outgoing—this will not serve in our case. Catrina was indeed outgoing, but Lianna was not particularly self-conscious. Lianna, however, had been taught English by a method that emphasized conscious memorization—learning—of the rules of the second language and had been tested on her explicit knowledge of these rules. Her teachers had provided her with a linguistic competence that could only be used as a monitor. Catrina, on the other hand, was taught English in a program that stressed communicating in the second language rather than knowing the rules of that language. Both were good students and learned what they were taught, and Lianna became an overuser and Catrina an underuser. In the last year of her second language education, Lianna was in the same program that Catrina was in; during that year her reliance on the monitor decreased as her acquired competence improved.

It is worth noting that many of the proposals for improving first language composing are also effective in helping second language learners develop acquired linguistic competence. They are effective because they emphasize the communicative aspect of composing rather than its formal aspect. Pappas and Sandilands (1983) and Jones and Pappas (1983) discuss the role of conferencing in the teaching of second language composing and present evidence that it develops acquired linguistic competence. Zamel (1983) examines a wide range of developments in first language teaching that appear to be effective in second language classrooms as well.

Second language writers do face problems because they are not fully proficient in the second language; but the form, as much as the degree, of that proficiency matters too. If the competence is learned rather than acquired, that proficiency does not serve the learner well. It does not allow the learner to use his or her competence efficiently, and it interferes with the accomplishment of other cognitive tasks. Not all students who overuse the monitor do so because that is their preferred strategy; they may not be able to use any other because they lack the acquired competence to do so.

ACKNOWLEDGMENTS

I want to thank Jacquie Tetroe, Janice Yalden, and Ian Pringle, who read and commented on parts of this chapter, and Aviva Freedman, who offered sound advice on several drafts. Joan Haire and Jane Hugo helped conduct the writing sessions and assisted with the analysis. The students who allowed us to observe and record their writing were more than generous with their time and patience. Research support from Carleton University is greatly appreciated.

NOTES

1. I will refer to writing problems as "linguistic," "cognitive," and "'affective," using these terms much as Rose does (1980, 1984). In general, "linguistic" refers to problems that result from lack of knowledge of the language, those that might be solved by reference to a traditional handbook. "Affective" problems are those caused by what writers perceive as potential reactions to their work. "Cognitive" problems are those related to unproductive strategies such as premature editing.

2. This theory has been developed over several years and in a number of papers. It has been most usefully summarized in Krashen's 1982 publication. I will not provide citations to support ideas developed from Krashen except where I use quotations. Readers interested in the theory and my presentation of it should consult Krashen (1982).

3. Unfortunately, Krashen has not been explicit about the nature of linguistic competence that is implied in his crucial distinction between learned and acquired competence. As a result, there has been considerable misunderstanding in the literature about the nature of this distinction (see, for example, McLaughlin, Rossman, & McLeod, 1983). What causes particular difficulty is Krashen's claim that the two modes of gaining competence are not only different but that *learning* cannot be transformed into *acquisition*.

This claim has been misunderstood by Krashen's critics because they have assumed that linguistic knowledge is of the same form as other forms of knowledge, such as knowledge of physics or automobile driving, and that it is obtained by the same process(es) as are these other forms. Thus "learning/acquisition" has been confused with such distinctions as "controlled/automatic" or "declarative/procedural." Were linguistic knowledge like these other processes, then the arguments against Krashen, particularly arguments against his claim that learned knowledge cannot be transformed into acquired knowledge, would have considerable weight because there is ample demonstration that what is controlled does become automatic and that declarative knowledge is a basis for procedural knowledge. However, the dominant understanding in linguistics is that linguistic knowledge is *not* like other knowledge, either in form or in acquisitional process, and it is this assumption that underlies Krashen's theory. (For the most recent, generally accessible argument that this linguistic assumption is not only a plausible one but the *most* plausible one, given our current knowledge about language, see Newmeyer, 1983.)

Let me continue this theoretical justification for Krashen's work by detailing what I believe to be the key elements in his distinction between learned and acquired competence. Linguistics assumes a system of linguistic knowledge and acquisition, of which there are three components, as follows.

a. *Linguistic competence:* This is knowledge about the grammatical structure of the language and how grammatical structures are paired with meanings. It does not include knowledge of which meaning is most likely in a given context, or of which form is socially appropriate in a given context, or of which form is most likely to be most effective, or of any other factor not solely concerned with grammatical form. Linguistic competence means exactly what Chomsky in *Syntactic Structures* (1957) says it means. The rules of linguistic competence are quite abstract, not simple summaries of surface structure regularities of the language, and they are thus not easily related to particular occurring forms or utterances. It must be noted that linguistic competence does not include everything systematic about language, only those things relating to knowledge of linguistic structure. This is not to say that there exists a clear and unambiguous criterion for deciding whether any particular linguistic phenomenon is an instance of linguistic competence or something else; the resolution of the status of such boundary phenomena is part of the theoretical work of linguistics.

b. *Linguistic production:* This component uses linguistic competence along with other knowledge (e.g., about what the user wants to say, socially appropriate form, rhetorical function) to produce utterances. The crucial assumption is that it is designed to use linguistic/grammatical knowledge only as it is organized in linguistic competence and not in some other form. Thus it is designed to work with quite abstract representations, not with representations close to surface structure. It is distinct from linguistic knowledge itself.

c. *Language acquisition device (LAD):* This system of learning is not a particular instance of some more general learning capability but a specific system designed to do but one job: acquire linguistic competence. It is designed to derive from the raw data, the utterances of the language, the abstract representations necessary for the linguistic production system. It is not designed to work with metalinguistic representations of the language, and so it cannot derive the necessary abstract representations from the summaries of surface structure features that are given as rules in all teaching grammars. It cannot even make use of the somewhat abstract representations that are provided by some teaching grammars based on transformational grammar. It "knows" only how to work with raw data.

These definitions are at the heart of Krashen's distinction between learned and acquired competence and are the basis for his claim that what is learned cannot be transformed into acquired competence. Since the LAD cannot turn surface summaries into abstract representations and since the linguistic production system can only use abstract representations, the surface summaries that are the essence of learned competence cannot be used by the linguistic production system. Instead, they can only be used to revise the products of the production system, to function as a monitor of linguistic form, just as Krashen claims. Acquired competence is just that, competence that results from the working of the LAD; learned competence results from being taught metalinguistic summaries.

Certainly, such superficial rules are part of the first language linguistic ability of every speaker, but they are only a minor part of that ability. And certainly, first language speakers monitor their output, but only occasionally do they resort to their conscious knowledge of these superficial rules to do so. In contrast, such rules are the principal part of the second language linguistic ability of many second language speakers because the language teaching they receive offers them nothing but simple summaries of data that refer only to the surface form of sentences.

4. Krashen lists a third factor, knowledge of the grammatical rule, but this is different in kind from the other two. This factor may determine whether a user monitors at a particular instance but does not generally determine whether a learner will monitor or not.

5. The basis for selection appears to have been simply familiarity with the learner.

6. In formal terms, acquisition is a Likert scale. The occurrence of an item high on the scale implies the occurrence of all items lower on the scale, but the occurrence of lower items does not imply the occurrence of items higher on the scale. Thus, in Dulay and Burt's study (1974), on the average, learners who had acquired the progressive had also acquired the article and the copula forms, but not all learners who had acquired the copula had acquired the progressive because the progressive is higher on the scale (later acquired) than the copula. And unmonitored performance will conform to this scale. Learning is not a Likert scale. Even if the presentation of items were to be universal, learning is not successful on every item presented, and a learner may not know some items that were presented before other items that he or she does know.

7. What follows must be understood to hold only for these second language, heavy monitor users. In general, I do not think that think-aloud protocols result in serious distortions of the normal process. Indeed, most of the work on composing that I have done, including that with Jacqueline Tetroe, has employed think-aloud techniques. Second language students, in our experience, do not find composing-aloud in the second language difficult, although some use a great deal of their first language while doing so (Jones & Tetroe, 1983).

8. The study was conducted in order to collect some basic data on second language composing. While we hoped to collect data relevant to monitor use, we did not design the study solely for that purpose. Consequently, the data reported in this paper are only part of those available from the study.

9. The students wrote with black pens so that the camera could easily pick up their writing. The students could not erase, but only cross out, their errors.

REFERENCES

Bailey, N., Madden, C., & Krashen, S. (1974). Is there a "natural sequence" in adult second language learning? *Language Learning, 24*, 235–243.

Carroll, B. (1980). *Testing communicative performance.* New York: Pergamon.

Chomsky, N. (1957). *Syntactic structures.* The Hague: Mouton.

Clark, H. & Clark, E. (1977). *Psychology and language: An introduction to psycholinguistics.* New York: Harcourt Brace Jovanovich.

Cohen, A., & Robbins, M. (1976). Towards assessing interlanguage performance: The relationship between selected errors, learner's characteristics, and learner's explanations. *Language Learning, 26,* 45–66.

Dulay, H., & Burt, M. (1974). Natural sequences in child second language acquisition. *Language Learning, 24,* 37–53.

Hatch, E. (1978). *Second language acquisition: A book of readings.* Rowley, MA: Newbury House.

Jones, S. (1982). Attention to rhetorical information while composing in a second language. In C. Campbell (Ed.), *Proceedings of the Fourth Los Angeles Second Language Research Forum.* Los Angeles: UCLA.

Jones, S., & Pappas, P. (1983). *Inside a conference.* Paper presented at the annual conference of TESL Ontario, Toronto, Ontario, Canada.

Jones, S., & Tetroe, J. (1983). Composing in a second language. In A. Matsuhashi (Ed.), *Writing in real time.* New York: Longman.

Krashen, S. (1978). Individual variation in the use of the monitor. In W. Ritchie (Ed.), *Second language acquisition research.* New York: Academic Press.

Krashen, S. (1982). *Principles and practice in second language acquisition.* New York: Pergamon.

Krashen, S., and Pon, P. (1975). An error analysis of an advanced ESL learner: The importance of the monitor. *Working Papers in Bilingualism, 7,* 125–129.

Matsuhashi, A. (1981). Pausing and planning: The tempo of written discourse production. *Research in the Teaching of English, 15,* 113–134.

McLaughlin, B., Rossman, T., & McLeod, B. (1983). Second language learning: An information-processing perspective. *Language Learning, 33,* 135–158.

Newmeyer, F., (1983). *Grammatical theory.* Chicago: University of Chicago Press.

Nold, E., & Davis, B. (1980). The discourse matrix. *College Composition and Communication, 31,* 141–152.

Pappas, P., & Sandilands, B. (1983). *Two heads are better than one.* Paper presented at the annual conference of TESOL, Toronto, Ontario, Canada.

Pianko, S. (1978). A description of the composing processes of college freshmen writers. *Research in the Teaching of English, 13,* 5–22.

Pringle, I. (1983). Why teach style? A review essay. *College Composition and Communication, 34,* 91–98.

Rose, M. (1980). Rigid rules, inflexible plans, and the stifling of language: A cognitivist analysis of writer's block. *College Composition and Communication, 31,* 389–401.

Rose, M. (1981). *The cognitive dimension of writer's block.* Paper read at the annual convention of the National Council of Teachers of English, San Francisco.

Rose, M. (1984). *Writer's block: The cognitive dimension.* Carbondale: Southern Illinois University Press.

Stafford, C., & Covitt, G. (1978). Monitor use in adult second language production. *ITL, 39/40,* 103–125.

Zamel, V. (1983). The composing process of advanced ESL students: Six case studies. *TESOL Quarterly, 17,* 165–187.

Anxious Writers in Context: Graduate School and Beyond

6

LYNN Z. BLOOM

An anxious writer out of context may be neither anxious nor a writer. The fundamental premise of social psychologist Kurt Lewin's classic *Field Theory in Social Science* (1951) is that behavior is the function of the interaction between the individual and his or her environment rather than a function of one or the other acting alone (see application in M. Bloom, 1980). And in "Meaning in Context: Is There Any Other Kind?" (1979, p. 2), Elliott G. Mishler makes a compelling case for researchers in the social and psychological sciences and in education to consider the context of the behavior they study as a necessary condition for understanding that behavior.[1]

Too often teachers or writing researchers focus on only a single context (such as the school-based. timed writing task) rather than on the multiple frames of reference in which the writer is operating. The more thoroughly that teachers, researchers, or the writers themselves get to know these contexts, which are nevertheless susceptible to change, the greater the chance not only to understand the difficulties but to resolve them.

Such a contextual approach has recently gained some popularity in research on writing processes, particularly in research with children, and with college students who are "basic" writers. Among the most notable investigations of children's writing processes are the longitudinal studies by Donald Graves (1975), Lucy Calkins (undated), and their

Lynn Z. Bloom. Department of English, Virginia Commonwealth University, Richmond, Virgina.

colleagues at the University of New Hampshire (Graves, Calkins, & Sowers, 1978–1979). These researchers spent months in elementary school classrooms gaining the confidence of their subjects and carefully noting the occasions for writing, the instructions the teachers gave, and the opportunities for spontaneous writing. They watched their subjects write and talked with them about their writing, sometimes while they were doing it, sometimes immediately afterward. Over time the omnipresent investigators became fixtures in the classroom, part of the context. Their careful observations, based on meticulous record-keeping, reflect numerous emotional, temperamental, and social aspects of the children's writing context, in addition to its intellectual features. When we read accounts of such investigations, we feel that we have gained a remarkably clear understanding of how schoolchildren write in different modes in the context of their classrooms.

Mina P. Shaughnessy's pioneering *Errors and Expectations* (1977) and David Bartholomae's "The Study of Error" (1980) make a convincing case for examining the writings of basic writers in their emotional, linguistic, rhetorical, and intellectual contexts. Bartholomae explains the theory of error analysis and justifies its contextual application:

> Error analysis begins with a theory of writing, a theory of language production and language development, that allows us to see errors as evidence of choice or strategy among a range of possible choices or strategies. . . . Errors, then, are stylistic features, information about this writer and this language; they are not necessarily . . . accidents of composing, or malfunctions in the language process. Consequently, we cannot identify errors without identifying them in context, and the context is not the text, but the activity of composing that presented the erroneous form as a possible solution to the problem of making a meaningful statement. (1980, p. 257)

Shaughnessy's taxonomy of error, Bartholomae points out, "identifies errors according to their source, not their type" (p. 257). A single type of error, such as subject-verb agreement, could have a variety of causes and might be variously categorized as "evidence of an intermediate system," an accident, or an "error of language transfer," such as dialect interference. A teacher familiar with the student writer's social and cultural contexts—such as the nature of his or her community and the language or dialect spoken at home—would be better able to identify the causes and provide appropriate solutions than would a teacher who focused merely on the errors and the "rules" for correcting them. Error cannot be accurately understood without an understanding of the student's history and current environment.

Considering the writer's immediate and broader social contexts, then, has proven valuable in understanding both how writers' abilities are developed and why errors are committed. And I have found that considering such contexts has deepened my understanding of the difficulties or successes that other populations have with writing.

To understand the difficulties of anxious writers we must examine them in context, for in the context may lie clues to the solutions, as well as to the problems. "Writing anxiety," as I use the term, is a label for one or a combination feelings, beliefs, or behaviors that interfere with a person's ability to start, work on, or finish a given writing task that he or she is intellectually capable of doing. The anxious writers who are the subjects of this and much other research are able to function well in other contexts; for them, the "inability to begin or continue writing for reasons other than a lack of skill or commitment" (Rose, 1981) is a particular and perhaps isolated problem. Nevertheless, its significance or intensity may be powerful enough to overwhelm the writer's whole life, especially if finishing a dissertation or writing articles or books is crucial to the writer's career. Since writing anxiety often appears as context-specific, it is clear that the particular context must intrinsically be part of the guiding conceptual framework we use to define, study, and resolve writing anxiety.

The Conceptual Framework: Individual Writers and Their Contexts

Before focusing on two case studies of academic women in context, I'd like to briefly identify the conceptual framework of this study.

Writers aren't simply the sum of their contexts. They bring individual differences in perception, ability, and disposition to their writing contexts—perceptions and abilities that were themselves developed through interactions with previous contexts. Some features of this complex interaction may be seen as internal to the writer (intellectual, temperamental, emotional), others as external (social, economic, academic), though to an extent these overlap. I will attempt to identify and illustrate some of these features.

INTERNAL FEATURES

Intellectual Factors. These consist of the writer's understanding of the subject, knowledge of appropriate methods and strategies to use in research and writing (such as how to find resources and organize notes from multiple sources), vocabulary, and writing skills. It may also, when relevant, include a knowledge of how to type, edit, or use a word processor. If the knowledge is incomplete or inappropriately applied (e.g., "Always grab your audience immediately") the writer may become enmeshed in a rigid, convoluted, or otherwise ineffective composing process (Rose, 1980, see also 1984).

Artistic Factors. A writer may be more or less creative, independent, insightful, willing to make or break rules and take other risks that, if successful, will result in good writing.

Temperamental Factors. The writer's motivation to start a particular piece of writing, and drive to continue and finish it, are critical factors. Whether a person can easily set goals, priorities, and time schedules and stick to them may well determine whether she finishes the work or not. A writer's self-confidence (or lack thereof) may also influence what the writer has to say and whether or not she says it.

Biological Factors. The writer's general level of energy and how much of that he expends on a given piece of writing are of central concern, as is his state of health. A writer's awareness of his daily biorhythmic pattern can enable him to schedule his writing when he's at his most energetic and creative and to avoid writing at those times of the day or night when he's not. The effect of the writer's gender will be discussed in the section on social context.

Emotional Factors. The research of John Daly and various associates on apprehensive writers has demonstrated the importance of writers' attitudes toward writing in general and toward their own writing in particular (see, for example, Chapter 3). They can hold mythical beliefs that make them fearful of writing: "Writing is easy for everyone else and hard for me." They may have been forced to write as punishment. Or they may harbor fears and resentments of past experiences with stifling writing assignments ("What I Did on My Summer Vacation"), with stultifying formats (fomulaic five-paragraph themes), and with scarifying writing evaluations (papers bleeding with red marks).

EXTERNAL CONTEXTS

The writer's individual factors interact with various social and cultural contexts. The two contexts of particular concern here are the broad social context and the more circumscribed academic context.

Social Context. Virginia Woolf and Tillie Olsen emphasize the difficulties that social contexts create to inhibit or curtail altogether their writing and that of their peers. Virginia Woolf gave *A Room of One's Own* (1929/1957) a metaphorical title for the literal context she considered essential for writing. She contends that "it would have been impossible, completely and entirely, for any woman to have written the plays of Shakespeare in the age of Shakespeare" (p. 48) because of the absence of supportive contexts and the presence of deterring ones. Women in that age would have had no educational context, no parental or social encouragement for writing. Their social context dictated early marriage, childrearing, and extinction of their literary talents, if not their very lives. Tillie Olsen, in *Silences* (1978), points out comparable difficulties for modern women, citing the frustrations of her own desire to write by the crushing needs to earn money, keep house, and care for children. And in *Alice James: A Biography* (1980), biographer Jean Strouse focuses on the delicate Alice James in the context of her parents and vigorous brothers. Strouse contends that Alice had enormous literary and intellectual talents and was as fully capable of being as fine a writer and thinker as were her famous brothers, William and Henry. Yet while her domineering father encouraged his sons to enter intellectual professions, Alice, ever the dutiful daughter, was encouraged to languish at home as a progressively deteriorating psychosomatic invalid. Clearly, the presence or absence of familial and social supports for writing can be crucial.

Academic Contexts. Academic contexts are consistently important as an encouragement or deterrent to writers, as is demonstrated by the research on elementary, high school, and college students cited above (see also Daly, 1979), and by the case studies of graduate students that I shall discuss in this chapter. These contexts, like others, have norms and expectations of the modes, style, extent, and sometimes content of student and faculty writing, often with rewards and punishments attached (grades, degrees, promotion and tenure). The same is true of much writing expected in the context of one's job. The pressure of deadlines, too much work, or the distractions by coworkers and a noisy or uncongenial environment may severely inhibit the writing, while the absence of such pressures may enhance it (L. Z. Bloom, 1981a, 1981c).

Two Case Studies of Graduate Student Writers

The case studies of graduate students, Sarah and Ellen, discussed below, offer long-term explorations of the relevant factors in their larger social and academic contexts in order to convey the situational reality behind the writing problems of these women. The solutions I've proposed are also related to these contexts.

Both Sarah and Ellen had completed their doctoral course work in English and in philosophy, respectively, at excellent universities but had become bogged down in their dissertations. Two and four years ago respectively, each came to my three-session series of workshops on Overcoming Writing Anxiety (L. Z. Bloom, 1980, in press) for help in finishing their work. Sarah succeeded, but in the four years since the workshops Ellen has yet to complete a single chapter. I have become friends with both women and converse with or see each separately every other month or so. Each knows that she is the basis for a case history and provides information on which I have taken detailed notes. I have watched each write—or try to write—sitting slightly behind her, out of her line of vision but where her face and the writing on the paper are visible. I've timed the various aspects of their writing processes—occasionally interrupting (alas, an artifact of the investigation; see Mishler, 1979, p. 5) to ask what they were thinking about, why they were pausing or doing something else—and have taken elaborate notes on this and on our conversations immediately following the writing sessions. Because these women were trying to write over a period of months or years, it did not seem feasible to try to videotape their writing.

SARAH, GRADUATE STUDENT AND ASSISTANT PROFESSOR: ROLE CONFLICTS AND CONTEXTUAL CONTINUITY

Sarah's first two years of her first teaching job were plagued by the conflicts between her role as a graduate student trying to finish a dissertation and her role as an assistant professor of English at a major state university. The demands of her teaching role were so pervasive and all-consuming that they overwhelmed the supports from that same academic context that might have enabled her to finish her dissertation during this time.

Sarah was well-prepared to fulfill both roles. With a bachelor's degree in Classical Studies, and a doctorate in English nearly completed, she had been well-trained in literary analysis. Yet, as is typical of many women, she lacked self-confidence and continually needed to receive external validation of her capability (Tavris & Offir, 1977, p. 189) through high grades, instructors' praise, and encouragement to publish. (Indeed, the publication of one chapter of her dissertation helped her to get her first academic job.) This supportive context was ideal for writing.

Sarah's excellent initial appointment validated the extra year she expected to spend writing the last chapter of her dissertation and preparing the entire work for publication. However, her new context, although academic, turned out to be anything but supportive of her writing aims because her professorial role dominated her student role to the point of oblivion. Sarah knew she was expected to excel in teaching, scholarship, and service to the university. Because she was conscientious and perfectionistic about every aspect of her work, she spent a great deal of time in class preparation and 15 to 20 minutes in grading every student paper.

Sarah also spent a great deal of time on committee work—which she felt obliged to perform—and a half day a week volunteering at the campus Women's Center. So the time she had initially set aside for writing, two days and two evenings a week, was continually eroded. Although she could keep up with the current scholarship on her dissertation topic by reading during the short blocks of time available, Sarah believed, erroneously, that for writing she needed a minimum of four hours of uninterrupted time, which was virtually nonexistent. Consequently, she postponed the actual writing until vacations, stopped trying to write during the academic year, and measured her progress instead by the stacks of notecards that continued to accumulate.

But when summer came, she took advantage of the opportunity to gain administrative experience, another facet of her professorial role, by directing a program for women returning to school. "It's only for five weeks," she rationalized. "I'll still have the rest of the summer to finish my dissertation, and I need the money." But by the time she got back to her dissertation, her fine critical eye was slightly out of focus, and to get up sufficient momentum to write she had to reread and rethink the preceding chapters. This led to several weeks of endless tinkering with what she had believed she'd already completed the year before, and all too soon it was time to prepare for the fall semester's classes.

Sarah spent the first semester of her second professorial year in a manner similar to the first. Procrastination in the name of preparation, either for her own classes or for her last chapter, was no crime, she continually repeated. Moreover, there was far more pressure from her chairman, peers, and students to function fully in her teaching role at the expense of her graduate work. What little counterpressure there was came not by her own instigation but from new members of her dissertation committee who, by long distance, were insisting on a number of fundamental changes in the existing manuscript before she could even get to the unwritten chapter. They, like most such committees, focused entirely on the text, unaware of and indifferent to the context in which the work wasn't getting done.

However, in January the university exerted pressure on Sarah to finish her dissertation or be fired; this impelled her to seek help in my workshop on Overcoming Writing Anxiety. Together we worked out a plan of action that allowed her to give appropriate emphasis to both student and teacher roles in order to complete the necessary writing.

This meant that Sarah had to change some of the dimensions of her current situation. She had to establish priorities and set goals that could be accomplished within a realistic time schedule. This meant allocating enough time, week by week, month by month, to fulfill her most pressing obligations. So she divided her worktime (including evening and weekend hours) about equally between teaching and dissertation writing, pared down her university committee work, greatly reduced her paper grading time (without loss of meaningful commentary—it can be done), and eliminated activities not directed toward her primary goals of finishing her dissertation and keeping her job.

Sarah's new, realistically demanding schedule provided a far more structured context than she had been working in before. It enabled her to balance her primary roles judiciously and to write about 20 hours per week during the academic year, a great deal more than had her earlier, vaguer schedule of "finish my dissertation by the end of the summer." She had to accomplish definite goals by the end of each week or month—for instance, to revise a chapter, or to write ten pages of the new chapter.

Her emphasis on the ends, on actually finishing the writing, led her to stop spending excessive time pursuing the means, and she stopped investigating materials that exceeded the boundaries of her research. She realized that such protracted reading had become an insidious form of procrastination. Her excessive reading on peripheral topics had also begun to drastically alter the shape of her dissertation as she tried to accommodate all of her diverse notes. Trained from childhood to be deferential to authority, a characteristic more common in women than in men (Maccoby & Jacklin, 1974), she had begun to believe she could say nothing as original or as perspicacious as her sources, nor could she write as elegantly.

Sarah was further inhibited at this point by a writing problem that had not appeared until the stakes for finishing her dissertation became so high. She grew perfectionistic, rigidly adhering to an inappropriate rule ("Always perfect each paragraph before you proceed to the next") that made her feel obliged to rewrite small blocks of text incessantly without notable improvement.

Neither perfectionism nor labor in excess of the demands of the task appears to be related to gender (Tavris & Offir, 1977, Chap. 6), nor is writing anxiety so related (Daly, 1979). In fact, since from the age of 10 or 11 through the high school years, girls outperform boys of the same age on both "lower" and "higher" measures of verbal skill (Maccoby & Jacklin, 1974), we might expect girls to be less anxious as writers than boys. We might also expect that this greater confidence—fostered, perhaps, by more writing experience—might carry over into adulthood. But such is not the case. It may be that, because women in general have lower self-confidence than men (Tavris & Offir, 1977, p. 189) and are socialized not to be risk-takers, the pressures of writing a dissertation affect them more strongly than men, though this remains to be explored in research.

However, women also appear to be more willing than men to try to reduce the pressures and more socialized toward getting help to do so. Nathanson (1977) has found that women are more oriented than men toward both preventing and relieving medical and psychological problems. This may explain why over twice as many women as men seek help from writing specialists, a ratio comparable to that of clients consulting physicians, social workers, and other professionals for advice on other problems (L. Z. Bloom, 1981b).

With my help, Sarah was able to regain some of her initial confidence in writing and to follow the manageable time schedule we established. Fortunately, her restructured academic context provided large blocks of time for writing and reinforced that writing with the normative expectation that it would not only be accomplished but rewarded. With two others struggling to finish their dissertations, she formed a support group (another type of context), an informal "Dissertations Anonymous." They met weekly to chart their progress, reinforce their writing goals, and encourage each other.

Sarah finished her dissertation on schedule, earned her PhD, and then followed the same schedule to write a related article. By ending her role as a graduate student, Sarah also ended her role conflict, and she learned to let the elements of her academic context that were conducive to writing function to support her writing as a continuing aspect of her academic career.

ELLEN: A STUDY IN CONTEXTUAL INTERFERENCE

Ellen, 38, has been a graduate student for nine years and is never likely to finish her dissertation, despite a great deal of good advice on how to do so. She cannot escape the many interferences from the contexts of her marriage, motherhood, and community, all of which interfere with her often postponed plans for extended research and writing.

Ellen, married at 19, spent four years as a part-time student while she reared her infant daughter. Divorced at 24, she worked for three years as a copy editor. During this time she became a meticulous corrector and reviser of others' writing but was sufficiently inhibited by this process to avoid writing on her own.

Ellen married again at 28 and started graduate work as a part-time doctoral student in philosophy, while Stan, her husband, began an assistant professorship in history. It was hard to write papers in her existing physical context—an apartment with no space to leave her materials out between writing sessions, no "room of one's own." As a hypercritical former editor, Ellen was left with a mental set that made it difficult to write and to evaluate her own work. Her marital context exacerbated these difficulties because both Ellen and Stan felt that, since Stan was the family breadwinner, his requirements for research and writing took priority over Ellen's.

Their family pattern called for Ellen to do nearly all the housework and to care for their two young children herself, generally unrelieved by Stan or a sitter. When the children were awake, they dominated the apartment and eliminated both the temporal and physical contexts conducive to writing. Ellen, temperamentally most alert in the morning, had no choice but to do most of her reading and writing at night after the children were in bed, when she was tired. Her family situation and her academic situation continually impinged on each other. Ellen's course work was prolonged over six years to accommodate her domestic situation. Nevertheless, the academic context provided some necessary supports: fixed deadlines for papers, easily accessible library facilities, professors and peers with whom she could discuss her work. She had just passed the qualifying exams when Stan took another job, still untenured because he himself had not finished the book he'd been working on during the entire time.

The move uprooted Ellen from her academic context and eliminated its supports. Her dissertation chairman let Ellen take the initiative in communicating with him. At a distance she was not only out of sight, but out of mind. She knew no one nearby with whom she could discuss her dissertation research. She had to get most of her research materials through interlibrary loan for short periods only, a time-consuming and frustrating process.

She was particularly hampered by an intellectual factor; she didn't know how to do research for a long work or how to write one. Nor did she know how to schedule her research and writing time to finish in an appropriate period. Her advisor never told her how to do it. A prolific writer himself, he simply assumed that all his graduate students knew how, and they didn't want to appear ignorant by asking him. Stan, mired hopelessly in his own work-in-progress, provided a poor model and no constructive advice. So, typical of many novice researchers, Ellen decided to read everything in the general field before focusing more precisely on her topic.

A year later, still reading in an increasingly desultory fashion, she came to my workshop for Overcoming Writing Anxiety. Several other factors became clear from our discussion. Her family situation was a consistent deterrent to her writing, for she continued to assume most of the responsibility for rearing the children and running the household; their needs always took precedence over her own. Her community involvement took second priority, as she performed many services for her neighbors and community organizations. Her emotions and temperament contributed to the setting of these priorities; she enjoyed these purposeful activities and found it far easier to complete those with their specific time limits than to work on her unstructured dissertation reading, which she kept postponing to an unspecified later time. When she did work on her preliminary research, it became less and less focused as every topic suggested a myriad of others.

My advice to Ellen centered on reestablishing her academic context and on structuring her intellectual and domestic contexts so she could work effectively. She should resume communication with her advisor (whom she'd been avoiding for over a year) to arrive at a clear understanding of the scope, emphasis, methodology, innovativeness, and length of her dissertation. With her advisor's assistance, Ellen should determine the appropriate resource materials for her first chapter, which she would write in a less-than-perfect draft and send to her advisor for comments before revising. She should feel free to ask him anything at any point, rather than struggling in isolation with problems she couldn't solve.

Moreover, Ellen and her advisor should also determine a realistic time schedule for writing the first draft of each chapter, for circulating it among her committee members, and for revising her writing. Ellen's schedule should accommodate the other essential demands on her time, and she should postpone less crucial community and domestic activities until after she had finished her dissertation. She should also try to write regularly when she was most alert—in her case, in the morning.

Yet despite Ellen's good intentions this plan, ambitious but realistic, did not work. There were many reasons, some personal, some contextual. Ellen's temperament undermined her schedule. Without sufficient self-motivation, there was no feasible way for her to remain accountable to either her schedule or her advisor. Although Ellen believed, "I need to finish my dissertation to get out from under my dependency on my advisor," she actually enjoyed the erratic but increasingly slower pace of her desultory reading and was reluctant to change it. She also enjoyed the activities of her family and community too much to put them aside, even temporarily; and so when she did try to write it was, she said, "only in small stretches," an inefficient pattern because of the large percentage of warmup time her particular writing process required.

Ellen's temporal and social contexts combined to contribute to her inertia. Why work so hard, as Stan continued to do, for the dubious rewards of an academic career, when jobs, scarce in any case, were even more difficult to obtain for a beginner with limited geographic mobility? Why work so hard when, at her age, her career span would be relatively short?

Trying to write in the context of her marriage was a particular deterrent because Stan's difficulties with his own writing had such a negative impact on Ellen's work as well. Each spouse interpreted the other's queries about work ("How's your writing going?") "as a form of nagging, no matter how well meant," said Ellen. "We haven't been able to discuss our work with each other in several years. When Stan's writing is not going well, he thinks of ways to interrupt me, and I can't write either. Or else I feel guilty if my work is going along better than his, and I stop."[2]

To resolve Ellen's writing problems would require a marriage therapist in addition to a writing specialist, to focus intensively on their family context as the source of some of the difficulties. Perhaps such therapy would stimulate in both partners a greater desire than either member of the couple currently possesses to complete their extended writing projects (see M. Bloom, 1980). Alas, in this case *carpe diem* has seemed preferable to *carpe dissertation.*

As Ellen's case illustrates, when contexts not conducive to writing interfere with those that are, the conflict may produce little writing—and little desire to do any. Even when writing teachers and researchers understand the scope of the problems, they may not be able to resolve the difficulties of approximately one quarter of the anxious writers who seek help. As Milton's Satan laments of his own context in *Paradise Lost*, "Which way I fly is hell; myself am hell." More psychologically oriented writing therapists (often, people with PhDs in English and several months of counseling training) often claim that after several months of therapy their clients feel a great deal more comfortable about writing, but to my knowledge there is no available data on whether or not the clients are actually completing the writing projects that drove them to the counselor in the first place. Yet, as Sarah's case reveals, by considering intellectual, emotional, temperamental, and other factors, teachers and researchers can often help anxious writers, providing specific solutions adapted to the social and academic contexts in which the difficulties occur.

Case studies, as has been implied throughout the exploration of the histories of Sarah and Ellen, reveal the importance of studying writing processes in the relevant contexts of the writer's life. Not only are the immediate writing contexts (such as the university and the home) of paramount influence on the performance of the writer; so are the writer's multiple roles in these contexts, among others, the roles of student, professor, spouse, parent, wage earner. Equally important is the writer's socialization into these roles, which determines how he or she is likely to perform in a given situation. For instance, the intensity with which the writer pursues the goals of working on and completing a particular writing task is inevitably influenced by his or her involvement in other roles and commitment to other activities perhaps unrelated to writing. When the aims and responsibilities of one role (say, wife, mother, or faculty member) conflict with another (say, student), the nature of the disequilibrium in its full context has to be understood before the person can be helped.

The dancer, the dance, and the place of performance are inextricably interrelated; they cannot be understood in isolation. Teachers, dissertation advisors, researchers, counselors, friends, or others working with anxious writers need to understand the writing problems as fully as possible in the appropriate contexts in order to provide specific, workable solutions adapted to the writer's temperament and to the performance of multiple roles in multiple contexts. An anxious writer, fully understood in context, can be more readily helped to be less anxious, more productive—to be simply, a writer.

NOTES

1. Mishler's view is reinforced by Janet Emig's theoretical "Inquiry Paradigms and Writing" (1982) and by Carol Berkenkotter's illuminating application of the "methodology of protocol analysis" combined with "the techniques of naturalistic inquiry" in her study of "The planning strategies of a publishing writer" (1983).

2. It should be noted here that coworkers in business settings may also impede each other's efforts in similar ways. Bosses can make their employees who have to write reports or memos highly anxious by failing to provide clear instructions for what they should do yet making them do the work over—and over, and over again—when it isn't right. Likewise, a perfectionist colleague who is never satisfied with the penultimate draft may slow down a rapid and capable writer.

REFERENCES

Bartholomae, D. (1980). The study of error. *College Composition and Communication, 31*, 253–269.

Berkenkotter, C. (1983). Decisions and revisions: The planning strategies of a publishing writer. *College Composition and Communication, 34*, 156–169.

Bloom, L. Z. (1980). The fear of writing. *Alumni Gazette, College of William and Mary, 47*, 25–29.

Bloom, L. Z. (1981a). Doctoring and mastering graduate writing. *Journal of English Teaching Techniques, 11*, 74–81.

Bloom, L. Z. (1981b, December). *When the muse is out to lunch: Professional women and writing anxiety.* Paper presented at the annual meeting of the Modern Language Association, New York.

Bloom, L. Z. (1981c). Why graduate students can't write: Implications of research on writing anxiety for graduate education. *Journal of Advanced Composition, 2*, 103–117.

Bloom, L. Z. (in press). Indentifying and reducing writing anxiety: Writing anxiety workshops. In D. Butturff (Ed.), *The psychology of composition.* Conway, AR: Language and Style Books.

Bloom, M. (1980). *Anxious writers: Distinguishing anxiety from pathology.* Washington, DC: Educational Resources Information Center. (ERIC Document Reproduction Service No. ED 172 254)

Calkins L. M. *Sequences of revision: Case study of a nine-year-old writer.* Durham: University of New Hampshire, Writing Process Laboratory. Undated manuscript.

Daly, J. A. (1979). Writing apprehension in the classroom: Teacher role expectancies of the apprehensive writer. *Research in the Teaching of English 13*, 37–44.

Emig, J. (1982). Inquiry paradigms and writing. *College Composition and Communication, 33*, 64–75.

Graves, D. (1975). An examination of the writing processes of seven-year-old children. *Research in the Teaching of English, 9*, 227–241.

Graves, D., Calkins, L., & Sowers, S. (1978–1979). *Research reports.* Durham: University of New Hampshire, Writing Process Laboratory.

Lewin, K. (1951). *Field theory in social science.* New York: Harper & Row.

Maccoby, E. E., & Jacklin, C. N. (1974). *The psychology of sex differences.* Stanford, CA: Stanford University Press.

Mishler, E. G. (1979). Meaning in context: Is there any other kind? *Harvard Educational Review, 49*, 1–19.

Nathanson, C. A. (1977). Sex roles as variables in preventive health behavior. *Journal of Community Health, 3*, 142–155.

Olsen, T. (1978). *Silences.* New York: Delacorte.

Rose, M. (1980). Rigid rules, inflexible plans, and the stifling of language: A cognitivist analysis of writer's block. *College Composition and Communication, 31*, 389–401.

Rose, M. (1981). *The cognitive dimension of writer's block: An examination of university students.* Unpublished doctoral dissertation, University of California, Los Angeles.

Rose, M. (1984). *Writer's block: The cognitive dimension.* Carbondale: Southern Illinois University Press.

Shaughnessy, M. P. (1977). *Errors and expectations: A guide for the teacher of basic writing.* New York: Oxford University Press.

Strouse, J. (1980). *Alice James, a biography.* Boston: Houghton Mifflin.

Tavris, C., & Offir, C. (1977). *The longest war: Sex differences in perspective.* New York: Harcourt Brace Jovanovich.

Woolf, V. (1957). *A room of one's own.* New York: Harcourt, Brace & World. (Originally published 1929)

Inventing the University 7

DAVID BARTHOLOMAE

Education may well be, as of right, the instrument whereby every individual, in a society like our own, can gain access to any kind of discourse. But we well know that in its distribution, in what it permits and in what it prevents, it follows the well-trodden battle-lines of social conflict. Every educational system is a political means of maintaining or of modifying the appropriation of discourse, with the knowledge and the powers it carries with it.
—Foucault, *The Discourse on Language*

. . . the text is the form of the social relationships made visible, palpable, material.
—Bernstein, *Codes, Modalities and the Process of Cultural Reproduction: A Model*

I.

Every time a student sits down to write for us, he has to invent the university for the occasion—invent the university, that is, or a branch of it, like history or anthropology or economics or English. The student has to learn to speak our language, to speak as we do, to try on the peculiar ways of knowing, selecting, evaluating, reporting, concluding, and arguing that define the discourse of our community. Or perhaps I should say the *various* discourses of our community, since it is in the nature of a liberal arts education that a student, after the first year or

David Bartholomae. Department of English, University of Pittsburgh, Pittsburgh, Pennsylvania.

two, must learn to try on a variety of voices and interpretive schemes—to write, for example, as a literary critic one day and as an experimental psychologist the next; to work within fields where the rules governing the presentation of examples or the development of an argument are both distinct and, even to a professional mysterious.

The student has to appropriate (or be appropriated by) a specialized discourse, and he has to do this as though he were easily and comfortably one with his audience, as though he were a member of the academy or an historian or an anthropologist or an economist; he has to invent the university by assembling and mimicking its language while finding some compromise between idiosyncracy, a personal history, on the one hand, and the requirements of convention, the history of a discipline, on the other. He must learn to speak our language. Or he must dare to speak it or to carry off the bluff, since speaking and writing will most certainly be required long before the skill is "learned." And this, understandably, causes problems.

Let me look quickly at an example. Here is an essay written by a college freshman.

> In the past time I thought that an incident was creative was when I had to make a clay model of the earth, but not of the classical or your everyday model of the earth which consists of the two cores, the mantle and the crust. I thought of these things in a dimension of which it would be unique, but easy to comprehend. Of course, your materials to work with were basic and limited at the same time, but thought help to put this limit into a right attitude or frame of mind to work with the clay.
>
> In the beginning of the clay model, I had to research and learn the different dimensions of the earth (in magnitude, quantity, state of matter, etc.) After this, I learned how to put this into the clay and come up with something different than any other person in my class at the time. In my opinion, color coordination and shape was the key to my creativity of the clay model of the earth.
>
> Creativity is the venture of the mind at work with the mechanics relay to the limbs from the cranium, which stores and triggers this action. It can be a burst of energy released at a precise time a thought is being transmitted. This can cause a frenzy of the human body, but it depends on the characteristics of the individual and how they can relay the message clearly enough through mechanics of the body to us as an observer. Then we must determine if it is creative or a learned process varied by the individuals thought process. Creativity is indeed a tool which has to exist, or our world will not succeed into the future and progress like it should.

I am continually impressed by the patience and goodwill of our students. This student was writing a placement essay during freshman orientation. (The problem set to him was: "Describe a time when you did something you felt to be creative. Then, on the basis of the incident you have described, go on to draw some general conclusions about 'creativity.'") He knew that university faculty would be reading and evaluating his essay, and so he wrote for them.

In some ways it is a remarkable performance. He is trying on the discourse even though he doesn't have the knowledge that would make the discourse more than a routine, a set of conventional rituals and gestures. And he is doing this, I think, even though he *knows* he doesn't have the knowledge that would make the discourse more than a routine. He defines himself as a researcher working systematically, and not as a kid in a high school class: "I thought of these things in a dimension of . . ."; "I had to research and learn the different dimensions of the earth (in magnitude, quantity, state of matter, etc.)." He moves quickly into a specialized language (his approximation of our jargon) and draws both a general, textbook-like conclusion—"Creativity is the venture of the mind at work . . ."—and a resounding peroration—"Creativity is indeed a tool which has to exist, or our world will not succeed into the future and progress like it should." The writer has even picked up the rhythm of our prose with that last "indeed" and with the qualifications and the parenthetical expressions of the opening paragraphs. And through it all he speaks with an impressive air of authority.

There is an elaborate but, I will argue, a necessary and enabling fiction at work here as the student dramatizes his experience in a "setting"—the setting required by the discourse—where he can speak to us as a companion, a fellow researcher. As I read the essay, there is only one moment when the fiction is broken, when we are addressed differently. The student says, "Of course, your materials to work with were basic and limited at the same time, but thought help to put this limit into a right attitude or frame of mind to work with the clay." At this point, I think, we become students and he the teacher giving us a lesson (as in, "You take your pencil in your right hand and put your paper in front of you"). This is, however, one of the most characteristic slips of basic writers. (I use the term "basic writers" to refer to university students traditionally placed in remedial composition courses.) It is very hard for them to take on the role—the voice, the persona—of an authority whose authority is rooted in scholarship, analysis, or research. They slip, then, into a more immediately available and realizable voice of authority, the voice of a teacher giving a lesson or the voice of a parent lecturing at the dinner table. They offer advice or homilies rather than "academic" conclusions. There is a similar break in the final paragraph, where the conclusion that pushes for a definition ("Creativity is the venture of the mind at work with the mechanics relay to the limbs from the cranium") is replaced by a conclusion that speaks in the voice of an elder ("Creativity is indeed a tool which has to exist, or our world will not succeed into the future and progress like it should").

It is not uncommon, then, to find such breaks in the concluding sections of essays written by basic writers. Here is the concluding section of an essay written by a student about his work as a mechanic. He had been asked to generalize about work after reviewing an on-the-job experience or incident that "stuck in his mind" as somehow significant.

> How could two repairmen miss a leak? Lack of pride? No incentive? Lazy? I don't know.

At this point the writer is in a perfect position to speculate, to move from the problem to an analysis of the problem. Here is how the paragraph continues, however (and notice the change in pronoun reference).

> From this point on, I take *my* time, do it right, and don't let customers get under *your* skin. If they have a complaint, tell them to call your boss and he'll be more than glad to handle it. Most important, worry about yourself, and keep a clear eye on everyone, for there's always someone trying to take advantage of you, anytime and anyplace. (Emphasis added)

We get neither a technical discussion nor an "academic" discussion but a Lesson on Life.[1] This is the language he uses to address the general question, "How could two repairmen miss a leak?" The other brand of conclusion, the more academic one, would have required him to speak of his experience in our terms; it would, that is, have required a special vocabulary, a special system of presentation, and an interpretive scheme (or a set of commonplaces) he could have used to identify and talk about the mystery of human error. The writer certainly had access to the range of acceptable commonplaces for such an explanation: "lack of pride," "no incentive," "lazy." Each commonplace would dictate its own set of phrases, examples, and conclusions; and we, his teachers, would know how to write out each argument, just as we know how to write out more specialized arguments of our own. A "commonplace," then, is a culturally or institutionally authorized concept or statement that carries with it its own necessary elaboration. We all use commonplaces to orient ourselves in the world; they provide points of reference and a set of "prearticulated" explanations that are readily available to organize and interpret experience. The phrase "lack of pride" carries with it its own account of the repairman's error, just as at another point in time a reference to "original sin" would have provided an explanation, or just as in certain university classrooms a reference to "alienation" would enable writers to continue and complete the discussion. While there is a way in which these terms are interchangeable, they are not all permissible: A student in a composition class would most likely be turned away from a discussion of original sin. Commonplaces are the "controlling ideas" of our composition textbooks, textbooks that not only insist on a set form for expository writing but a set view of public life.[2]

When the writer says, "I don't know," then, he is not saying that he has nothing to say. He is saying that he is not in a position to carry on this discussion. And so we are addressed as apprentices rather than as teachers or scholars. In order to speak as a person of status or privilege, the writer can either speak to us in our terms—in the privileged language of university discourse—or, in default (or in defiance) of that, he can speak to us as though we were children, offering us the wisdom of experience.

I think it is possible to say that the language of the "Clay Model" paper has come *through* the writer and not from the writer. The writer has located himself (more precisely, he has located the self that is represented by the "I" on the page) in a context that is finally beyond him, not his own and not available to his immediate procedures for inventing and arranging text. I would not, that is, call this essay an example of "writer-based" prose. I would not say that it is egocentric or that it represents the "interior monologue or a writer thinking and talking to himself" (Flower, 1981, p. 63). It is, rather, the record of a writer who has lost himself in the discourse of his readers. There is a context beyond the intended reader that is not the world but a way of talking about the world, a way of talking that determines the use of examples, the possible conclusions, acceptable commonplaces, and key words for an essay on the construction of a clay model of the earth. This writer has entered the discourse without successfully approximating it.

Linda Flower (1981) has argued that the difficulty inexperienced writers have with writing can be understood as a difficulty in negotiating the transition between "writer-based" and "reader-based" prose. Expert writers, in other words, can better imagine how a reader will respond to a text and can transform or restructure what they have to say around a goal shared with a reader. Teaching students to revise for readers, then, will better prepare them to write initially with a reader in mind. The success of this pedagogy depends on the degree to which a writer can imagine and conform to a reader's goals. The difficulty of this act of imagination and the burden of such conformity are so much at the heart of the problem that a teacher must pause and take stock before offering revision as a solution. A student like the one who wrote the "Clay Model" paper is not so much trapped in a private language as he is shut out from one of the privileged languages of public life, a language he is aware of but cannot control.

II.

Our students, I've said, have to appropriate (or be appropriated by) a specialized discourse, and they have to do this as though they were easily or comfortably one with their audience. If you look at the situation this way, suddenly the problem of audience awareness becomes enormously complicated. One of the common assumptions of both composition research and composition teaching is that at some "stage" in the process of composing an essay a writer's ideas or his motives must be tailored to the needs and expectations of his audience. Writers have to "build bridges" between their point of view and the reader's. They have to anticipate and acknowledge the reader's assumptions and biases. They must begin with "common points of departure" before introducing new or controversial arguments. Here is what one of the most popular college textbooks says to students.

> Once you have your purpose clearly in mind, your next task is to define and analyze your audience. A sure sense of your audience—knowing who it is and what assumptions you can reasonably make about it—is crucial to the success of your rhetoric. (Hairston, 1978, p. 107)

It is difficult to imagine, however, how writers can have a purpose before they are located in a discourse, since it is the discourse with its projects and agendas that determines what writers can and will do. The writer who can successfully manipulate an audience (or, to use a less pointed language, the writer who can accommodate her motives to her reader's expectations) is a writer who can both imagine and write from a position of privilege. She must, that is, see herself within a privileged discourse, one that already includes and excludes groups of readers. She must be either equal to or more powerful than those she would address. The writing, then, must somehow transform the political and social relationships between students and teachers.

If my students are going to write for me by knowing who I am—and if this means more than knowing my prejudices, psyching me out—it means knowing what I know; it means having the knowledge of a professor of English. They have, then, to know what I know and how I know what I know (the interpretive schemes that define the way I would work out the problems I set for them); they have to learn to write what I would write or to offer up some approximation of that discourse. The problem of audience awareness, then, is a problem of power and finesse. It cannot be addressed, as it is in most classroom exercises, by giving students privilege and denying the situation of the classroom—usually, that is, by having students write to an outsider, someone excluded from their privileged circle: "Write about 'To His Coy Mistress,' not for your teacher but for the students in your class"; "Describe Pittsburgh to someone who has never been there"; "Explain to a high school senior how best to prepare for college"; "Describe baseball to an Eskimo." Exercises such as these allow students to imagine the needs and goals of a reader, and they bring those needs and goals forward as a dominant constraint in the construction of an essay. And they argue, implicitly, what is generally true about writing—that it is an act of aggression disguised as an act of charity. What these assignments fail to address is the central problem of academic writing, where a student must assume the right of speaking to someone who knows more about baseball or "To His Coy Mistress" than the student does, a reader for whom the general commonplaces and the readily available utterances about a subject are inadequate.

Linda Flower and John Hayes, in an often quoted article (1981), reported on a study of a protocol of an expert writer (an English teacher) writing about his job for readers of *Seventeen* magazine. The key moment for this writer, who seems to have been having trouble getting started, came when he decided that teenage girls read *Seventeen*; that some teenage girls like English because it is tidy ("some of them will have wrong reasons in that English is good because it's tidy—can be a neat tidy little girl"); that some don't like it because it is "prim" and that, "By God, I can change that notion for them." Flower and Hayes's conclusion is that this effort of "exploration and consolidation" gave the writer "a new, relatively complex, rhetorically sophisticated working goal, one which encompasses plans for a topic, a persona, and the audience" (p. 383).[3]

Flower and Hayes give us a picture of a writer solving a problem, and the problem as they present it is a cognitive one. It is rooted in the way the writer's knowledge is represented in the writer's mind. The problem resides there, not in the nature of knowledge or in the nature of discourse but in a mental state prior to writing. It is possible, however, to see the problem as (perhaps simultaneously) a problem in the way subjects are located in a field of discourse.

Flower and Hayes divide up the composing process into three distinct activities: "planning or goal-setting," "translating," and "reviewing." The last of these, reviewing (which is further divided into two subprocesses, "evaluating" and "revising"), is particularly powerful, for as a writer continually reviews his goals, plans, and the text he is producing, and as he continually generates new goals, plans, and text, he is engaging in a process of learning and discovery. Let me quote Flower and Hayes's conclusion at length.

> If one studies the process by which a writer uses a goal to generate ideas, then consolidates those ideas and uses them to revise or regenerate new, more complex goals, one can see this learning process in action. Furthermore, one sees why the process of revising and clarifying goals has such a broad effect, since it is through setting these new goals that the fruits of discovery come back to inform the continuing process of writing. In this instance, some of our most complex and imaginative acts can depend on the elegant simplicity of a few powerful thinking processes. We feel that a cognitive process explanation of discovery, toward which this theory is only a start, will have another special strength. By placing emphasis on the inventive power of the writer, who is able to explore ideas, to develop, act on, test, and regenerate his or her own goals, we are putting an important part of creativity where it belongs—in the hands of the working, thinking writer. (1981, p. 386)

While this conclusion is inspiring, the references to invention and creativity seem to refer to something other than an act of writing—if writing is, finally, words on a page. Flower and Hayes locate the act of writing solely within the mind of the writer. The act of writing, here, has a personal, cognitive history but not a history as a text, as a text that is made possible by prior texts. When located in the perspective afforded by prior texts, writing is seen to exist separate from the writer and his intentions; it is seen in the context of other articles in *Seventeen*, of all articles written for or about women, of all articles written about English teaching, and so on. Reading research has made it possible to say that these prior texts, or a reader's experience with these prior texts, have bearing on how the text is read. Intentions, then, are part of the history of the language itself. I am arguing that these prior texts determine not only how a text like the *Seventeen* article will be read but also how it will be written. Flower and Hayes show us what happens in the writer's mind but not what happens to the writer as his motives are located within our language, a language with its own requirements and agendas, a language that limits what we might say and that makes us write and sound, finally, also like someone else. If you think of other accounts of the composing process—and I'm thinking of accounts as diverse as Richard Rodriguez's *Hunger or Memory* (1983) and Edward Said's *Beginnings* (1975)—you get a very different account of what happens when private motive enters into public discourse, when a personal history becomes a public account. These accounts place the writer in a history that is not of the writer's own invention; and they are chronicles of loss, violence, and compromise.

It is one thing to see the *Seventeen* writer making and revising his plans for a topic, a persona, and an audience; it is another thing to talk about discovery, invention, and creativity. Whatever plans the writer had must finally have been located in language and, it is possible to argue, in a language that is persistently conventional and formulaic. We do not, after all, get to see the *Seventeen* article. We see only the elaborate mental procedures that accompanied the writing of the essay. We see a writer's plans for a persona; we don't see that persona in action. If writing is a process, it is also a product; and it is the product, and not the plan for writing, that locates a writer on the page, that locates him in a text and a style and the codes or conventions that make both of them readable.

Contemporary rhetorical theory has been concerned with the "codes" that constitute discourse (or specialized forms of discourse). These codes determine not only what might be said but also who might be speaking or reading. Barthes (1974), for example, has argued that the moment of writing, where private goals and plans become subject to a public language, is the moment when the writer becomes subject to a language he can neither command nor control. A text, he says, in being written passes through the codes that govern writing and becomes "de-originated," becomes a fragment of something that has "always been *already* read, seen, done, experienced" (p. 21). Alongside a text we have always the presence of "off-stage voices," the oversound of all that has been said (e.g., about girls, about English). These voices, the presence of the "already written," stand in defiance of a writer's desire for originality and determine what might be said. A writer does not write (and this is Barthes's famous paradox) but is, himself, written by the languages available to him.

It is possible to see the writer of the *Seventeen* article solving his problem of where to begin by appropriating an available discourse. Perhaps what enabled that writer to write was the moment he located himself as a writer in a familiar field of stereotypes: Readers of *Seventeen* are teenage girls; teenage girls think of English (and English teachers) as "tidy" and "prim," and, "By God, I can change that notion for them." The moment of eureka was not simply a moment of breaking through a cognitive jumble in that individual writer's mind but a moment of breaking into a familiar and established territory—one with insiders and outsiders; one with set phrases, examples, and conclusions.

I'm not offering a criticism of the morals or manners of the teacher who wrote the *Seventeen* article. I think that all writers, in order to write, must imagine for themselves the privilege of being "insiders"—that is, the privilege both of being inside an established and powerful discourse and of being granted a special right to speak. But I think that right to speak is seldom conferred on us—on any of us, teachers or students—by virtue of that fact that we have invented or discovered an original idea. Leading students to believe that they are responsible for something new or original, unless they understand what those words mean with regard to writing, is a dangerous and counterproductive practice. We do have the right to expect students to be active and engaged, but that is a matter of continually and stylistically working against the inevitable presence of conventional language; it is not a matter of inventing a language that is new.

When a student is writing for a teacher, writing becomes more problematic than it was for the *Seventeen* writer (who was writing a version of the "Describe baseball to an Eskimo" exercise). The student, in effect, has to assume privilege without having any. And since students assumes privilege by locating themselves within the discourse of a particular community—within a set of specifically acceptable gestures and commonplaces—learning, at least as it is defined in the liberal arts curriculum, becomes more a matter of imitation or parody than a matter of invention and discovery.

To argue that writing problems are also social and political problems is not to break faith with the enterprise of cognitive science. In a recent paper reviewing the tremendous range of research directed at identifying general cognitive skills, David Perkins (in press) has argued that "the higher the level of competence concerned," as in the case of adult learning, "the fewer *general* cognitive control strategies there are." There comes a point, that is, where "field-specific" or "domain-specific" schemata (what I have called "interpretive strategies") become more important than general problem-solving processes. Thinking, learning, writing—all these become bound to the context of a particular discourse. And Perkins concludes:

> Instruction in cognitive control strategies tends to be organized around problem-solving tasks. However, the isolated problem is a creature largely of the classroom. The nonstudent, whether operating in scholarly or more everyday contexts, is likely to find himself or herself involved in what might be called "projects"—which might be anything from writing a novel to designing a shoe to starting a business.

It is interesting to note that Perkins defines the classroom as the place of artificial tasks and, as a consequence, has to place scholarly projects outside the classroom, where they are carried out by the "nonstudent." It is true, I think, that education has failed to involve students in scholarly projects, projects that allow students to act as though they were colleagues in an academic enterprise. Much of the written work that students do is test-taking, report or summary—

work that places them outside the official discourse of the academic community, where they are expected to admire and report on what we do, rather than inside that discourse, where they can do its work and participate in a common enterprise.[4] This, however, is a failure of teachers and curriculum designers, who speak of writing as a mode of learning but all too often represent writing as a "tool" to be used by an (hopefully) educated mind.

It could be said, then, that there is a bastard discourse peculiar to the writing most often required of students. Carl Bereiter and Marlene Scardamalia (in press) have written about this discourse (they call it "knowledge-telling"; students who are good at it have learned to cope with academic tasks by developing a "knowledge-telling strategy"), and they have argued that insistence on knowledge-telling discourse undermines educational efforts to extend the variety of discourse schemata available to students.[5] What they actually say is this:

> When we think of knowledge stored in memory we tend these days to think of it as situated in three-dimensional space, with vertical and horizontal connections between sites. Learning is thought to add not only

> new elements to memory but also new connections, and it is the richness and structure of these connections that would seem . . . to spell the difference between inert and usable knowledge. On this account, the knowledge-telling strategy is educationally faulty because it specifically avoids the forming of connections between previously separated knowledge sites.

It should be clear by now that when I think of "knowledge" I think of it as situated in the discourse that constitutes "knowledge" in a particular discourse community, rather than as situated in mental "knowledge sites." One can remember a discourse, just as one can remember an essay or the movement of a professor's lecture; but this discourse, in effect, also has a memory of its own, its own rich network of structures and connections beyond the deliberate control of any individual imagination.

There is, to be sure, an important distinction to be made between learning history, say, and learning to write as an historian. A student can learn to command and reproduce a set of names, dates, places, and canonical interpretations (to "tell" somebody else's knowledge); but this is not the same thing as learning to "think" (by learning to write) as an historian. The former requires efforts of memory; the latter requires a student to compose a text out of the texts that represent the primary materials of history and in accordance with the texts that define history as an act of report and interpretation.

Let me draw on an example from my own teaching. I don't expect my students to *be* literary critics when they write about *Bleak House*. If a literary critic is a person who wins publication in a professional journal (or if he or she is one who could), the students aren't critics. I do, however, expect my students to be, themselves, invented as literary critics by approximating the language of a literary critic writing about *Bleak House*. My students, then, don't invent the language of literary criticism (they don't, that is, act on their own) but they are, themselves, invented by it. Their papers don't begin with a moment of insight, a "by God" moment that is outside of language. They begin with a moment of appropriation, a moment when they can offer up a sentence that is not theirs as though it were their own. (I can remember when, as a graduate student, I would begin papers by sitting down to write literally in the voice—with the syntax and the key words—of the strongest teacher I had met.)

What I am saying about my students' essays is that they are

approximate, not that they are wrong or invalid. They are evidence of a discourse that lies between what I might call the students' primary discourse (what the students might write about *Bleak House* were they not in my class or in any class, and were they not imagining that they were in my class or in any class—if you can imagine any student doing any such thing) and standard, official literary criticism (which is imaginable but impossible to find). The students' essays are evidence of a discourse that lies between these two hypothetical poles. The writing is limited as much by a student's ability to imagine "what might be said" as it is by cognitive control strategies.[6] The act of writing takes the student away from where he is and what he knows and allows him to imagine something else. The approximate discourse, therefore, is evidence of a change, a change that, because we are teachers, we call "development." What our beginning students need to learn is to extend themselves, by successive approximations, into the commonplaces, set phrases, rituals and gestures, habits of mind, tricks of persuasion, obligatory conclusions and necessary connections that determine the "what might be said" and constitute knowledge within the various branches of our academic community.[7]

Pat Bizzell is, I think, one of the most important scholars writing now on "basic writers" (and this is the common name we use for students who are refused unrestrained access to the academic community) and on the special characteristics of academic discourse. In a recent essay, "Cognition, Convention, and Certainty: What We Need to Know about Writing" (1982a), she looks at two schools of composition research and the way they represent the problems that writing poses for writers.[8] For one group, the "inner-directed theorists," the problems are internal, cognitive, rooted in the way the mind represents knowledge to itself. These researchers are concerned with discovering the "universal, fundamental structures of thought and language" and with developing pedagogies to teach or facilitate both basic, general cognitive skills and specific cognitive strategies, or heuristics, directed to serve more specialized needs. Of the second group, the "outer-directed theorists," she says that they are "more interested in the social processes whereby language-learning and thinking capacities are shaped and used in particular communities."

> The staple activity of outer-directed writing instruction will be analysis of the conventions of particular discourse communities. For example, a main focus of writing-across-the-curriculum programs is to demystify the conventions of the academic discourse community. (1982a, pp. 218)

The essay offers a detailed analysis of the way the two theoretical camps can best serve the general enterprise of composition research and composition teaching. Its agenda, however, seems to be to counter the influence of the cognitivists and to provide bibliography and encouragement to those interested in the social dimension of language learning.

As far as basic writers are concerned, Bizzell argues that the cognitivists' failure to acknowledge the primary, shaping role of convention in the act of composing makes them "particularly insensitive to the problems of poor writers." She argues that some of those problems, like the problem of establishing and monitoring overall goals for a piece of writing, can be

> better understood in terms of their unfamiliarity with the academic discourse community, combined, perhaps, with such limited experience outside their native discourse communities that they are unaware that there is such a thing as a discourse community with conventions to be mastered. What is underdeveloped is their knowledge both of the ways experience is constituted and interpreted in the academic discourse community and of the fact that all discourse communities constitute and interpret experience. (1982a, p. 230)

One response to the problems of basic writers, then, would be to determine just what the community's conventions are, so that those conventions could be written out, "demystified" and taught in our classrooms. Teachers, as a result, could be more precise and helpful when they ask students to "think," "argue," "describe," or "define." Another response would be to examine the essays written by basic writers—their approximations of academic discourse—to determine more clearly where the problems lie. If we look at their writing, and if we look at it in the context of other student writing, we can better see the points of discord that arise when students try to write their way into the university.

The purpose of the remainder of this chapter will be to examine some of the most striking and characteristic of these problems as they are presented in the expository essays of first-year college students. I will be concerned, then, with university discourse in its most generalized form—as it is represented by introductory courses—and not with the special conventions required by advanced work in the various disciplines. And I will be concerned with the difficult, and often violent accommodations that occur when students locate themselves in a discourse that is not "naturally" or immediately theirs.

III.

I have reviewed 500 essays written, as the "Clay Model" essay was, in response to a question used during one of our placement exams at the University of Pittsburgh: "Describe a time when you did something you felt to be creative. Then, on the basis of the incident you have described, go on to draw some general conclusions about "creativity." Some of the essays were written by basic writers (or, more properly, those essays led readers to identify the writers as basic writers); some were written by students who "passed" (who were granted immediate access to the community of writers at the university). As I read these essays, I was looking to determine the stylistic resources that enabled writers to locate themselves within an "academic" discourse. My bias as a reader should be clear by now. I was not looking to see how a writer might represent the skills demanded by a neutral language (a language whose key features were paragraphs, topic sentences, transitions, and the like—features of a clear and orderly mind). I was looking to see what happened when a writer entered into a language to locate himself (a textual self) and his subject; and I was looking to see how, once entered, that language made or unmade the writer.

Here is one essay. Its writer was classified as a basic writer and, since the essay is relatively free of sentence level errors, that decision must have been rooted in some perceived failure of the discourse itself.

> I am very interested in music, and I try to be creative in my interpretation of music. While in highschool, I was a member of a jazz ensemble. The members of the ensemble were given chances to improvise and be creative in various songs. I feel that this was a great experience for me, as well as the other members. I was proud to know that I could use my imagination and feelings to create music other than what was written.
>
> Creativity to me, means being free to express yourself in a way that is unique to you, not having to conform to certain rules and guidelines. Music is only one of the many areas in which people are given opportunities to show their creativity. Sculpting, carving, building, art, and acting are just a few more areas where people can show their creativity.
>
> Through my music I conveyed feelings and thoughts which were important to me. Music was my means of showing creativity. In whatever form creativity takes, whether it be music, art, or science, it is an important aspect of our lives because it enables us to be individuals.

Notice the key gesture in this essay, one that appears in all but a few of the essays I read. The student defines as his own that which is a commonplace. "Creativity, *to me*, means being free to express yourself in a way that is unique to you, not having to conform to certain rules and guidelines." This act of appropriation constitutes his authority; it constitutes his authority as a writer and not just as a musician (that is, as someone with a story to tell). There were many essays in the set that told only a story—where the writer established his presence as a musician or a skier or someone who painted designs on a van, but not as a person at a remove from that experience interpreting it, treating it as a metaphor for something else (creativity). Unless those stories were long, detailed, and very well told—unless the writer was doing more than saying, "I am a skier" or a musician or a van-painter—those writers were all given low ratings.

Notice also that the writer of the "Jazz" paper locates himself and his experience in relation to the commonplace (creativity is unique expression; it is not having to conform to rules or guidelines) regardless of whether the commonplace is true or not. Anyone who improvises "knows" that improvisation follows rules and guidelines. It is the power of the commonplace—its truth as a recognizable and, the writer believes, as a final statement—that justifies the example and completes the essay. The example, in other words, has value because it stands within the field of the commonplace.[9] It is not the occasion for what one might call an "objective" analysis or a "close" reading. It could also be said that the essay stops with the articulation of the commonplace. The following sections speak only to the power of that statement. The reference to "sculpting, carving, building, art, and acting" attest to the universality of the commonplace (and it attests the writer's nervousness with the status he has appropriated for himself—he is saying, "Now, I'm not the only one here who has done something unique"). The commonplace stands by itself. For this writer, it does not need to be elaborated. By virtue of having written it, he has completed the essay and established the contract by which we may be spoken to as equals: "In whatever form creativity takes, whether it be music, art, or science, it is an important aspect of *our* lives because it enables *us* to be individuals." (For me to break that contract, to argue that *my* life is not represented in that essay, is one way for me to begin as a teacher with that student in that essay.)

All of the papers I read were built around one of three commonplaces: (1) creativity is self-expression, (2) creativity is doing something new or unique, and (3) creativity is using old things in new ways. These are clearly, then, key phrases from the storehouse of things to say about creativity. I've listed them in the order of the students' ratings: A student with the highest rating was more likely to use number three than number one, although each commonplace ran across the range of possible ratings. One could argue that some standard assertions are more powerful than others, but I think the ranking simply represents the power of assertions within our community of readers. Every student was able to offer up an experience that was meant as an example of "creativity"; the lowest range of writers, then, was not represented by students who could not imagine themselves as creative people.[10]

I said that the writer of the "Jazz" paper offered up a commonplace regardless of whether it was true or not; and this, I said, was an instance of the power of a commonplace to determine the meaning of an example. A commonplace determines a system of interpretation that can be used to "place" an example within a standard system of belief. You can see a similar process at work in this essay.

> During the football season, the team was supposed to wear the same type of cleats and the same type socks, I figured that I would change this a little by wearing my white shoes instead of black and to cover up the team socks with a pair of my own white ones. I thought that this looked better than what we were wearing, and I told a few of the other people on the team to change too. They agreed that it did look better and they changed there combination to go along with mine. After the game people came up to us and said that it looked very good the way we wore our socks, and they wanted to know why we changed from the rest of the team.
>
> I feel that creativity comes from when a person lets his imagination come up with ideas and he is not afraid to express them. Once you create something to do it will be original and unique because it came about from your own imagination and if any one else tries to copy it, it won't be the same because you thought of it first from your own ideas.

This is not an elegant paper, but it seems seamless, tidy. If the paper on the clay model of the earth showed an ill fit between the writer and his project, here the discourse seems natural, smooth. You could reproduce this paper and hand it out to a class, and it would take a lot of prompting before the students sensed something fishy and one of the more aggressive ones said something like, "Sure he came up with the idea of wearing white shoes and white socks. Him and Billy 'White-Shoes' Johnson. Come on. He copied the very thing he said was his own idea, 'original and unique.'"

The "I" of this text—the "I" who "figured," "thought," and "felt"—is located in a conventional rhetoric of the self that turns imagination into origination (I made it), that argues an ethic of production (I made it and it is mine), and that argues a tight scheme of intention (I made it because I decided to make it). The rhetoric seems invisible because it is so common. This "I" (the maker) is also located in a version of history that dominates classrooms, the "great man" theory: History is rolling along (the English novel is dominated by a central, intrustive narrative presence; America is in the throes of a Great Depression; during football season the team was supposed to wear the same kind of cleats and socks) until a figure appears, one who can shape history (Henry James, FDR, the writer of the "White Shoes" paper), and everything is changed. In the argument of the "White Shoes" paper, the history goes "I figured . . . I thought . . . I told . . . They agreed . . ." and, as a consequence, "I feel that creativity *comes from when* a person lets his imagination come up with ideas and he is not afraid to express them." The act of appropriation becomes a narrative of courage and conquest. The writer was able to write that story when he was able to imagine himself in that discourse. Getting him out of it will be a difficult matter indeed.

There are ways, I think, that a writer can shape history in the very act of writing it. Some students are able to enter into a discourse but, by stylistic maneuvers, to take possession of it at the same time. They don't originate a discourse, but they locate themselves within it aggressively, self-consciously. Here is another essay on jazz, which for sake of convenience I've shortened. It received a higher rating than the first essay on jazz.

> Jazz has always been thought of as a very original creative field in music. Improvisation, the spontaneous creation of original melodies in a piece of music, makes up a large part of jazz as a musical style. I had the opportunity to be a member of my high school's jazz ensemble for three years, and became an improvisation soloist this year. Throughout the years, I have seen and heard many jazz players, both proffessional and amateur. The solos performed by these artists were each flavored with that particular individual's style and ideas, along with some of the conventional premises behind improvisation. This particular type of solo work is creative because it is, done on the spur of the moment and blends the performer's ideas with basic guidelines.
>
> I realized my own creative potential when I began soloing. . . .
>
> My solos, just as all the solos generated by others, were original because I combined and shaped other's ideas with mine to create something completely new. Creativity is combining the practical knowledge and guidelines of a discipline with one's original ideas to bring about a new, original end result, one that is different from everyone else's. Creativity is based on the individual. Two artists can interpret the same scene differently. Each person who creates something does so by bringing out something individual in himself.

The essay is different in some important ways from the first essay on jazz. The writer of the second is more easily able to place himself in the context of an "academic" discussion. The second essay contains an "I" who realized his "creative potential" by soloing; the first contained an "I" who had "a great experience." In the second essay, before the phrase, "I had the opportunity to be a member of my high school's jazz ensemble," there is an introduction that offers a general definition of improvisation and an acknowledgment that other people have thought about jazz and creativity. In fact, throughout the essay the writer offers definitions and counterdefinitions. He is placing himself in the context of what has been said and what might be said. In the first paper, before a similar statement about being a member of a jazz ensemble, there was in introduction that locates jazz solely in the context of this individual's experience: "I am very interested in music." The writer of this first paper was authorized by who he is, a musician, rather than by what he can say about music in the context of what is generally said. The writer of the second essay uses a more specialized vocabulary; he talks about "conventional premises," "creative potential," "musical style," and "practical knowledge." And this is not just a matter of using bigger words, since these terms locate the experience in the context of a recognizable interpretive scheme—on the one hand there is tradition and, on the other, individual talent.

It could be said, then, that this essay is also framed and completed by a commonplace: "Creativity is combining the practical knowledge and guidelines of a discipline with one's original ideas to bring about a new, original end result, one that is different from everyone else's." Here, however, the argument is a more powerful one; and I mean "powerful" in the political sense, since it is an argument that complicates a "naive" assumption (it makes scholarly work possible, in other words), and it does so in terms that come close to those used in current academic debates (over the relation between convention and idiosyncracy or between rules and creativity). The assertion is almost consumed by the pleas for originality at the end of the sentence; but the point remains that the terms "original" and "different," as they are used at the end of the essay, are problematic, since they must be thought of in the context of "practical knowledge and guidelines of a discipline."

The key distinguishing gesture of this essay, that which makes it "better" than the other, is the way the writer works against a conventional point of view, one that is represented within the essay by conventional phrases that the writer must then work against. In his practice he demonstrates that a writer, and not just a musician, works within "conventional premises." The "I" who comments in this paper (not the "I" of the narrative about a time when he soloed) places himself

self-consciously within the context of a conventional discourse about the subject, even as he struggles against the language of that conventional dicourse. The opening definition of improvisation, where improvisation is defined as spontaneous creation, is rejected when the writer begins talking about "the conventional premises behind improvisation." The earlier definition is part of the conventional language of those who "have always thought" of jazz as a "very original creative field in music." The paper begins with what "has been said" and then works itself out against the force and logic of what has been said, of what is not only an argument but also a collection of phrases, examples, and definitions.

I had a teacher who once told us that whenever we were stuck for something to say, we should use the following as a "machine" for producing a paper: "While most readers of ______ have said ______, a close and careful reading shows that ______." The writer of the second paper on jazz is using a standard opening gambit, even if it is not announced with flourish. The essay becomes possible when he sets himself against what must become a "naive" assumption—what "most people think." He has defined a closed circle for himself. In fact, you could say that he has laid the ground work for a discipline with its own key terms ("practical knowledge," "disciplinary guidelines," and "original ideas"), with its own agenda and with its own investigative procedures (looking for common features in the work of individual soloists).

The history represented by this student's essay, then, is not the history of a musician and it is not the history of a thought being worked out within an individual mind; it is the history of work being done within and against conventional systems.

In general, as I reviewed the essays for this study, I found that the more successful writers set themselves in their essays against what they defined as some more naive way of talking about their subject—against "those who think that . . ."—or against earlier, more naive versions of themselves—"once I thought that. . . ." By trading in one set of commonplaces at the expense of another, they could win themselves status as members of what is taken to be some more privileged group. The ability to imagine privilege enabled writing. Here is one particularly successful essay. Notice the specialized vocabularly, but notice also the way in which the text continually refers to its own language and to the language of others.

Throughout my life, I have been interested and intrigued by music. My mother has often told me of the times, before I went to school, when I would "conduct" the orchestra on her records. I continued to listen to music and eventually started to play the guitar and the clarinet. Finally, at about the age of twelve, I started to sit down and to try to write songs. Even though my instrumental skills were far from my own high standards, I would spend much of my spare time during the day with a guitar around my neck, trying to produce a piece of music.

Each of these sessions, as I remember them, had a rather set format. I would sit in my bedroom, strumming different combinations of the five or six chords I could play, until I heard a series of which sounded particularly good to me. After this, I set the music to a suitable rhythm, (usually dependent on my mood at the time), and ran through the tune until I could play it fairly easily. Only after this section was complete did I go on to writing lyrics, which generally followed along the lines of the current popular songs on the radio.

At the time of the writing, I felt that my songs were, in themselves, an original creation of my own; that is, I, alone, made them. However, I now see that, in this sense of the word, I was not creative. The songs themselves seem to be an oversimplified form of the music I listed to at the time.

In a more fitting sense, however, I *was* being creative. Since I did not purposely copy my favorite songs, I was, effectively, originating my songs from my own "process of creativity." To achieve my goal, I needed what a composer would call "inspiration" for my piece. In this case the inspiration was the current hit on the radio. Perhaps, with my present point of view, I feel that I used too much "inspiration" in my songs, but, at that time, I did not.

Creativity, therefore, is a process which, in my case, involved a certain series of "small creations" if you like. As well, it is something, the appreciation of which varies with one's point of view, that point of view being set by the person's experience, tastes, and his own personal view of creativity. The less experienced tend to allow for less originality, while the more experienced demand real originality to classify something a "creation." Either way, a term as abstract as this is perfectly correct, and open to interpretation.

This writer is consistently and dramatically conscious of herself forming something to say out of what has been said *and* out of what she has been saying in the act of writing this paper. "Creativity" begins in this paper as "original creation." What she thought was "creativity," however, she now says was imitation; and, as she says, "in this sense of the word" she was not "creative." In another sense, however, she says that she *was* creative, since she didn't purposefully copy the songs but used them as "inspiration."

While the elaborate stylistic display—the pauses, qualifications, and the use of quotation marks—is in part a performance for our benefit, at a more obvious level we as readers are directly addressed in the first sentence of the last paragraph: "Creativity, therefore, is a process which, in my case, involved a certain series of 'small creations' if you like." We are addressed here as adults who can share her perspective on what she has said and who can be expected to understand her terms. If she gets into trouble after this sentence, and I think she does, it is because she doesn't have the courage to generalize from her assertion. Since she has rhetorically separated herself from her younger "self," and since she argues that she has gotten smarter, she assumes that there is some developmental sequence at work here and that, in the world of adults (which must be more complete than the world of children) there must be something like "real creativity." If her world is imperfect (if she can only talk about creation by putting the word in quotation marks), it must be because she is young. When she looks beyond herself to us, she cannot see our work as an extension of her project. She cannot assume that we too will be concerned with the problem of creativity and originality. At least she is not willing to challenge us on those grounds, to generalize her argument, and to argue that even for adults creations are really only "small creations." The sense of privilege that has allowed her to expose her own language cannot be extended to expose ours.

The writing in this piece—that is, the work of the writer within the essay—goes on in spite of, or against, the language that keeps pressing to give another name to her experience as a songwriter and to bring the discussion to closure. (In comparison, think of the quick closure of the "White Shoes" paper.) Its style is difficult, highly qualified. It relies on quotation marks and parody to set off the language and attitudes that belong to the discourse (or the discourses) that it would reject, that it would not take as its own proper location.

David Olson (1981) has argued that the key difference between oral language and written language is that written language separates both the producer and the receiver from the text. For my student writers, this means that they had to learn that what they said (the code) was more important than what they meant (the intention). A writer, in other words, loses his primacy at the moment of writing and must begin to attend to his and his words' conventional, even physical presence on the page. And, Olson says, the writer must learn that his authority is not established through his presence but through his absence—through his ability, that is, to speak as a god-like source beyond the limitations of any particular social or historical moment; to speak by means of the wisdom of convention, through the oversounds of official or authoritative utterance, as the voice of logic or the voice of the community. He concludes:

> The child's growing competence with this distinctive register of language in which both the meaning and the authority are displaced from the

> intentions of the speaker and lodged "in the text" may contribute to the similarly specialized and distinctive mode of thought we have come to associate with literacy and formal education. (1918, p. 110)

Olson is writing about children. His generalizations, I think I've shown, can be extended to students writing their way into the academic community. These are educated and literate individuals, to be sure, but they are individuals still outside the peculiar boundaries of the academic community. In the papers I've examined in this chapter, the writers have shown an increasing awareness of the codes (or the competing codes) that operate within a discourse. To speak with authority they have to speak not only in another's voice but through another's code; and they not only have to do this, they have to speak in the voice and through the codes of those of us with power and wisdom; and they not only have to do this, they have to do it before they know what they are doing, before they have a project to participate in, and before, at least in terms of our disciplines, they have anything to say. Our students may be able to enter into a conventional discourse and speak, not as themselves, but through the voice of the community; the university, however, is the place where "common" wisdom is only of negative values—it is something to work against. The movement toward a more specialized discourse begins (or, perhaps, best begins) both when a student can define a position of privilege, a position that sets him against a "common" discourse, and when he or she can work self-consciously, critically, against not only the "common" code but his or her own.

IV.

Pat Bizzell, you will recall, argues that the problems of poor writers can be attributed both to their unfamiliarity with the conventions of academic discourse and to their ignorance that there are such things as discourse communities with conventions to be mastered. If the latter is true, I think it is true only in rare cases. All the student writers I've discussed (and, in fact, most of the student writers whose work I've seen) have shown an awareness that something special or something different is required when one writes for an academic classroom. The essays that I have presented in this chapter all, I think, give evidence of writers trying to write their way into a new community. To some degree, however, all of them can be said to be unfamiliar with the conventions of academic discourse.

Problems of convention are both problems of finish and problems of substance. The most substantial academic tasks for students, learning history or sociology or literary criticism, are matters of many courses, much reading and writing, and several years of education. Our students, however, must have a place to begin. They cannot sit through lectures and read textbooks and, as a consequence, write as sociologists or write literary criticism. There must be steps along the way. Some of these steps will be marked by drafts and revisions. Some will be marked by courses, and in an ideal curriculum the preliminary courses would be writing courses, whether housed in an English department or not. For some students, students we call "basic writers," these courses will be in a sense the most basic introduction to the language and methods of academic writing.

Our students, as I've said, must have a place to begin. If the problem of a beginning is the problem of establishing authority, of defining rhetorically or stylistically a position from which one may speak, then the papers I have examined show characteristic student responses to that problem and show levels of approximation or stages in the development of writers who are writing their way into a position of privilege.

As I look over the papers I've discussed, I would arrange them in the following order: the "White Shoes" paper; the first "Jazz" essay; the "Clay Model" paper; the second "Jazz" essay; and, as the most successful paper, the essay on "Composing Songs." The more advanced essay for me, then, are those that are set against the "naive" codes of "everyday" life. (I put the terms "naive" and "everyday" in quotation marks because they are, of course, arbitrary terms.) In the advanced essays one can see a writer claiming an "inside" position of privilege by rejecting the language and commonplaces of a "naive" discourse, the language of "outsiders." The "I" of those essays locates itself against one discourse (what it claims to be a naive discourse) and approximates the specialized language of what is presumed to be a more powerful and more privileged community. There are two gestures present, then—one imitative and one critical. The writer continually audits and pushes against a language that would render him "like everyone else" and mimics the language and interpretive systems of the privileged community.

At a first level, then, a student might establish his authority by simply stating his own presence within the field of a subject. A student, for example, writes about creativity by telling a story about a time he went skiing. Nothing more. The "I" on the page is a skier, and skiing stands as a representation of a creative act. Neither the skier nor skiing are available for interpretation; they cannot be located in an essay that is not a narrative essay (where skiing might serve metaphorically as an example of, say, a sport where set movements also allow for a personal style). Or a student, as did the one who wrote the "White Shoes" paper, locates a narrative in an unconnected rehearsal of commonplaces about creativity. In both cases, the writers have finessed the requirement to set themselves against the available utterances of the world outside the closed world of the academy. And, again, in the first "Jazz" paper, we have the example of a writer who locates himself within an available commonplace and carries out only rudimentary procedures for elaboration, procedures driven by the commplace itself and not set against it. Elaboration, in this latter case, is not the opening up of a system but a justification of it.

At a next level I would place student writers who establish their authority by mimicking the rhythm and texture, the "sound," of academic prose, without there being any recognizable interpretive or academic project under way. I'm thinking, here, of the "Clay Model" essay. At an advanced stage, I would place students who establish their authority as *writers;* they claim their authority, not by simply claiming that they are skiers or that they have done something creative, but by placing themselves both within and against a discourse, or within and against competing discourses, and working self-consciously to claim an interpretive project of their own, one that grants them their privilege to speak. This is true, I think, in the case of the second "Jazz" paper and, to a greater degree, in the case of the "Composing Songs" paper.

The levels of development that I've suggested are not marked by corresponding levels in the type or frequency of error, at least not by the type or frequency of sentence-level error. I am arguing, then, that a basic writer is not necessarily a writer who makes a lot of mistakes. In fact, one of the problems with curricula designed to aid basic writers is that they too often begin with the assumption that the key distinguishing feature of a basic writer is the presence of sentence-level error. Students are placed in courses because their placement essays show a high frequency of such errors, and those courses are designed with the goal of making those errors go away. This approach to the problems of the basic writer ignores the degree to which error is less often a constant feature than a marker in the development of a writer. A student who can write a reasonably correct narrative may fall to pieces when faced with a more unfamiliar assignment. More important, however, such courses fail to serve the rest of the curriculum. On every campus there is a significant number of college freshmen who require a course to introduce them to the kinds of writing that are required for a university education. Some of these students can write correct sentences and some cannot; but, as a group, they lack the facility other freshmen possess when they are faced with an academic writing task.

The "White Shoes" essay, for example, shows fewer sentence-level errors than the "Clay Model" paper. This may well be due to the fact that the writer of the "White Shoes" paper stayed well within safe, familiar territory. He kept himself out of trouble by doing what he could easily do. The tortuous syntax of the more advanced papers on my list is a syntax that represents a writer's struggle with a difficult and unfamiliar language, and it is a syntax that can quickly lead an inexperienced writer into trouble. The syntax and punctuation of the "Composing Songs" essay, for example, shows the effort that is required when a writer works against the pressure of conventional discourse. If the prose is inelegant (although I confess I admire those dense sentences) it is still correct. This writer has a command of the linguistic and stylistic resources—the highly embedded sentences, the use of parentheses and quotation marks—required to complete the act of writing. It is easy to imagine the possible pitfalls for a writer working without this facility.

There was no camera trained on the "Clay Model" writer while he was writing, and I have no protocol of what was going through his mind, but it is possible to speculate on the syntactic difficulties of sentences like these: "In the past time I thought that an incident was creative was when I had to make a clay model of the earth, but not of the classical or your everyday model of the earth which consists of the two cores, the mantle and the crust. I thought of these things in a dimension of which it would be unique, but easy to comprehend." The syntactic difficulties appear to be the result of the writer's attempt to use an unusual vocabulary and to extend his sentences beyond the boundaries of what would have been "normal" in his speech or writing. There is reason to believe, that is, that the problem was with *this* kind of sentence, in this context. If the problem of the last sentence is that of holding together the units "I thought," "dimension," "unique" and "easy to comprehend," then the linquistic problem was not a simple matter of sentence construction. I am arguing, then, that such sentences fall apart not because the writer lacked the necessary syntax to glue the pieces together but because he lacked the full statement within which these key words were already operating. While writing, and in the thrust of his need to complete the sentence, he had the key words but not the utterance. (And to recover the utterance, I suspect, he would need to do more than revise the sentence.) The invisible conventions, the prepared phrases remained too distant for the statement to be completed. The writer would have needed to get inside of a discourse that he could in fact only partially imagine. The act of constructing a sentence, then, became something like an act of transcription in which the voice on the tape unexpectedly faded away and became inaudible.

Shaughnessy (1977) speaks of the advanced writer as one who often has a more facile but still incomplete possession of this prior discourse. In the case of the advanced writer, the evidence of a problem is the presence of dissonant, redundant, or imprecise language, as in a sentence such as this: "No education can be *total*, it must be *continuous*." Such a student, Shaughnessy says, could be said to hear the "melody of formal English" while still unable to make precise or exact distinctions. And, she says,

> the pre-packaging feature of language, the possibility of taking over phrases and whole sentences without much thought about them, threatens the writer now as before. The writer, as we have said, inherits the language out of which he must fabricate his own messages. He is therefore in a constant tangle with the language, obliged to recognize its public, communal nature and yet driven to invent out of this language his own statements. (1977, pp. 207–208)

For the unskilled writer, the problem is different in degree and not in kind. The inexperienced writer is left with a more fragmentary record of the comings and goings of academic discourse. Or, as I said above, he or she often has the key words without the complete statements within which they are already operating.

Let me provide one final example of this kind of syntactic difficulty in another piece of student writing. The writer of this paper seems to be able to sustain a discussion only by continually repeating his first step, producing a litany of strong, general, authoritative assertions that trail quickly into confusion. Notice how the writer seems to stabilize his movement through the paper by returning again and again to recognizable and available commonplace utterances. When he has to move away from them, however, away from the familiar to statements that would extend those utterances, where he, too, must speak, the writing—that is, both the syntax and the structure of the discourse—falls to pieces.

> Many times the times drives a person's life depends on how he uses it. I would like to think about if time is twenty-five hours a day rather than twenty-four hours. Some people think it's the boaring or some people might say it's the pleasure to take one more hour for their life. But I think the time is passing and coming, still we are standing on same position. We should use time as best as we can use about the good way in our life. Everything we do, such as sleep, eat, study, play and doing something for ourselves. These take the time to do and we could find the individual ability and may process own. It is the important for us and our society. As time going on the world changes therefor we are changing, too. When these situation changes we should follow the suitable case of own. But many times we should decide what's the better way to do so by using time. Sometimes like this kind of situation can cause the success of our lives or ruin. I think every individual of his own thought drive how to use time. These affect are done from environmental causes. So we should work on the better way of our life recognizing the importance of time.

There is a general pattern of disintegration when the writer moves off from standard phrases. This sentence, for example, starts out coherently and then falls apart: "*We should use time as best as we can* use about the good way in our life." The difficulty seems to be one of extending those standard phrases or of connecting them to the main subject reference, "time" (or "the time," a construction that causes many of the problems in the paper). Here is an example of a sentence that shows, in miniature, this problem of connection: "*I think every individual* of his own thought drive how to use *time*."

One of the remarkable things about this paper is that, in spite of all the synatic confusion, there is the hint of an academic project here. The writer sets out to discuss how to creatively use one's time. The text seems to allude to examples and to stages in an argument, even if in the end it is all pretty incoherent. The gestures of academic authority, however, are clearly present, and present in a form that echoes the procedures in other, more successful papers. The writer sets himself against what "some people think"; he speaks with the air of authority: "But I think. . . . Everything we do. . . . When these situation changes . . . ." And he speaks as though there were a project underway, one where he proposes what he thinks, turns to evidence, and offers a conclusion: "These affect are done from enviornmental causes. So we should work. . . ." This is the case of a student with the ability to imagine the general outline and rhythm of academic prose but without the ability to carry it out, to complete the sentences. And when he gets lost in the new, in the unknown, in the responsibility of his own commitment to speak, he returns again to the familiar ground of the commonplace.

The challenge to researchers, it seems to me, is to turn their attention again to products, to student writing, since the drama in a student's essay, as he or she struggles with and against the languages of our contemporary life, is as intense and telling as the drama of an essay's mental preparation or physical production. A written text, too, can be a compelling model of the "composing process" once we conceive of a writer as at work within a text and simultaneously, then, within a society, a history, and a culture.

It may very well be that some students will need to learn to crudely mimic the "distinctive register" of academic discourse before they are prepared to actually and legitimately do the work of the discourse, and before they are sophisticated enough with the refinements of tone and gesture to do it with grace or elegance. To say this, however, is to say that our students must be our students. Their initial progress will be marked by their abilities to take on the role of privilege, by their abilities to establish authority. From this point of view, the student who wrote about constructing the clay model of the earth is better prepared for his education than the student who wrote about playing football in white shoes, even though the "White Shoes" paper is relatively error-free and the "Clay Model" paper is not. It will be hard to pry loose the writer of the "White Shoes" paper from the tidy, pat discourse that allows him to dispose of the question of creativity in such a quick and efficient manner. He will have to be convinced that it is better to write sentences he might not so easily control, and he will have to be convinced that it is better to write muddier and more confusing prose (in order that it may sound like ours), and this will be harder than convincing the "Clay Model" writer to continue what he has already begun.

ACKNOWLEDGEMENTS

Preparation of this chapter was supported by the Learning Research and Development Center of the University of Pittsburgh, which is supported in part by the National Institute of Education.

NOTES

1. David Olson (1981) has made a similar observation about school-related problems of language learning in younger children. Here is his conclusion: "Hence, depending upon whether children assumed language was primarily suitable for making assertions and conjectures or primarily for making direct or indirect commands, they will either find school texts easy or difficult" (p. 107).

2. For Aristotle, there were both general and specific commonplaces. A speaker, says Aristotle, has a "stock of arguments to which he may turn for a particular need."

> If he knows the *topoi* (regions, places, lines or argument)—and a skilled speaker will know them—he will know where to find what he wants for a special case. The general topics, or *common*places, are regions containing arguments that are common to all branches of knowledge. . . . But there are also special topics (regions, places, *loci*) in which one looks for arguments appertaining to particular branches of knowledge, special sciences, such as ethics or politics. (1932, pp. 154–155)

And, he says, "the topics or places, then, may be indifferently thought of as in the science that is concerned, or in the mind of the speaker." But the question of location is "indifferent" *only* if the mind of the speaker is in line with set opinion, general assumption. For the speaker (or writer) who is not situated so comfortably in the privileged public realm, this is indeed not an indifferent matter at all. If he does not have the commonplace at hand, he will not, in Aristotle's terms, know where to go at all.

3. Pat Bizzell has argued that the *Seventeen* writer's process of goal-setting

> can be better understood if we see it in terms of writing for a discourse community. His initial problem . . . is to find a way to include these readers in a discourse community for which he is comfortable writing. He places them in the academic discourse community by imagining the girls as students. . . . Once he has included them in a familiar discourse community, he can find a way to address them that is common in the community: he will argue with them, puttting a new interpretation on information they possess in order to correct misconceptions. (1982a, p. 228)

4. See Bartholomae (1979, 1983) and Rose (1983) for articles on curricula designed to move students into university discourse. The movement to extend writing "across the curriculum" is evidence of a general concern for locating students within the work of the university; see Bizzell (1982a) and Maimon *et al.* (1981). For longer works directed specifically at basic writing, see Ponsot and Deen (1982) and Shaughnessy (1977). For a book describing a course for more advanced students, see Coles (1978).

5. In spite of my misgivings about Bereiter and Scardamalia's interpretation of the cognitive nature of the problem of "inert knowledge," this is an essay I regularly recommend to teachers. It has much to say about the dangers of what seem to be "neutral" forms of classroom discourse and provides, in its final section, a set of recommendations on how a teacher might undo discourse conventions that have become part of the institution of teaching.

6. Stanley Fish (1980) argues that the basis for distinguishing novice from expert readings is the persuasiveness of the discourse used to present and defend a given reading. In particular, see the chapter, "Demonstration vs. Persuasion: Two Models of Critical Activity" (pp. 356–373).

7. Some students, when they come to the university, can do this better than others. When Jonathan Culler says, "the possibility of bringing someone to see that a particular interpretation is a good one assumes shared points of departure and common notions of how to read," he is acknowledging that teaching, at least in English classes, has had to assume that students, to be students, were already to some degree participat-

ing in the structures of reading and writing that constitute English studies (quoted in Fish, 1980, p. 366).

Stanley Fish tells us "not to worry" that students will violate our enterprise by offering idiosyncratic readings of standard texts:

> The fear of solipsism, of the imposition by the unconstrained self of its own prejudices, is unfounded because the self does not exist apart from the communal or conventional categories of thought that enable its operations (of thinking, seeing, reading). Once we realize that the conceptions that fill consciousness, including any conception of its own status, are culturally derived, the very notion of an unconstrained self, of a consciousness wholly and dangerously free, becomes incomprehensible. (1980, p. 335)

He, too, is assuming that students, to be students (and not "dangerously free"), must be members in good standing of the community whose immediate head is the English teacher. It is interesting that his parenthetical catalogue of the "operations" of thought, "thinking, seeing, reading," excludes writing, since it is only through written records that we have any real indication of how a student thinks, sees, and reads. (Perhaps "real" is an inappropriate word to use here, since there is certainly a "real" intellectual life that goes on, independent of writing. Let me say that thinking, seeing, and reading are valued in the academic community *only* as they are represented by extended, elaborated written records.) Writing, I presume, is a given for Fish. It is the card of entry into this closed community that constrains and excludes dangerous characters. Students who are excluded from this community are students who do poorly on written placement exams or in freshman composition. They do not, that is, move easily into the privileged discourse of the community, represented by the English literature class.

8. My debt to Bizzell's work should be evident everywhere in this essay. See also Bizzell (1978, 1982b) and Bizzell and Herzberg (1980).

9. Fish says the following about the relationship between student and an object under study:

> we are not to imagine a moment when my students "simply see" a physical configuration of atoms and *then* assign that configuration a significance, according to the situation they happen to be in. To be in the situation (this or any other) is to "see" with the eyes of its interests, its goals, its understood practices, values, and norms, and so to be conferring significance *by* seeing, not after it. The categories of my students' vision are the categories by which they understand themselves to be functioning as students . . . and objects will appear to them in forms related to that way of functioning rather than in some objective or preinterpretive form. (1980, p. 334)

10. I am aware that the papers given the highest rankings offer arguments about creativity and originality similar to my own. If there is a conspiracy here, that is one of the points of my chapter. I should add that my reading of the "content" of basic writers' essays is quite different from Lunsford's (1980).

REFERENCES

Aristotle. (1932). *The "Rhetoric of Aristotle* (L. Cooper, Trans.). Englewood Cliffs, NJ: Prentice-Hall.

Barthes, R. (1974). *S/Z* (R. Howard, Trans.). New York: Hill & Wang.

Bartholomae, D. (1979). Teaching basic writing: An alternative to basic skills. *Journal of Basic Writing, 2*, 85–109.

Bartholomae, D. (1983). Writing assignments: Where writing begins. In P. Stock (Ed.), *Forum* (pp. 300–312). Montclair, NJ: Boynton/Cook.

Bereiter, C., & Scardamalia, M. (in press). Cognitive coping strategies and the problem of "inert knowledge." In S. S. Chipman, J. W. Segal, & R. Glaser (Eds.), *Thinking and learning skills: Research and open questions* (Vol. 2). Hillsdale, NJ: Erlbaum.

Bizzell, P. (1978). The ethos of academic discourse. *College Composition and Communication, 29*, 351–355.

Bizzell, P. (1982a). Cognition, convention, and certainty: What we need to know about writing. *Pre/text, 3*, 213–244.

Bizzell, P. (1982b). College composition: Initiation into the academic discourse community. *Curriculum Inquiry, 12*, 191–207.

Bizzell, P., & Herzberg, B. (1980). "Inherent" ideology, "universal" history, "empirical" evidence, and "context-free" writing: Some problems with E. D. Hirsch's *The Philosophy of Composition. Modern Language Notes, 95*, 1181–1202.

Coles, W. E., Jr. (1978). *The plural I.* New York: Holt, Rinehart & Winston.

Fish, S. (1980). *Is there a text in this class? The authority of interpretive communities.* Cambridge, MA: Harvard University Press.

Flower, L. S. (1981). Revising writer-based prose. *Journal of Basic Writing, 3*, 62–74.

Flower, L., & Hayes, J. (1981). A cognitive process theory of writing. *College Composition and Communication, 32*, 365–387.

Hairston, M. (1978). *A contemporary rhetoric.* Boston: Houghton Mifflin.

Lunsford, A. A. (1980). The content of basic writers' essays. *College Composition and Communication, 31*, 278–290.

Maimon, E. P., Belcher, G. L., Hearn, G. W., Nodine, B. F., & O'Connor, F. X. (1981). *Writing in the arts and sciences.* Cambridge, MA: Winthrop.

Olson, D. R. (1981). Writing: The divorce of the author from the text. In B. M. Kroll & R. J. Vann (Eds.), *Exploring speaking–writing relationships: Connections and contrasts.* Urbana, IL: National Council of Teachers of English.

Perkins, D. N. (in press). General cognitive skills: Why not? In S. S. Chipman, J. W. Segal, & R. Glaser (Eds.), *Thinking and learning skills: Research and open questions* (Vol. 2). Hillsdale, NJ: Earlbaum.

Ponsot, M., & Deen, R. (1982). *Beat not the poor desk.* Montclair, NJ: Boynton/Cook.

Rodriquez, R. (1983). *Hunger of memory.* New York: Bantam.

Rose, M. (1983). Remedial writing courses: A critique and a proposal. *College English, 45*, 109–128.

Said, E. W. (1975). *Beginnings: Intention and method.* Baltimore: The Johns Hopkins University Press.

Shaughnessy, M. (1977). *Errors and expectations.* New York: Oxford University Press.

Diagnosing Writing-Process Problems: A Pedagogical Application of Speaking-Aloud Protocol Analysis 8

MURIEL HARRIS

Introduction: Practitioners and Researchers

It's a truism that doing research doesn't necessarily include finding methods for applying the results of that research. It's equally obvious that unless ways are found to translate research results into common practice, researchers may well speed down one road while practitioners (the potential users of those results) travel their own highways. In industry, research and development teams are set up to offset this problem, but "R & D" is not normally an academic pastime, or at least not in the humanities. This split between research and practice is a particularly crucial problem in the teaching of composition because new models of the writing process are being shaped by research. However, unless pedagogies are built on these results, composition research is in danger of being relegated to the pages of journals read only by other researchers—despite the potential riches for the classroom practitioner.

The outcome of such a parting of ways is too often a sense of hostility on both sides. On one hand, composition researchers are likely to view their colleagues who are not actively engaged in scholarly research as merely "nuts-and-bolts" or "what-do-I-do-on-Monday"

Muriel Harris. Department of English, Purdue University, West Lafayette, Indiana.

sorts of people. On the other hand, those who are leery of quantifiable results or unfamiliar with chi-squares and significance levels tend to view research in general as irrelevant to what teaching writing is all about. Symptoms of this two-camps mentality have been recorded by A. M. Tibbetts (1982) in his survey of attitudes and practices of college teachers of writing. Tibbetts's conclusion is that research is not being used in any consistent fashion and in fact is often simply being ignored. Says Tibbetts, "The scholar-researcher and the teacher of writing are pulling farther apart every day. If you judge by what he does in his daily work, the teacher no longer believes that researchers can give him valuable advice" (p. 127). As a teacher of writing, I'm sometimes inclined to applaud such sentiments—about some research—but every field has its vacuous nit-picking as well as its truly useful, invigorating work. Certainly, the whole set of new notions about writing that focus on illuminating composing processes offers great potential benefits. But the problem is to find teaching and tutoring strategies to match, strategies that are process-oriented, consistent with current models of composing, and not grounded in or dependent on product scrutiny alone.

Teachers of writing, then, have a special kind of responsibility to their students. For it is their task, and not that of others outside their classrooms, to sift through the results of research to find what is useful to them and to think about how to use those results. As more is learned about composing processes, teachers will not only be able to guide students to compose more effectively but will also be able to get at process dysfunctions which were previously unreachable and mysterious. We will rummage around in the tool kits used by researchers and borrow some of the strategies they use to peer more closely into cognitive processes. This selecting and borrowing can encourage a mutually beneficial relationship, for it can surely help in closing the gap between research and pedagogy.

Three Research Strategies for Observing Writing Processes

Among the methods used to gain access to writing processes, Mike Rose (1981) has identified three of the most promising: post hoc questioning, stimulated recall, and speaking-aloud protocols. Of these three, "post hoc questioning" has the advantage of being the least intrusive, for it does not disturb the writer's production of a piece of writing. Instead, the observer watches the writer as he or she writes and then afterward asks questions about behavior that was observed during writing. The disadvantages are equally apparent: Subjects may not remember why they wrote what they did, what mental processes they called upon, or how they produced what was recorded on paper. Our memories are too limited to recall every mental decision afterward, and some students are as likely to recall what they think they ought to have done as what they actually did. Linda Flower (1982) has noted not only the evaluative tendency of writers to focus their reports on their own strengths and weaknesses but also the abstract nature of such reports. That is, the writer tends to offer a generalized synthesis of what he or she had thought about. But, despite these limitations, post hoc questioning can bring to light distinctive behaviors and habitual composing methods, as the work of Stallard (1974) and Pianko (1979) has shown us.

"Stimulated recall" is a slightly more intrusive technique but does offer assistance to the writer's memory. When used for composing, the method involves videotaping the page as the writer writes. When the videotape is replayed immediately afterward, the writer is invited to comment on his or her actions, and the researcher questions and probes. Both the writer and researcher can stop the tape if necessary. This dialogue is audiotaped, transcribed, and then analyzed by the researcher. While videotape units, tape recorders, and other recording devices do not substantially interfere with composing, they can be distractions as the writer writes. A more critical disadvantage, though, is that the writer still cannot recall all of the mental activities that occurred during the composing stage. Some distortions are possible also because writers are not consistently able to label with total accuracy what they were doing or to summarize the process correctly. Moreover, the method requires hardware not immediately available to everyone. But, despite the difficulties, Mike Rose's work on writer's block (1980, 1981, 1984) shows us how much can be uncovered by employing stimulated recall.

A third method, the use of "speaking-aloud protocols," is the one I am most familiar with, having used it both for teaching and for diagnostic purposes in writing lab tutorials. "Protocols," the verbal reports writers offer of what they are thinking about as they write, are the source of data which are tape-recorded, typed, and subsequently analyzed. The work of Flower and Hayes (Flower & Hayes, 1979; Hayes & Flower, 1980) in developing a model of the composing process is an indication of the enormous power of this tool. It is the most direct and unimpeded of the three methods for viewing the composing process, unimpeded in the sense that it reduces the opportunities for the writer to interpret or generalize for the observer. Instead, the observer watches (and hears) the writer at work and draws conclusions from what is seen and heard. Despite the richness of what is uncovered through protocol analysis, there are inherent weaknesses in this method that must also be acknowledged. As anyone who has given protocols while writing can testify, the act of speaking aloud interferes with thinking and, in the view of some researchers, distorts processes of thought. There are also charges that protocols reveal only those cognitive processes that are easy to report (Atlas, undated). And, of course, some students cannot readily talk aloud while writing, though a short training program can help (Selfe, 1982).

While the obtrusiveness of protocols is a major weakness, Ericsson and Simon (1979, pp. 30–31, 37) stress the need to remember primarily the incompleteness of such reports when examining evidence. This incompleteness, they explain, is due in part to limitations connected with short-term memory and also to the writer's tendency to stop verbalizing when working under heavy cognitive loads. However, as Ericsson and Simon point out, though the incompleteness of verbal reports may make some information unavailable, this does not invalidate information that is present; thus, protocols are reliable sources for what they do contain, but not for what they omit. And what is reported is indeed useful.

Despite the incompleteness, the artificiality, the intrusiveness, and the potential need for training, protocols are extremely rich sources of information, information that the student often doesn't even realize is valuable. And because the student is unlikely to report such bits of data afterward, the immediacy and the richness of protocols make them a useful diagnostic tool for uncovering individual composing-process problems. Thus, I have found this tool to be highly useful in the writing lab. For when students come to a writing lab for individualized help, they have left behind the institution's approach to their problems that Ross Winterowd (1981) has characterized as that of a "penicillin clinic": In a penicillin clinic, he explains, everyone is given penicillin, the person with influenza, the person with pneumonia—even the person with a cracked rib. The lab, then, is the place where the student's uniqueness can be stressed rather than his or her area of overlap with or general fit to the group. The protocols students offer are extremely helpful in getting at individual composing problems. And by thinking about these individual protocols, we can arrive at pedagogies that help students to alter more general dysfunctional processes, for the silent processes behind the written product are made manifest.

The Uses of Protocols: The Discovery of Five Students' Problems and Some Solutions

SHANNON: AN INDECISIVE WRITER

Shannon came to our Writing Lab complaining about the length of time it took her to write anything: "It probably only takes some people only . . . an hour to write some things, and it takes me five years," she explained. Shannon, a highly articulate student placed in an accelerated composition course because of her high Scholastic Aptitude Test (SAT) scores, could describe her problem generally, and she could eliminate some common possible causes such as "not having anything to write about" or "worrying too much about an opening sentence." However, she could not pinpoint where she did bog down or elaborate on why she would labor over a paper for a whole evening or two before producing even a useful paragraph.

After listening to Shannon compose aloud, I began to hear how her time was spent. When she had choices to make, perhaps about a word or even about subject matter, she cycled around and around, unable to choose an option. Instead, she spent additional time generating more options. For example, in the midst of a short piece of writing that focused on the tyranny of the computer in students' lives, she produced this sentence: "For example—the computer reserves full rights on running schedules." By reading Shannon's protocol for this sentence—that is, the thoughts she spoke aloud as she composed—we can observe the extent of her indecisiveness.

> What are the exact—are things done by computers? Schedules classes and consequences, and late registration fees, things that a computer will do to you, computer grading of the most, um— One opportunity—which a computer takes most advantage of is scheduling classes—um— One example,—the computer—ah—

Shannon then stopped to reread a phrase from the previous sentence: "grief and sorrow." She then returned to composing the sentence she had been working on.

> . . . what things can happen when you're trying to schedule classes? You can get closed out of a class that's vital to your major, computers can go down right before your schedule can be run,—computer going down as it's about to run, computer going down, computer down, um—ah—can lose your identity because of wrong social security number, and that's pretty—computer down, lose social security numbers. What else can it do? Putting out great demands, number two pencils, fill in the eraser marks completely, uh, refusing to grade something, no number two pencils, more than one, ummm—

Again, Shannon paused to reread a portion of what she had previously written: "Everything is done by computers. Purdue's campus is no exception. Here the mastermind . . . finds great pleasure in bringing grief and sorrow to students." She then returned to the sentence she was working on and finally began transcribing words on paper. The italicized words are those being transcribed as she spoke them.

> Um—one opportunity—ah—the computer takes—for instance—much better—the computer reserves full rights in scheduling classes. *For* example, *example—the computer reserves full rights* on scheduling classes, on—on *running schedules*, um—a variety of things can go wrong in this area—

Shannon then paused to reread the sentence she had just transcribed on paper: "the computer reserves full rights on running schedules." Though she had now written the sentence, she tried out a few more options aloud.

> . . . um—close out classes vital to your major, computer will go down day before classes, ah—I'm having trouble in what to say—um running schedules—ah—ah—what can I say? I think I ought to organize this different—terrible—

Of all the examples Shannon generated, only the one in the sentence she wrote remained as part of the text. This behavior was habitual for Shannon, as she showed by continuing to produce numerous choices for every sentence. Suspended in doubt, she seemed to keep producing yet more options without deciding on any, rejecting any, or setting up criteria for judging them.

For this student, writing was a "frustrating experience," a term she used repeatedly to explain why she avoided writing. In the 24-item questionnaire devised by Mike Rose to identify writer's block (Rose, 1984), Shannon's reponse to questions about the frequency of blocking varied from "often" to "almost always." Yet her scores for the verbal skills portion of the SAT were high; and her ability to generate outlines and to analyze a topic were competent, as I heard and saw. The problem seemed to be her indecisiveness, her lack of evaluation criteria to use in deciding what to include and what to toss away. Since one of our goals as teachers is to help students gain control over their own composing processes, my approach to helping Shannon was, first, to describe to her what I had seen. As we talked, she was able to put the problem in a larger context of consistent behavior—for example, the agonizing hours she spent shopping when she couldn't decide which sweater to buy, or the time she wasted in exams deciding which questions to answer.

Though recognition of a problem is a necessary first step, our work together was not through because Shannon still had no strategies for making decisions. However, after being introduced to the simple problem-solving technique of selecting a reasonable option and pushing it until it fails or succeeds, Shannon began to work her way out of her indecisiveness. To help her experience this trial-and-error process, I sat with her as she planned her next essay, a particularly difficult assignment that required analyzing a short story. Each time she produced several options for a part of a rough outline, I prodded her into making a "best guess" and running with it. Some choices worked, some didn't. However, at the rough draft/outline stage, she began to see how easily and cheaply her less productive guesses could be abandoned. Within 25 minutes she had that paper planned, and Shannon was awed. More work was needed, but she had experienced a process she was not previously adept at.

TODD: ANOTHER KIND OF INDECISIVE WRITER

While Shannon's wheel-spinning appeared to be part of a more general inability to choose between options, the same observable problem in the writing of another student, Todd, seemed to have more localized causes. Todd's responses to the Rose questionnaire indicated a high degree of blocking, particularly a major difficulty in getting started with an assignment. When confronted with a short writing task I gave him, Todd began by reading and rereading the assignment. When prompted to think aloud, he continued to stare at the assignment and to offer the following thoughts aloud.

> This is the indecision part— I just sit here changing my mind— What can I write about? How should I start? Of course—this is the way it always is.

> I sit there, I just sit there, and I'll say, What can I write?—I just sit there going in circles. It's so dumb.

After a short spurt of composing a few sentences, Todd proceeded to scratch them out and to return to thinking about his problem:

> I think one of the hardest things here is like trying to pinpoint something you want to write about. I have a lot of trouble—I have so many thoughts—I want to— It's like I could make this ten pages long. I don't want to do that, so—I'm sitting here trying to figure a way to narrow it down, I think. It's weird—

Though Todd appeared to think he had numerous choices at his fingertips as he composed, he did not offer aloud long lists of options as Shannon did, nor did his writing indicate a rich variety of directions. However, there was also no evidence that Todd was in need of help with invention; and when he came to our Writing Lab he had been in a freshman composition course for almost three months, a class in which invention strategies were heavily stressed, particularly tagmemic heuristics. Perhaps that had added to Todd's problems by giving him a way to generate more options than he could deal with, but I could not confirm his self-diagnosis by anything I could see or hear as he composed aloud. Yet something was wrong, something so disabling that this student intensely disliked writing and avoided it if at all possible. When asked why he felt so negative, Todd responded, "It's so hard. No way. I hate it."

Forced back to the tape of Todd's protocol, I kept in mind Ericsson and Simon's warning about the incompleteness of protocols. I listened repeatedly, more aware of what I was not hearing than of what I did hear. Of course, since not enough is known about composing processes that are enabling, I was also feeling at a loss to recognize dysfunctional processes that might also be present. But as I listened I began to hear a pattern to some of the comments interspersed throughout Todd's composing. At one point he asked himself, "What's right here?" Later, he reread a phrase and commented, "don't know if this is going to be right or not." Later, another comment indicated that he didn't know what would be the "right thing here—what the teacher wants." Such comments seemed to indicate an overdependence on the teacher's criteria, rather than the writer's, to select what was recorded on the page.

We are all familiar with such dependence at the revision stage as students attempt to follow suggestions as if they were commandments in an effort to give the teacher "what she wants." This view of the teacher as an examiner who knows "what is right" is often reinforced at the secondary level where, as Arthur Applebee and associates have demonstrated (Applebee, Lehr, & Auten, 1981), most writing is composed of mechanical tasks which bypass the problem of creating information. Most student writing in high school involves, as Applebee says, "organizing and reporting back information the teacher [has] provided. Delineating the topic [is] straightforward, and students [know] what they [are] supposed to do" (p. 79). It may well be that some students in college courses have not moved beyond that notion of the teacher as the receiver of "correct" writing, whatever they think that might be. For students caught in the notion of trying to write what the teacher wants, the world of college essay writing seems a frustratingly vague and ill-defined place to work.

If this was a contributing cause in Todd's indecision, then I could confirm it by giving him another writing assignment in which the information was given and his task was simply to present it in a few paragraphs. When Todd returned to our lab, I tried such an assignment and found that he composed far more easily and progressed with far fewer comments on his inability to decide on what to say. He even concluded the session with comments on how much more he had enjoyed that writing task than the first one. We hadn't yet begun to work constructively on Todd's writing difficulties, but the protocol did help in defining what was involved in his writing problems. In an oversimplified sense, what seemed to plague Todd was having to create material when he didn't know what was "right," that is, what the teacher wanted. Using his writing to deliver his own messages was not a procedure Todd was familiar with, at least not in his writing for composition courses.

MIKE: AN INCESSANT EDITOR

For both Todd and Shannon, the long, agonizing, unproductive hours spent trying to compose were a common denominator, a symptom they shared with many other students with blocking problems. Both the frustration of such students and the time they waste often lead to the attitudes they express, usually a blunt admission of how much they dislike writing, though such attitudes do not always deter them from planning on careers that involve writing. Mike, a student with severe blocking problems, planned eventually to apply to law school despite the long hours it took him to write even a two or three-paragraph assignment. In Mike's case, the major difficulty indicated in his protocols was an incessant tendency to edit prematurely. Though I have described Mike's composing problems in great detail elsewhere (Harris, 1983), it is useful here to contrast this type of blocking with, for example, Shannon's difficulties. Mike's continual revising, changing, planning, criticizing, scratching out, and launching in again was a more difficult dysfunctional behavior to work with than was Shannon's because he lacked any sense of a better way to proceed. Merely describing to him the freewriting approach of pushing ahead without editing did not result in his being able to do it. Instead, Mike needed to see, to observe at first hand, more productive writing processes; and he also needed to try them with an observer at hand to remind him not to slip into old habits.

The method that proved to be effective with Mike was "modeling," a standard and well-researched technique frequently used with success in behavior modification therapy. Modeling can be a valuable teaching technique because it allows a teacher to demonstrate processes and not merely to talk about them. With Mike, this meant several sessions of first having him watch me as I composed aloud and then having him compose aloud using the same techniques that I had tried to demonstrate. After three sessions of his copying the behaviors he observed in me, his total writing time was slightly less than half that of his first session, though the total number of words he produced was almost the same. Moreover, I had his paper evaluated by nine experienced teachers of writing, and they agreed unanimously that his last piece of writing was far superior to his first one. In Mike's case protocols served as a diagnostic tool, in that I could hear his incessant editing and revising, and also as a teaching tool, in that Mike could hear and observe—different composing processes.

BETH: MISGUIDED ABOUT A USEFUL STRATEGY

Another of the many values of watching students composing is that such observation is a window on all the ways students can misinterpret well-meaning instruction. For example, the outline as a means to impose order on the chaos of invention is commonly a useful strategy. Yet, in the hands of some students, the outline becomes an inhibiting device, a structure that by its rigidity can limit further invention or by its complexity hamper the writer's progress (Rose,

1980, p. 394). Or, as I discovered when observing another student, Beth, composing aloud, the outline can impede a student's composing when it is misunderstood as a disorganized listing procedure. In high school Beth had been shown outlining techniques, most probably to help her impose order on her rambling, disorganized prose. However, for Beth the outline was merely a listing or record of what she thought of, a memory dump of ideas as they occurred to her. Rather than being a device or structure to impose order, an outline served merely as a reminder to keep her from forgetting what she wanted to include in a piece of writing. Given a short assignment, Beth spent the first few minutes drawing up this type of "outline" or list. The outline had no overall coherence, and Beth did not stop to evaluate its organization, development, or direction. Instead, when she had listed what she felt was enough material, she plunged into writing—checking the outline only to be sure she had included everything, not to follow any pattern it set up. In fact, as she progressed, she would stop to "correct" the outline to reflect the direction her writing had taken. In several instances, the act of "fixing up the outline" interrupted her composing so much that she lost her train of thought.

Had I examined only the paper that resulted from that session, I would not have suspected that part of its general lack of coherence was due to interruptions to redo an outline. The protocols were also useful in allowing me to hear evidence that Beth generally lacked strategies to bring coherence to her writing and to see that she did not reread her papers, a procedure that would have given her a sense of their direction and development. What Beth needed were better, more effective composing strategies. For example, to help impose structure on her ideas after generating material, she needed a problem-solving strategy such as building the kind of "issue tree" described by Flower and Hayes (Flower & Hayes, 1977, pp. 456–457).

CAROL: AN INCESSANT REREADER

One last example will help to indicate the diversity of writing problems uncovered by protocols. While Beth had to learn the need for rereading her writing to gain an overall sense of structure, another student, Carol, needed assistance in getting over the habit of incessantly rereading as she composed. Up to what point is rereading productive, and at what point does it become unproductive? For Carol, this was a crucially important question because she seemed to spend too much of her time rereading and used that rereading as her only observable heuristic. The excerpt below from one of Carol's protocols is typical in including seemingly excessive rereading but untypical in that, as she produced a sentence, she did not (as she frequently did elsewhere) reread previous sentences in the paragraph or previous paragraphs. This more moderate excerpt is offered here because it is easier to follow. The sentence that Carol produced was this: "The opening of the SGA bookstore was prompted by numerous student complaints of high textbook prices in existing bookstores." In the protocol for this sentence, I've placed each rereading of the sentence on a new line to indicate more clearly the extent of Carol's rereading. Worlds transcribed on the page as Carol spoke them aloud are underlined.

> First of all—let's see—first of all—I don't like "First of all"—let's see—um—
>
> The SGA bookstore was—no, how about—
>
> The opening of the SGA bookstore—
>
> The opening of the SGA bookstore was prompted by several—by numerous—makes it sound a little bit more effective—
>
> The opening of the SGA bookstore was prompted by numerous student complaints of—
>
> The opening of the SGA bookstore was prompted by numerous student complaints of high textbook prices and low—um—let's see—
>
> The opening of the SGA bookstore was prompted by numerous student complaints of high textbook prices and low—I don't know what you call them—return—low sellback—low—low—cash return—low prices—that doesn't even make sense—
>
> The opening of the SGA bookstore was prompted by numerous student complaints of high textbook prices and low prices for selling back books—
>
> The opening of the SGA bookstore was prompted by numerous student complaints of high textbook prices and low prices for selling back books—um—
>
> The opening of the SGA bookstore was prompted by numerous student complaints of high textbook prices in the existing bookstores.
>
> The opening of the SGA bookstore was prompted by numerous student complaints of high textbook prices in existing bookstores.

While rereading does help a writer to gain a sense of how the text is developing and does help in generating material, Carol's habit of reading every sentence eight or ten times tied her so closely to her text that she did not stop to evaluate or to formulate larger goals as she wrote.

Carol needed to learn other invention strategies such as "brainstorming," "cubing," "looping," or using a set of heuristic questions; and she required help in seeing the need to pause, to break away from her word-by-word development of the text, in order to refine or clarify larger goals. Locked into her one approach, Carol was convinced she "knew how to write." Before Carol could be taught new strategies, she had to see the need to learn.

Conclusions: Drawing General Guidelines from Specific Cases

Whether or not the problems of the students described here are common, these examples are of interest because they offer clues for using protocols as a diagnostic tool. On one hand, we can use protocols to search for possible problems that have already been identified for us. For example, we can draw on Sondra Perl's work that identifies some composing-process problems of unskilled writers, problems such as the incessant tendency to interrupt composing in order to edit for grammatical or spelling errors (Perl, 1979). But it is unlikely, given the complexity of composing processes, that we will ever be able to draw up a universally workable short checklist to keep at the side of our desks. As we have seen with Shannon, Todd, Mike, Beth, and Carol, some students display idiosyncratic behaviors that cannot easily be generalized into neat categories. However, we ought not feel lost in a sea of uniqueness, for there are approaches we can all use, general questions that we can ask ourselves as we listen to and analyze what our students say as they compose aloud:

1. *Are the student's composing strategies sufficiently varied, flexible, and complex?*

- Lack of variety: Is there an overdependence on one strategy to the exclusion of others?
- Lack of flexibility: Is there a rigidity that turns a strategy or heuristic into an inflexible rule?
- Lack of complexity: Is there an oversimplification or a reduction of a strategy to a simplistic tool?

2. *Are the student's composing strategies productive?* As we listen and watch, we need to assess whether the student's strategies seem to work well for him or her and seem to result in effective writing. Or are the strategies inhibiting in some way? For example, generating options

as we compose is certainly a useful process in writing; but in Shannon's case that process was neither useful nor productive, but truly disabling. It hindered her composing, just as the use of an outline had become for Beth a disruptive device rather than an effective tool. Given the variety of approaches to writing, we may find it too formidable a task to evaluate whether any particular technique is generally enabling or not; but when watching and listening to a single student, it is far easier to judge whether that student is progressing well with a particular technique or not. For example, the debate swirling around the merits of freewriting may rage on indefinitely; but I have observed students for whom it works well as a generating strategy, and I have seen students seriously hampered by having to write without structure or planning. And some heuristics seem to open hitherto closed avenues of exploratory thought for some students while they stymie others or bring them to a screeching halt.

3. *Is there anything missing or inadequate in the student's composing processes?* As we observe students, we need to ask ourselves if there are composing stages or strategies that ought to be evident but aren't. Reminding ourselves of the incompleteness of protocols, we need to look for what is not there as well as to analyze what is present. Though a definitive model of the composing process may not yet have been delivered from some burning bush, we now know enough about it that we can work with what we have: We know about the recursiveness of writing; the planning, translating, and reviewing stages; the need for setting and reevaluating goals, and so on. We can ask ourselves if we see some evidence in a student's protocol of missing processes and subprocesses. Has the writer asked himself or herself inadequate questions, set skimpy goals, settled for undeveloped (or underdeveloped) ideas? Does the student lack adequate means to record fleeting thoughts as they occur or lack techniques for reorganizing material retrieved from long-term memory?

Once we have begun to identify these composing problems, there are pedagogical tools to help us fix them, tools available for general classroom use as well as for tutorial or conference teaching. We can model composing processes we want our students to try—and for those teachers less eager to attempt composing aloud in front of their students, research has shown that videotapes and films are also effective ways to demonstrate various kinds of behaviors, (Feltz, Landers, & Raeder, 1979, p. 117; Perry & Furukawa, 1980, p. 138). Actual demonstrations of composing in all its messy reality will not only help student writers to learn better ways to generate, organize, and revise, but will also help them to understand their own composing processes. And we can combine demonstrations with classroom discussions, ask students to observe and record their own composing processes, or suggest that they observe fellow students composing. There is no way we can expect students to recognize that they may have problems—or what kinds of problems they have—unless they have some sense of what constitutes the more common or usual writing behaviors. Lacking that familiarity, students have come to our Writing Lab convinced that they are poor writers because of some peculiar inability to "get it right the first time" or some free-floating anxiety about "not being able to follow my outline." Worse still, of course, are the students who never seek help because they've assigned themselves to the limbo of the hopeless, the "bad writer." Only by knowing something about composing processes can students begin to articulate for themselves and for us what they want to learn. And as we work with students, watching, listening, teaching, and demonstrating, we too can learn more about composing and the various ways composing goes awry. Once we unearth these problems from the silent depths of the writer's mind, we can then set ourselves the task of offering instruction that is truly needed.

REFERENCES

Applebee, A., Lehr, F., & Auten, A. (1981). Learning to write in the secondary school: How and where. *English Journal, 70*, 78–82.

Atlas, M. A. *A brief overview of research methods for the writing researcher.* Undated manuscript, Carnegie-Mellon University, Pittsburgh, PA.

Ericsson, K. A., & Simon, H. A. (1979, December). *Verbal reports as data* (C.I.P. Working Paper No. 402). Pittsburgh, PA: Carnegie-Mellon University.

Feltz, D., Landers, D., & Raeder, U. (1979). Enhancing self-efficacy in high avoidance motor tasks: A comparison of modeling techniques. *Journal of Sport Psychology, 1*, 112–122.

Flower, L. (1982, April). Lecture presented at a graduate seminar, Purdue University.

Flower, L. S., & Hayes, J. R. (1977). Problem solving strategies and the writing process. *College English, 39*, 449–461.

Flower, L. S., & Hayes, J. R. (1979, August 15). *A process method of composition* (Tech. Rep. No. 1). Pittsburgh, PA: Carnegie-Mellon University, Document Design Project.

Harris, M. (1983). Modeling: A process method of teaching. *College English, 45*, 74–84.

Hayes, J. R., & Flower, L. S. (1980). Identifying the organization of writing processes. In L. W. Gregg & E. R. Steinberg (Eds.), *Cognitive processes in writing* (pp. 3–30). Hillsdale, NJ: Erlbaum.

Perl, S. (1979). The composing processes of unskilled college writers. *Research in the Teaching of English, 13*, 317–336.

Perry, M., & Furukawa, M. J. (1980). Modeling methods. In F. Kanfer & A. Goldstein (Eds.), *Helping people change* (2nd ed., pp. 131–171). New York: Pergamon.

Pianko, S. (1979). A description of the composing processes of college freshman writers. *Research in the Teaching of English, 13*, 5–22.

Rose, M. (1980). Rigid rules, inflexible plans, and the stifling of language: A cognitivist analysis of writer's block. *College Composition and Communication, 31*, 389–401.

Rose, M. (1981). *The cognitive dimension of writer's block: An examination of university students.* Unpublished doctoral dissertation, University of California, Los Angeles.

Rose, M. (1984). *Writer's block: The cognitive dimension.* Carbondale: Southern Illinois University Press.

Selfe, C. (1982). *Training subjects to compose aloud.* Unpublished manuscript. (Available from Department of Humanities, Michigan Technological University, Houghton, Michigan 49931)

Stallard, C. (1974). An analysis of the writing behavior of good student writers. *Research in the Teaching of English, 8*, 206–218.

Tibbetts, A. (1982). *Working papers: A teacher's observations on composition.* Glenview, IL: Scott, Foresman.

Winterowd, R. (1981, June). Rhetoric Seminar lecture, Purdue University.

Psychotherapies for Writing Blocks 9

ROBERT BOICE

In a sense, psychology has much to offer the blocked or stymied writer, if one considers the venerableness of the problem in the literaure: Psychologists have been interested in writing and in ways of facilitating it since before the days of Freud and Janet. Some of the earliest accounts are about fascinating treatments such as automatic writing, a semihypnotic task in which the writer is not consciously aware of writing, and about intriguing symptoms such as writer's cramp, a paralytic condition in which the writer cannot move the writing arm while attempting to compose.

But in another sense, psychotherapeutic treatments of writing blocks are limited: Compared to treatments of fairly common problems, writing-block therapies have infrequently appeared. Of the published accounts, most have been anecdotal—many are based entirely on the author's self-treatment of a block—and almost all have been narrowly tied to a doctrinaire approach. There is, to complete this negative preview, little clear sense of what writing blocks are or even of whether psychotherapists who employ, say, psychoanalytic versus cognitive approaches are treating the same problem as are writing specialists.

Still, the story of psychologists' interest in writing blocks has much to offer teachers, researchers, and clinicians. It is a story that promises to get better. Psychologists working with writing skills and problems are, I believe, on the threshold of an area that is just beginning to flourish. Our appreciation of that promise rests in part on an awareness of how psychologists have thus far developed treatments for writing blocks. My taxonomy of this scattered literature produces

Robert Boice. Department of Psychology, State University of New York, Albany, New York.

seven different types of approaches. With each, I will attempt to review how writing blocks are conceptualized, how they are illuminated by that particular approach, and what is helpful about that approach when compared to the others. I also illustrate the treatment potential of each approach by citing recent developments in research as well as cases from my own 12 years of clinical experience as a psychologist working with stymied writers in academia.

Psychoanalysis and the Treatment of Writer's Block

FREUD ON CREATIVITY

Freud was not only an exemplar as a theorist and therapist but also a model for writing habits that help forestall blocking (Ellenberger, 1970): He wrote regularly, regardless of mood; he taught himself to love his native language and to revel in a rich vocabulary; he forgave himself for taking ideas from the minds of others; and he learned that writing a first draft proceeds much more easily when attention is directed at concepts rather than at the correctness of all facts. Moreover, Freud provided a psychotherapeutic system that is congenial to literary interests and to the analysis of writing problems; specifically, he dealt with themes from classical mythology and with concepts like "defensive structures" and "guilt in liberating fantasy," ideas that can illuminate blocks in the creative process (M. Rosenberg, 1976).

Although he does not speak directly about writing blocks, Freud uses a metaphor from another literary giant, Schiller, that serves as an explanation of blocking. The first part of Schiller's metaphor describes what must ordinarily occur in creative productions: "In the case of a creative mind, however, the intelligence had withdrawn its watchers from the gates, the ideas rush in pell-mell and only then the great heap is looked over and critically examined." The second part is an apt description of what can inhibit creativity: "You are ashamed or afraid of the momentary and transitory madness which is found in all real creators, and whose longer or shorter duration distinguishes the thinking artist from the dreamer . . . you reject too soon and discriminate too severely" (Freud, 1900/1913, p. 80).

Thinking about the allegory of a watcher at the gates seem to have helped many writers to forestall blocking. Virginia Woolf, for instance, got past her "watcher" by writing at a "rapid haphazard gallop."

Not many of Freud's circle shared his interest in or his flair for writing (Ellenberger, 1970). But Rank (1934) did make a contribution to the psychology of writing by attempting to change traditionally negative beliefs about artists as neurotics. By explaining neurotics as failed artists, Rank set the stage for recent demonstrations that creativity is correlated with healthy qualities such as the ability to cope with affect-charged thinking and an openness to novel experience (Suler, 1980).

BERGLER AS PIONEER

Only one psychoanalyst has reported extensive work with writing blocks. Bergler assumed, perhaps incorrectly, that he had pioneered the concept of "writing blocks" (1950b; but cf. Brande, 1934); he was, in any case, the first to write about the topic at length. His definition of a writing block as a "euphemism for sterility of productivitiy" has not found popular usage, nor, evidently, have his treatment methods. Although Bergler claimed a nearly 100 percent cure rate for 36 patients with writing blocks, he did not share any details of how he treated patients except to hint that they might be handled as oral regressives (i.e., individuals who still need the equivalent of a mother's breast). What Bergler did provide, at length, was a disparaging picture of writers in general and of blocked writers in particular. None of us, Bergler concludes, can fathom our own reasons for wanting to write:

> All statements to the contrary, no "real" writer writes because of conscious palpable reasons. Since the writer himself is ignorant of his unconscious conflicts which push him into writing, he is uncapable of answering the question of what "made him write." (1950b, p. 2)

What does make us write, or at least hope to? In Bergler's view, writers have an unconscious need to be refused—they are "injustice collectors" who despise their audiences and critics but who continue to submit to their mistreatment, usually in the form of disappointing reviews and misunderstanding. The "motor" or motive for artistic production, he asserts, is an immense sense of guilt. Put simply, "Normal people just don't feel impelled to write" (1950b, p. 220).

Because reviewers chided him for not saying much about the nature of blocking, Bergler responded with an article entitled "Does 'Writer's Block' Exist?" (1950a). Here too, details are elusive. He seems to allow the interpretations of his critics to create the explanation of blocking and of treatment, as in this review of his book that he quotes from *Time*:

> . . . the adult writer's flow of words is a psychological substitute for the flow of milk he wanted and did not get, plus a recompense for all the guilt he subconsciously felt since his diaper days. Once the analyst has worked the anxious writer back to the point where he can endorse mother's product without fear, shame or remorse, it's simply a matter of putting a fresh sheet of paper into the machine and hitting the keys. (1950a, p. 49)

Bergler is more direct in stating the outcome of unblocking: The patient will likely prove to be a poor writer and be better suited to another pursuit.

Despite Bergler's dismissal of his critics as "ignoramuses" who were unwilling to eat their well-deserved "humble pie," he eventually published some specifics on causes of writing blocks (1955). He posits four hurdles to creative writing: (a) oral refusal as defense (i.e., refusing to need the mother's milk by refusing to write), (b) too little distance between the repressed wish and defenses (i.e., actually attempting to write about a repressed wish such as masochism that could elicit an even stronger defense), (c) scopophilia (i.e., a tendency to voyeurism and its relative, exhibitionism, that can elict inner defenses against public behaviors, writing included), and (d) increase of the neurosis (i.e., blocked writers suffering from other difficulties such as alcoholism that sap the energies needed to resolve the block).

Bergler was, then, a pioneer psychologist in publicizing writing blocks. One of his explanations, scopophilia, found some currency among other writing-block therapists; at the least, he helped bring the idea of writing blocks to the public and professional awareness. His failing, in my view, was his insistence on promoting the notion that writers are necessarily neurotic. So it was, I suspect, that he devoted so much of his book and two articles on writing blocks to criticisms of his patients and reviewers and so little to therapeutic methods for unblocking.

OTHER REPORTS OF PSYCHOANALYTIC TREATMENT

Psychoanalysts after Bergler who have reported cures of writers' blocks have added surprisingly little to our theoretical or practical knowledge. This failure is not, as I hope to demonstrate, due to inherent shortcomings of psychoanalysis.

Goodman (1952) published a vague account of how writing blocks in playwrights might be due to the uncomfortable similarity of dramatic characterization to real social interactions. The cure, Goodman claims, consists of inducing writers to tell their own actual stories so they may thereby learn that drama is fictional instead of real interaction. If, conversely, playwrights do not overcome this inhibition via disclosure, they presumably will not be able to "play" while composing and their writing will be "over particularized" and heavy.

Meyer (1953), who like Goodman shows little awareness of Bergler's work, seems to be speaking about his own tendencies to block. It is the growth of information in psychoanalysis, he assumes, that produces the feeling that one cannot know enough to publish. So it is, Meyer concludes, that psychoanalysts are more likely to seek psychotherapy for help with writing problems than are other professionals. Quaytman (1969) also writes about his own writing block and echoes the opinion that writers are hard-pressed to believe that they can match the significance of what has already been published. But he lists additional reasons for blocking that are much like those in contemporary use: One problem with writing is that it, unlike verbalizing, receives little immediate feedback on the correctness or acceptability of a message; another problem is the irreversibility of printed words—once in print they cannot be retracted as easily as spoken words.

In a sequel, Quaytman (1973) writes about the letters he got from other analysts concerning difficulties in writing for publication. The gist of their anecdotes is an account of writing blocks in more analytically oriented terminology: for example, writing anxiety based on the fear of competing with colleagues becomes "castration anxiety." More important, writing blocks acquire a kind of characterological quality of "passivity." Quaytman's most unique and important contribution is an emphasis on the need for "healthy exhibitionism" to avoid writing blocks; that is, a writer must be willing to step out and say "this is who I am."

Schuman's 1981 article in the *Psychoanalytic Review* is the most recent of this genre. It unfortunately displays all the faults of its predecessors. Schuman reveals his deficiency as a scholar when he claims to be the first to prescribe a treatment for writer's block. At the time his article appeared, at least three successful treatments had already appeared in the Gestalt and transactional literature and four in the behavioral literature. Worse still, Schuman (after meandering among unrelated topics) reveals little about his own cure for writing blocks. Almost as an afterthought he mentions having gotten a resistant patient to write by making him furious. No mention is made of whether that patient met his goal of completing a dissertation.

UNDEVELOPED POTENTIAL OF PSYCHOANALYSIS FOR TREATING WRITER'S BLOCK

In this era in which psychoanalysis has fallen from favor among practicing psychotherapists, it would be easy to dismiss analytic treatments of writing blocks as anachronistic and irrelevant. But in fact writers like Bergler and Schuman do not represent the best of the tradition established by Freud. They cannot, it seems to me, do justice to writing blocks with such negative attitudes about blocked writers or without specifying techniques for unblocking. Psychoanalysis cannot be dismissed without considering how more mainstream therapists might approach writing blocks.

Since the 1940s, the psychoanalytic movement has been shifting, for the most part, to an "ego psychology" (Fine, 1979). This evolution away from an id-oriented psychology has resuted in two important changes. First, ego psychology takes a more positive stance about behaviors being rational and autonomous from id influences and as being susceptible to cultural influences. Thus, modern psychoanalysis can deal with writing as something more than the product of deep-seated conflicts, as something shaped also by sociocultural factors (such as the expectation that women will not be successful writers). Second, psychoanalysts are dropping their bias against empirical research. Silverman's studies (1976) of how experimentally implanted and unconscious motives can affect behavioral conflicts provide an exemplar of how psychoanalytic research on writing blocks might begin.

Finally, I am convinced by my own experience as a therapist of the potential usefulness of psychoanalysis for treating blocked writers. Most of my clients with writing blocks are academicians, some of whom are already "imprinted" on psychoanalysis through reading and as a result of having been in analysis. These people tend to reject more behavioral treatments and are quite skilled at shaping the content of sessions toward analytic concepts and interpretations. As a result, I developed enough interest to complete two extended cases from an entirely psychoanalytic approach. Both were treated in a framework established by Erik Erikson (1964). His approach is like that of more traditional psychoanalysis in that it places a heavy emphasis on life history and on psychosocial stages. But what makes Erikson's approach more contemporary is his emphasis on endowing the ego with trust and hope, autonomy and will, industry and competence, generativity and care, and other qualities, all of which are involved in finding creative solutions to problems that accompany each stage of life. As do earlier varieties of psychoanalysis, Erikson's method directs attention to the vulnerability of the ego, to irrational ego defenses, and to problems created by guilt, anxiety, and trauma. But what marks Erikson as an ego psychologist is his insistence that a patient can, with psychotherapy, develop an ego capable of handling those problems.

I chose Erikson as a model in part because he values some of the things I believe are critical to fluent writing, such as "factuality." Factuality is one of his "dimensions of reality" that a new ego identity might take; it refers to verification of real-world events and their interrelatedness with careful observation (Erikson, 1974). In practice, this form of psychotherapy produced some sessions strikingly different from my usual sessions with a behavioral emphasis. The patient and I began by talking much less about current writing problems and anxieties and much more about early experiences. I did much less problem-formulating and much more listening, while the patient sooner or later evoked the insights about why he or she was blocking. And, perhaps because a psychoanalytic approach doesn't involve precise interventions and directives, it seemed that unblocking occurred rather imperceptibly.

Nonetheless, I did discover some striking commonalities between the psychoanalytic and behaviorally oriented sessions. In either case, patients came to the same basic conclusions about what was causing them to block—usually some combination of negative expectations (e.g., writing will be criticized), perfectionism, impatience, and poor time management. And in both cases, patients began writing shortly after weekly sessions had begun. More regular writing came once insights about blocking had induced changes in attitudes and habits connected with writing.

It seems that ego psychology deserves much more attention in the literature on writing skills. For instance, Erikson's methods are ideally suited to psychohistorical interpretations of writers as personalities. I am currently working with the autobiographical materials of Isaac Asimov (1979) to learn more about how an exceptionally prolific author persists through numerous crises, conflicts, and complexes.

Why is there so little of substance about writing published by psychoanalysts? One reason is that psychoanalysis has never been a part of the American psychological establishment, the dominant influence on psychotherapeutic practice. A second reason is that psychoanalytic therapies do not easily lend themselves to description as do behavioral techniques; psychoanalysis seems easier to communicate via training and modeling than detailed writing. A third reason, odd as it may seem, is that many of the psychoanalysts who treat blocked writers claim to be blocked themselves (e.g., Quaytman, 1969, 1973). Perhaps they are blocked for reasons similar to those attributed by Elbow (1981) to English teachers who rarely write for publication; they are so accustomed to a superior and somewhat critical role that risking public errors in their own writing is threatening. The fourth reason is a matter of practicality: Psychoanalysts tend to work in applied settings where case loads are heavy and where writing and research are not encouraged (Boice & Jones, 1984).

Automatic Writing/Free Writing

Automatic writing is an activity during which the subject is aware of writing but not of what is being written (Ellenberger, 1970). Its origins were in early forms of hypnotherapy, perhaps dating back to the Mesmerists. It owed its greatest popularity to spiritualists of a century ago, who believed that automatic writing was a means of communicating with departed spirits. Some automatic writers or mediums produced best-selling books (e.g., Worth, 1917), one of which included accounts and pictures of houses on the planet Jupiter (Bois, 1907). Like other forms of hypnosis, automatic writing lends itself to the exaggerated and mystical interpretations of zealots but is subject to the skepticism of respectable professionals (Boice & Meyers, 1983).

But even in the hands of spiritualists, automatic writing showed promise for helping problem writers. Records of automatic writers indicate that they wrote at a remarkable pace. Gardiner (1908) witnessed an automatic writer who produced from 7 to 14 poems an hour, "rarely trivial in subject" and without erasures. Eventually, the use of automatic writing developed in two somewhat independent directions. The first remained wholly tied to psychoanalysis; the other had various literary applications.

PSYCHOTHERAPEUTIC APPLICATIONS

Prince (1905) saw the value of automatic writing in terms of spontaneity of expressions and of freedom from "artifacts" unwillingly manufactured by the observer. Muhl (1930) tried to correct some of the negative impressions that had caused other analysts to shy away from this technique (e.g., the view that it was potentially addictive for patients who practiced it on their own). Milton Erickson (1937), the hypnotherapist, was influential in demonstrating that automatic writing follows ordinary laws of expression. The few reports of automatic writing in therapy that followed (e.g., Lindner, 1944; Muhl, 1956; Wohlberg, 1945), suggest that it worked nicely as a means of preparing patients to tolerate repressed ideas.

The best experimental analysis in a psychoanalytic framework may be Harriman's demonstration (1951) that hypnotically induced conflicts later show up in the patient's automatic writing. More recently, psychoanalysts seem to have confirmed the prediction of LeCron (1956) that automatic writing would be seen as dangerous (e.g., Earle & Theye, 1968). When it is practiced without careful supervision, automatic writing may induce an addiction to the activity or the revelation of unmanageable ideas from the unconscious.

LITERARY AND OTHER ARTISTIC APPLICATIONS

The second direction in which automatic writing developed can be attributed at least in part to William James. Like Janet (1889), he argued that careful analysis of automatic writings suggested their source to be in a writer's mind that was in "an abstracted state," and not in "another intelligence." James's greater impact in this regard came indirectly, by involving his graduate student, Gertrude Stein, in an obscure experiment (Stein & Solomons, 1896). Stein along with a second researcher, Solomons, showed that automatic writing by "normals" produced the same sort of material usually verbalized by patients with multiple personalities. In the view of Stein and Solomons, the factor producing this disassociation of normal ideas was the state of distraction induced in automatic writing. Stein elaborated this experience into a technique she called "experimental writing" and into the writing style that helped make her famous (cf. Skinner, 1934).

The artistic use of automatic writing had its origins not only in early psychology but also among some writers and artists. Surrealists in Paris of the 1920s and 1930s used a form of free-intuitive writing that they called automatic writing (Rainer, 1978). André Breton, in particular, was influential in promoting the use of a technique that relied on hypnagogic images; that is, he placed himself in a hypnotic state in which his observation was directed almost exclusively at his own thoughts. Ellenberger describes the result:

> Breton's attention was drawn to these mysterious sentences in which he saw the very essence of poetry . . . [and] then noted that there is in man, not only in the hypnagogic state but permanently, an "inner discourse" (*discours intérieur*) which can be perceived if sufficient attention is paid. This inner voice is quite different from what . . . James Joyce called the interior monologue, which is rather an imitation of ordinary speech. Breton's inner discourse is intermittent and appears in short sentences and groups of words that are disconnected from one another. Moreover, there can be several simultaneous verbal streams, each carrying a flow of images that vie for supremacy. (1970, p. 835)

The method used by Breton for tapping this inner discourse was different from that used by the spiritualists. For surrealists, automatic writing was not a matter of unconscious writing but of careful listening to inner discourse and of recording that discourse without changing a word. In this form, automatic writing is clearly akin to what contemporary teachers of composition (Elbow, 1973) and therapists (Rainer, 1978) call "free writing." I will return to the topic of free writing momentarily.

APPLICATIONS TO TREATING WRITING BLOCKS

One thing that is missing in the interesting story of automatic writing is an application to blocked writers. That this was an unexplored possibility with obvious promise for getting clients writing motivated me to treat some of my blocked colleagues with various forms of automatic writing. It proved to be an especially useful technique with clients who resisted behavioral methods for philosophical reasons or who did not want to take responsibility for what they had written.

I used the same induction procedure with all clients that I exposed to automatic writing, one based on methods developed by William James. Details of this procedure and additional information about automatic writing appear elsewhere (Boice & Myers, 1983), but I'll summarize the techniques and results here. I supervised all sessions—all automatic writing should be guided by an experienced clinician. I had writers place their heads in the crook of their nonwriting arm, rest their writing arm in a supportive sling, and listen to me read them a piece of prose unrelated to what they wrote. In the first few sessions, a third person was present who acted as a "coach" to help keep the writer's hand on the page and help keep him or her from writing over already written material.

One subject was an academician who sought treatment for a writing block but who agreed to behavioral treatment only if it was combined with a more "humanistic" procedure. He liked the idea of automatic writing as the second technique and stated an intention to prove it more effective than the behavioral technique we used of "contingency management" (i.e., earning basic daily rewards such as a morning shower by first completing a specified number of pages—thus making the reward contingent on writing). Following the baseline phase in which writing was spontaneous (no contingency management) he was shifted to a contingency phase designed to "force" him to write. As he had predicted, he did not write.

The apparent failure of contingency management brought him the desired result: access to five daily, hour-long sessions of automatic writing. This completed, he returned to contingency management *and* to a productive record of writing output. At that point, of course, the effective agent in unblocking this writer had not been specified. Only later, long after the contingency had been removed and following his spontaneous reblocking, did he engage in a second installment of automatic writing. The results suggest that the effect of the second installment of automatic writing was to reestablish writing but not in a stable or persistent form. Only when this writer reinstituted the external contingency was he able to remain unblocked for extended periods of time.

A second writer opted for a procedure whereby she spent two sessions a week with me, each Monday and Tuesday, doing automatic writing. On each of the three remaining weekdays, she worked on scholarly writing projects. The expectation was that by starting each week with a guided and successful writing experience, she would be unblocked in her attempts to write for publication. The graphs she kept of daily output suggest a reasonable amount of success in unblocking, one that met her stated needs. Her graphs also indicate a general tendency for writing productivity to decrease as the workweek progressed.

A third subject was a blocked writer who wanted to begin each scheduled writing day with a 20-minute period of automatic writing. She and I began her treatment by training her spouse, a clinical psychologist, to supervise sessions of automatic writing at home. While her graphs show that she clearly became unblocked and able to complete some writing projects, she did not write as much or as regularly as clients who chose contingency management interventions (Boice, 1982b).

These and related therapeutic applications suggest that automatic writing is an effective therapeutic intervention for writing blocks. My impression is that it owes its effectiveness to three related factors: (a) Automatic writing gives a writer permission to write without taking responsibility for errors; (b) it establishes momentum in writing that can be transferred to other, more inherently difficult writing tasks; and (c) it can show a writer that he or she is capable of composing competent and creative copy. Similar points about the inspirational and informational potentials of placing blocked clients into trance states have been made by therapists using more conventional hypnotic inductions with creatively blocked playwrights and artists (Mellgren, 1976; Rosenberg, 1976).

USES OF FREE WRITING

Teachers of composition have a long-standing tradition of advocating free writing as a means of building momentum and generating ideas. Brande (1934) described a technique in which writers were encouraged to write anything that comes to mind, to write early in the morning, and to write quickly. With practice, she assured readers, free writing transforms writing into a task that is no longer arduous or dull. The idea of free writing is apparently quite a bit older than other tactics for unblocking. Börne (1958), who seems to have influenced Freud's techniques for free association, advocated a brainstorming approach to writing in which everything that came to mind was written down. The physicist Haym (1870) offered a more sophisticated form of free writing. He began by writing out his thoughts in unclear and incomplete form and used those notes to generate experiments and formal writing.

Free writing was not well-known, however, until Elbow (1973, 1981) popularized it. What Elbow has done for free writing is to present its advantages with unprecedented charm and clarity.

> The most effective way I know to improve your writing is to do free writing exercises regularly. At least three times a week. They are sometimes called "automatic writing," "babbling," or "jabbering" exercises. The idea is simply to write for ten minutes (later on, perhaps fifteen or

> twenty). Don't stop for anything. Go quickly without rushing. (1973, p. 3)

Equally important, Elbow anticipates the objections to his simple but effective method and, in so doing, provides this insight about a cause of writing blocks: "The reason it feels like chaos and disorientation to write freely is because you are giving up a good deal of control" (1973, p. 31). And, to complete this brief overview, Elbow explains why free writing can help unblock and improve writing:

> Free writing makes writing easier by helping you with the root psychological or existential difficultly in writing: finding words in your head and putting them down on a blank piece of paper. So much writing time and energy is spent *not* writing. . . . Frequent free writing exercises help you learn simply to *get* on with it and not be held back by worries about whether these words are good words or the right words. Thus, free writing is the best way to learn—in practice, not just in theory—to separate the producing process from the revising process. (1981, p. 14)

The notion that generativity must be separated from editing seems to be widely accepted (e.g., Mandel, 1980; Rainer, 1978). But I know of only one published account of this sort of free writing being used therapeutically with a blocked writer (Galbraith, 1980). This single case study of a blocked dissertation writer is interesting, but it does not provide clear information about which of this therapist's therapy components caused the writer to increase production or why the client was so resistant to revising her writing.

Free writing of a somewhat different variety, journal writing, is used by a variety of psychotherapists as a means to get patients to describe and analyze their problems more thoroughly than they might do in verbal interactions (e.g., Domash, 1970). Rainer (1978) has developed what may be the most sophisticated system of diary writing. Her treatment for blocked writers consists of having clients practice "free-intuitive writing" as a means of outwitting the "censor" (who likes to make judgments on the writer writing) and the "critic" (whose role as a useful commentator must be withheld during a first draft).

But here and in related approaches that emphasize "right-brained"—that is, intuitive, unthinking, nonanalytic—approaches for getting past the stiffness and obsessiveness that may block creativity (Edwards, 1979), there is disappointingly little objective evidence for the effectiveness of specific techniques. Sears (1979) did, however, prescribe a specific, 11-step process (e.g., narrowing the writing topic, peer evaluations) in a letter-writing technique for treating writing blocks in freshman composition students. The virtue of her article is that another teacher or therapist can easily replicate her strategy, thus confirming or disconfirming its utility.

Therapies for Writer's Cramp

Treatments for writer's cramp, like automatic writing and free writing, represent another tradition that predates Freud. Writer's cramp was described as long ago as 1883 (Sanavio, 1980). Until recently, this group of spasms, tremors, or paralyses that occur each time a patient attempts to write was considered difficult to treat. Earlier forms of psychotherapy such as Janet's attempts (1919) to progressively strengthen the writer's hand muscles were not impressive, perhaps because they overlooked the roles of anxiety and of writing avoidance in writer's cramp.

The advent of behavioral techniques has produced consistent success in treating this relatively rare form of writing block (e.g., Liversedge & Sylvester, 1960, p. 34). Biofeedback seems to be the most effective of these new techniques (e.g., Reavley, 1975): Electrodes are attached to the cramped muscles, electronic feedback is used to train patients to lower muscle tension "at will," and writing is reestablished while conditions of muscle relaxation are maintained. A surprising amount of theorizing and study have been devoted to writer's cramp, almost all of it in Europe. The incidence of writer's cramp seems to be even lower in America than the low rates cited in British and Italian journals.

Patients with writer's cramp, although not judged as neurotic, do seem to manifest neurotic traits such as hypersensitivity, conscientiousness, and dependency (Crisp & Moldofsky, 1965). The consensus of researchers is that writer's cramp is learned, possibly via conditioned anxiety (Sanavio, 1980). Other hypotheses do persist, including psychosomatic explanations, but add little new explanatory power to those based on feedback mechanisms.

My own experience with treating writer's cramp is limited, but I can add two observations to those available in the literature just reviewed. One is that about a third of my writing-block clients admit to having suffered some mild form of writer's cramp at some earlier time, usually in pressure situations such as exams. This frequency seems to be much higher than that for consistently successful writers I have surveyed. It seems clear to me that cramps and blocks are related and that similar therapeutic techniques might be used with both. The second observation is that writer's cramp may be treated successfully with nonbehavioral techniques. I treated one academician who complained of severe muscle cramps in his writing arm with five weekly sessions of automatic writing. These not only proved to the patient that he could write painlessly but that he could write acceptable copy for a scholarly project he had planned.

Transactional and Gestalt Therapies

Some of the most interesting psychotherapies occur outside the mainstream, in tributaries related to humanistic and existential psychology. Articles about creative blocks in journals like *Art Psychotherapy* provide good examples. Kronsky (1979) is a Gestalt therapist who begins her account with a reminder that artists need to learn an "attitude of respectful letting-be." That is, writers or any other artists must train themselves to work in nothing more than a moment-by-moment awareness. But the therapist's role consists of more than teaching clients a Taoistic attitude of living in the present. It also includes coaching them to give up negative attitudes about themselves implanted by authoritarian educators. It includes teaching ways of detecting what Kronsky calls "turning-off actions," whereby the artist begins to think in old, blocking ways. And the teaching emphasizes overcoming fears of one's own excitement and energy—or of losing the support of important others.

Henning (1981) relies on another technique common to Gestalt therapy, "paradoxical treatment" (e.g., by stating a doubt that the client can succeed, the therapist motivates the client to prove him or her wrong). The paradox seems to have inspired his client to produce the "badly written" copy he dreaded and to have led him to discover that he didn't write badly even when he "tried." Thus, stripped of his reason for not doing scholarly writing, the client abandoned his block.

Transactional therapists tend to place the cause of writing blocks in intimidating authority figures such as teachers. The solution is to retrain writers in situations where criticism is minimized, where exploration and play are safe, and where nonstop writing can be arranged (Scanlon, 1979). Minninger provides a sense of how transactionalists describe their work:

> During the exploratory phase participants have permission to give up, temporarily, all sense of responsibility for what they write. . . . The old teachers are banished from the old classroom kingdom. Participants are encouraged to explore their unique writing voice and no one is allowed to criticize. Anything is OK—here no one can fail. (1977, p. 71)

Although such articles by transactional therapists are refreshingly different, they do not in fact add much that is novel to psychotherapies for writing blocks. The biggest difference is in terminology—in the use of labels such as "reteachering." Moreover, the most successful and most frequently imitated treatments in this area have borrowed heavily from the very behaviorists that transactional and Gestalt therapists purport to oppose. Consider an article by Jones (1975). She begins with the usual transactionalist terms such as "discounting" (i.e., blocked writers seem to procrastinate because they play down their abilities to write). But she quickly moves to an analysis that would please B. F. Skinner. Blocking, according to Jones, always includes two components: grandiose but fluctuating expectations of success, and a vaguely planned project. The solution is a matter of defining expectations and specifying plans by drawing up an exacting contract: The writer composes a statement of the subject to be covered, works out a schedule of pages to be written per day with an estimate of completion dates for various sections of the paper, and specifies provisions for giving himself or herself "strokes" (rewards) for completing each step of the program. There is nothing wrong, of course, with transactional therapists using behavioral techniques that work. My only reservation is that these authors seem reluctant to admit their eclecticism and to acknowledge writing-block treatments beyond their own theoretical specialities.

Behaviorist Therapies

Many people involved in composition teaching and research seem to have a strong bias against behaviorism (e.g., DeBeaugrande, 1982). My concern is to get humanistic readers to see that some behavioral interventions for writing blocks deserve patient consideration.

One of the problems, I suppose, is to get past Skinner's well-known claims that all verbal behavior is learned in exactly the same way as any other behavior. His articles, such as "On Having a Poem" (1972), are evidently designed to combatively annoy humanists who might suppose that creative inspiration and internally generated ideas are the major factors in writing. But if possible I'd like to suspend philosophical issues and discuss behavioral tactics, including cognitive therapies, that are proving effective in relieving writer's block. And, while doing this, I will attempt to show how all these techniques derive from commonsense strategies that have long ago been established by successful writers who cared nothing about debates between behaviorists and humanists.

THE FIRST CASE STUDIES OF WRITERS BY BEHAVIORISTS

The best-known article on writing blocks in the behavioral literature is Upper's (1974). His title, "An Unsuccessful Self-Treatment of a Case of 'Writer's Block,'" is followed by a blank page. This represents, all too clearly, the kind of nervous humor with which psychologists typically approach this subject; we can feel comfortably different from a patient who is schizophrenic but not always so from one who complains of an inability to write.

Behaviorists have been publishing accounts of successful case histories since 1970. Nurnberger and Zimmerman (1970) began the series with evidence that an especially strong form of contingency management can get a blocked writer writing. They devised a "productive avoidance" technique that virtually ensures writing by having the client write out checks for a meaningful sum to a hated organization (e.g., the Ku Klux Klan) which are to be mailed on any scheduled writing day when the preset number of pages are not completed. Not only did Nurnberger and Zimmerman produce a reliable increase in the writing output of their patient but also his related problems, including marital dissatisfaction, showed parallel improvements.

Other case histories of blocked clients treated with contingency management have helped confirm that original study. Boudin (1972) motivated a client to meet her goals of completing scholarly papers by arranging her life-style so that she earned ordinary rewards like cigarettes and food for each scheduled bit of writing she completed. Similar papers (Harris, 1974; Passman, 1976; Rosenberg & Lah, 1982) make the point that having clients contract to complete small, sequential components in a project is a powerful aid to unblocking.

Another case history of the 1970s more clearly indicates the concern of behaviorists with writing problems. Pear (1977) took the novel step of reanalyzing the writing records of the novelist Irving Wallace. When Pear translated Wallace's charts into graphs of pages completed per day, he was able to show that they followed remarkably clear patterns. The essential result, one that would delight a behaviorist, was a "fixed-ratio" pattern of writing output: In writing novel after novel, Wallace's rate of production followed the pattern expected of someone responding to contingent rewards occurring after a fixed ratio of writing behavior; that is, as a manuscript progressed, rates of writing increased, evidently because the completion of each ratio (e.g., chapters per book manuscript) signaled the nearer approach of a reward (i.e., completion of the task). Moreover, productivity dropped off in time intervals proportional to the lengths of units just completed (e.g., a chapter versus an entire draft of a novel). Pear's point was not to show that a pigeon, that can also master a fixed-ratio schedule, could have written Wallace's novels. Instead, the interpretation was that writing, heretofore considered a behavior under mysterious controls, may be subject to ordinary laws of reinforcement.

Wallace was able to help provide these data because he, like many other prolific writers, had established his own program of charting and of external contingencies to "create discipline." He had also anticipated some of the insights to be gained by behaviorists, notably that writers become successful not through flashes of inspiration but by dint of hard and uniform labor. Wallace (1971), like anyone schooled in Romantic notions, had to unlearn his prejudice against the use of "mechanical" devices to aid writing. Only later, he reports, did he gratefully discover that many literary geniuses had "stooped" to using similar devices. In retelling Wallace's story, Pear implies that the same self-management techniques used by the successful writers might be used to help unproductive writers (Goldiamond, 1977).

In spite of the successful work I have cited, behavioral treatments of writing blocks did not achieve much status in the 1970s. Many behaviorists felt that such studies lacked tight experimental controls. The single case studies, while interesting and suggestive, did not eliminate possibilities that factors other than contingency management (e.g., amount of therapist contact) were responsible for unblocking (e.g., Menks, 1979). The more systematic clinical treatment studies of the 1980s have provided the methodological safeguards so important to behavioral researchers.

METHODICAL PROOFS THAT CONTINGENCY MANAGEMENT WORKS FOR WRITERS

I am not by nature a behaviorist. But I work in a clinical psychology that is increasingly dominated by behavioral research. So it was that I decided to rely on behavioral strategies for my clinical treatments of writing blocks in order to increase the likelihood that other clinicians would be able to duplicate my work and consider blocked writers as treatable clients.

I began my quest to gain scientific respectability for clinical research on writing blocks with a multiple case study (Boice, 1982a). While each of the six academicians involved received individualized treatment, all were exposed to the same experimental design in order to test the ability of contingency management to effect stable increases in writing productivity. Figure 9-1 helps make the point.

The subject depicted in this graph was exposed to a treatment plan of contingency management called an "ABAB design." That is, a period of noncontingent writing (A) was followed by a period in which daily rewards like showers were contingent in writing (B), and so on. The initial period of noncontingent or spontaneous writing (A) is considered a baseline phase because it reveals a subject's rate of writing prior to the implementation of contingency management. The increase during phase B, where writing is encouraged via external rewards, can then be contrasted to the output recorded during the baseline phase. The second A-phase in Figure 9-1 represents a return to noncontingent conditions. If the contingency management intervention was indeed responsible for a subject's stable writing output, then rates were expected to drop off during the second A-phase—perhaps to levels like those in the baseline phase, unless factors other than contingency

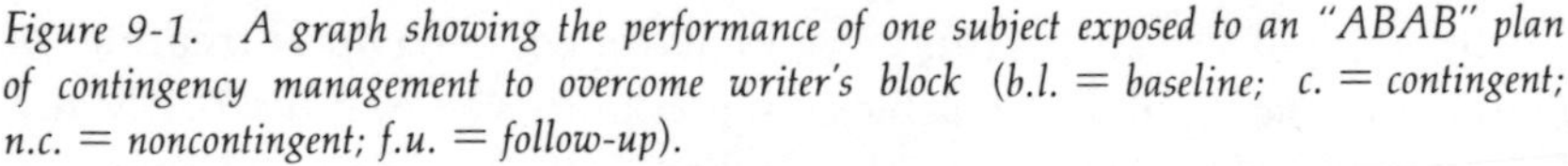

Figure 9-1. A graph showing the performance of one subject exposed to an "ABAB" plan of contingency management to overcome writer's block (b.l. = baseline; c. = contingent; n.c. = noncontingent; f.u. = follow-up).

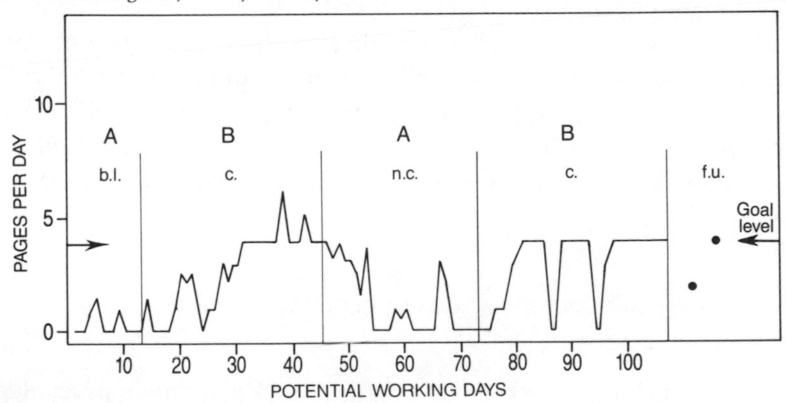

management were now in effect. The second B-phase simply shows that reestablishment of the contingency in this case reinstated a strong writing habit. Behaviorists delight in demonstrating "stimulus control" where the behavioral improvement seemingly can be turned on and off and on again with some precision.

In my experience, contingency management invariably works in a manner similar to that illustrated in Figure 9-1. Initial therapy sessions, during which reasons for blocking are discussed, are typically sufficient to elicit small and sporadic amounts of writing (this in itself impresses clients; many blocked writers enter treatment with strong convictions that they can write nothing scholarly). But the kind of spontaneous output characteristic of baseline phases is rarely sufficient to meet the clients' stated needs for completing written projects. In the second stage, once they have agreed on an effective contingency, most clients write regularly because "they have to." The writer depicted in Figure 9-1 was atypically slow in adjusting to contingency management. For the first few weeks of his contract to earn showers by writing four pages a day, he simply remained unbathed and somewhat miserable.

Some clients begin by insisting on contingencies that have little chance of succeeding. A professor turned administrator, for instance, decided to earn his lunches by meeting writing goals; that way, he reasoned, he would either write or lose weight. Once the ineffectiveness of this contingency plan had been demonstrated, he agreed to establish separate rewards for writing and dieting programs, both with good results.

One question that occurs immediately to nonbehaviorists regards the seeming rigidity of behavioral research designs. If a clinician is conscientiously collecting systematic data, will emergency needs of clients be given humane consideration? One of the subjects in the study just described was an academician referred to me for treatment after a serious suicidal gesture. Her distress seemed clearly related to her inability to write and to the prospect that she would not gain tenure. The priority, obviously, was to get her writing quickly; I omitted the baseline phase and settled for a "BAB design"; that is, she began with a contingency phase.

I also decided not to expose her directly to usual contingency management conditions. Instead, she and I devised a program of "successive approximations" to formal writing to help ensure that she would experience the immediate completion of writing tasks. Because this client expressed an inability to carry out even the simplest writing tasks such as professional correspondence, we began by contracting for minimal amounts of letter writing to earn the right to leave her office at the end of each workday. She began by having to complete only one piece of correspondence; subsequently, the goal level was increased by one unit per day. When she had become proficient at this simple task, we moved to successively closer approximations of formal writing: putting ideas on cards, constructing outlines and then "filled" outlines, and drafting rough compositions. When she had reached the sixth level of "shaping," to formal composition and to contingency management, she had long since ceased to report any suicidal thoughts or to show signs of severe depression. After establishing stable and high levels of writing in scholarly projects, she, like the other subjects in this study, was exposed to phases where contingency mangement was removed and then reintroduced. This tactic, incidentally, is not only useful for convincing behaviorists of a research clinician's scientific merits; it also shows clients how important contingency management is for *maintaining* consistent and substantial levels of writing output.

Two more questions about this sort of behavioral treatment follow from what I have just said: To what are the treatment effects attributable, and do treatment effects persist beyond the weekly therapy sessions? The answer to the first is presumably provided by the ABAB design mentioned earlier; that is, the relative superiority of contingent to noncontingent phases of treatment for the same client suggests that contingency management is the effective "change agent." A subsequent study provided even clearer evidence of this (Boice, 1983a). Blocked academicians, whether with or without "therapeutic" assistance, achieved the same stable levels of writing productivity but only when contingencies were in effect. The answer to the second question is that the subjects in the earlier study were continuing to write regularly and to submit articles that were being accepted for publication at follow-up checks a year or more after treatment (Boice, 1982a). Success in maintenance, not surprisingly, appeared to be directly linked to the prolonged use of external contingencies.

A fourth question about contingency management is usually the most urgent. Doesn't forcing writers to write result in writing that is artificial and uncreative? In a sense this question is as old as concerns about the superficiality of behavioral techniques that treat symptoms but ignore underlying causes of problems. Skinner (1972) has devoted considerable effort to defending his conviction that behavior can be creative when it is "produced." And behavioral researchers have shown that contingency management of classroom writing was associated with independent judges' higher ratings of quality and creativity (e.g., Ballard & Glynn, 1975). But such defenses of "produced" writing have not been influential. Skinner's arguments seem logical, but they are conjectural. The classroom experiments have dealt with writing in fairly limited ways; for example, elementary students were shaped to use more action verbs in ten-sentence compositions. Overall, psychologists remain strongly convinced that meaningful behavior change must be internally motivated (e.g., McKeachie, 1979) and that creativity cannot occur without spontaneity (e.g., Henning, 1981).

I attempted to find out whether forced writing is less creative than spontaneous writing in another study of blocked colleagues (Boice, in press). Of the 27 academicians who completed this project, 9 each were assigned to a condition where they (a) were forced to write five days a week by strong external contingencies, or (b) were left to write spontaneously, or (c) agreed to put off all but emergency writing until the ten-week experiment had ended. All 27 clients carried out the same essential charting and logging activities: They kept graphs of numbers of pages completed; they made daily entries of their creative ideas in a log; and, by making logged entries, they provided an index of their creative output related to writing.

The decision to use clients' own estimates of their creativity was based on two related issues in research on creativity. One is the difficulty in deciding what would be a novel and useful idea for professors writing in specialized areas. The second is that self-reports of creativity are evidently the most defensible basis on which to rate creativity (Hocevar, 1981). Each thought-listing sheet was headed with these instructions:

> Ideas to be listed here must be useful and relevant to your professional writing projects, they must be novel or original in your usage, they must have occurred since the last scheduled writing day, and they must be entered at the time of day when writing would ordinarily begin. Do not enter ideas that you have already listed in similar form. Try to express the idea succinctly and add a brief note about its possible significance.

In weekly sessions with clients I verified entries for written pages by perusing their materials, and I gave them feedback on the appropriateness of listings for creative ideas. Acceptable listings were often about a connection between ideas. A clearly inappropriate listing was, for example, a concern about not writing enough.

Over the course of this ten-week program of experimental therapy, striking differences developed between the three groups. "Contingency" clients were by far the most productive writers; they went from an average baseline output of .4 pages per writing day to 3.2 pages under contingency management. "Spontaneous" clients, who began at a comparable level of .3 pages per day, showed only a moderate increase to .9 pages even when reminded to write more. The "abstention" group, not surprisingly, wrote almost nothing.

This same pattern of productivity also held for output of creative ideas. The graph in Figure 9-2 shows that reports of creativity were highest in "contingency" writers (broken line), moderate in "spontaneous" writers (solid line), and low in nonwriters (dotted line). These data suggest that contingency management fosters rather than impedes the appearance of creative ideas. Clients who were forced to write by powerful external contingencies not only produced more writing, but they also conjured more novel and useful ideas than did clients who wrote when they felt like it.

What is it about contingency management that facilitates creative thinking? Part of the answer might be that regular writing habits establish ideal conditions for thinking about writing (Zoellner, 1969). Gould (1980) found that a common trait of successful writers is the regularity with which they think about writing. Another explanation of why forced writing could be more creative derives from research on

Figure 9-2. Patterns of productivity of creative ideas that were logged by writers on a contingency management plan (broken line), by writers left to write spontaneously (solid line), and by writers who agreed to put off all but emergency writing. Numbers on the negative side of the scale refer to days before *the start of sustained writing.*

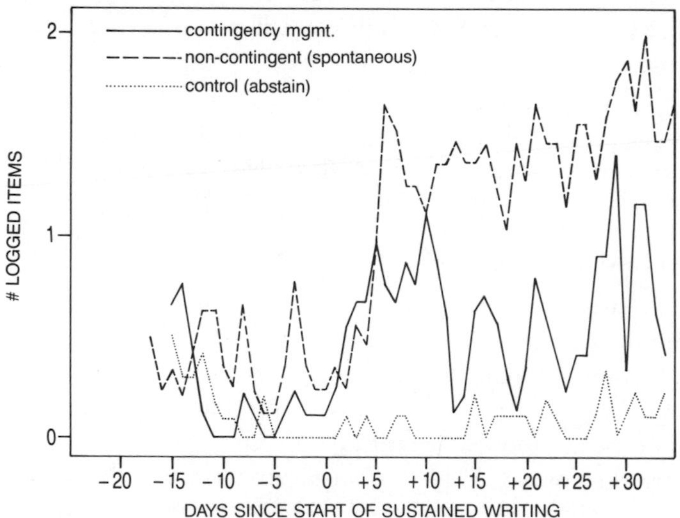

observational skills (Boice, 1983b). Writing is a task that, like observational skills, must be practiced regularly for good effect (Applebee, 1981; Hull, 1981). It requires—just as do other arts, including observation—perceiving deeply and in great detail (Edwards, 1979). And the result, once writing becomes regular, is an elaboration of thinking processes (such as a readiness to perceive the unexpected) that comprise creative thinking (Perkins, 1981).

A fifth question typically asked by humanists about this sort of behavioral methodology is whether the writers enjoy forced productivity. Eventually, almost all seem to. The uniform report of my clients on contingency programs is that as writing becomes habitual it is both easier and more enjoyable. Contingency writers also claim that external contingencies can be seen in the positive light of decisions already made for them; having committed themselves to complete projects at a steady and automatic rate, they no longer have to struggle with themselves each time they sit down to write.

A sixth, and final, question concerns the process of writing. Why do I, as a writing-block therapist, not teach techniques for generating, organizing, and conveying ideas? To the extent that I do ignore giving such instructions, it is because I work mostly with colleagues who already possess reasonably sound writing skills. What they seem to need, at least at the outset, is to learn what more productive writers already know: that writing is best done habitually and in regular amounts, regardless of mood and without awaiting inspiration. But because I do see many clients for a year or more, I have many opportunities to work on process matters; getting my clients to write materials acceptable to editors and reviewers is clearly an important part of keeping them unblocked (Boice & Jones, 1984). In those instances I emphasize the problem-solving techniques advocated by Flower and Hayes (1977).

COGNITIVE-BEHAVIOR MODIFICATION

If the litany of questions about the limitations of behavioral therapies for treating writing blocks was allowed to continue, one other query would surely arise. It would concern cognition. Given the overdue shift in psychology to the study of cognitive processes, have behaviorists incorporated cognitively oriented therapies into their treatments of writing blocks? The answer is a qualified yes.

The greater part of clinical research with a cognitive orientation is being carried out by behaviorists. Pioneers in this rapidly growing area (e.g., in Mahoney & Thoresen, 1974) make the point that traditional behavioral therapy has failed in one critical respect: It has overemphasized environmental influences on behavior and underemphasized the fact that people don't just react to the environment, but perceive and evaluate it as well. Cognitive-behavior therapists continue to emphasize behavioral notions such as contingent rewards but also emphasize methods to modify the maladaptive "self-talk" common among clients with phobias—and such clients would include blocked writers.

Consider, as an example of maladaptive self-talk, the manner in which test-anxious people carry on implicit conversations in evaluative situations: (a) They question their own performance and worry about the performance of others; (b) they devalue the task or situation and wonder about alternatives; and (c) they are preoccupied with anticipations of punishment and loss of esteem (Meichenbaum & Cameron, 1974). Much the same pattern of cognitions, in my experience, is characteristic of blocked writers trying to write.

Even though this sort of negative self-talk clearly interferes with test performance, many test-anxious people are either unaware of how much they engage in it or else conclude they are powerless to control it. The first step in most cognitive-behavioral therapies is to make clients aware of the negative statements they make to themselves. This is often a gradual process. At first, many clients deny that they talk to themselves: They are unused to observing their own cognitions; and, in any case, they have little insight into how closely their negative self-talk corresponds to negative states such as depression or tension. The second step consists of teaching clients to teach themselves techniques of supplanting negative self-statements with self-talk that will facilitate performance. These "thought substitution" procedures include "modeling" (i.e., the therapist demonstrates the tactic as she or he might use it personally), "rehearsal" (e.g., the therapist has the client imagine he or she is in an evaluative situation and is coping with negative self-statements), and "covert self-rewards" (e.g., the therapist encourages the client to verbally pat himself or herself on the back). The third step is a matter of substituting the most adaptive self-statements for negative cognition. Meichenbaum, a leading cognitive-behavior therapist, advises the use of statements of these types: (a) "If I push myself, I can do this properly"; (b) "I will enforce a no-stop rule and defer judgments;" (c) "I will begin by sizing up the problem and deciding exactly what needs to be done"; and (d) "I will relax and go slowly. There is no need to hurry; I'll just let it happen."

I am now in the process of using this cognitive–behavioral approach with a group of faculty, each of whom are coming to me for individual treatment of writer's block. I have seen these six clients once a week for a year. The treatment consists of the stages just described along with another device now in common use: thought-listing sheets. These clients begin each of five scheduled writing sessions every week by listing on standardized forms their ongoing self-statements.

Initially, the cognitions of these blocked writers were typically counterproductive to writing. Clients at this stage tended to list thoughts that encouraged avoidance (e.g., "I really have to get the car washed"), that demeaned the task (e.g., "most of what gets published is garbage; why should I add to it?"), or that simply distracted them (e.g., "I wonder what I'll make for dinner tomorrow?"). Emphasis in early therapy sessions was placed on recognizing how these thoughts interfered with writing by competing for time and/or by inducing anxiety and self-doubt. Later, attention was shifted toward thought substitution. Clients were taught, via modeling and the other tactics just mentioned, to substitute more positive and relaxing thoughts that would help get them on task.

Overall, the cognitive–behavioral paradigm has worked well. All the clients were quickly unblocked. All have maintained reasonably productive levels of writing. And in every instance, they have been delightful clients because they have learned to be their own therapists, anticipating my comments and often "carrying sessions." However, their consistent complaint, one that never occurs with my contingency management clients, has been resentment about someone tampering with their thoughts; it occasionally has seemed to them that I am imposing my "values" on them. Of course they're right. Therapists do just that, usually with some precautions to determine that the values—in this case, of writing regularly and learning to put limits on other activities such as office hours—are shared by the client (Hatterer, 1965).

The results thus far suggest that cognitive-modification techniques are about as effective as the automatic-writing techniques discussed earlier. Cognitive-modification subjects do unblock, do report getting over most of their anxiety about writing, and do complete important projects. But they consistently complain about not doing enough writing because of missing scheduled sessions when other activities have taken priority. In this respect, cognitive techniques seem inferior to contingency management regimens where subjects do write regularly and invariably report satisfaction with their writing. Obviously, not all writers need to work regularly; for them, cognitive-behavioral techniques may be ideal. In my private practice, where my clients are not always research subjects, I prefer to combine techniques including cognitive modification and contingency management.

Cognitive Psychology

Another approach to the psychotherapy of writing blocks is the application of nonbehavioral studies of cognitive processes to writing problems. This is the area of cognitive psychology familiar to composition researchers and teachers (e.g., Gregg & Steinberg, 1980). Problem-solving techniques, as cognitive strategies, have been particularly promoted as a means of helping problem writers (Flower & Hayes, 1977; Rose, 1980). With one partial exception, though, cognitive-psychological techniques have not yet been tested in clinical settings.

Both DeBeaugrande (1982) and Rose (1981) provide an account of cognitive psychology as it pertains to writing. Research and theory on cognitive rules and plans can be used to construct models of the writing process and thus can provide insights into what skilled and unskilled or blocked and unblocked writers do (Oliver, 1982). Rose (1980) compared the cognitive styles of rule and plan application in ten undergraduates. Five of his student subjects wrote with ease, and five were immobilized with blocks that

> usually resulted in rushed, often late papers and resultant grades that did not truly reflect these students' writing ability. And then, of course, there were other less measurable but probably more serious results: a growing distrust of their abilities and an aversion toward the composing process itself. (1980, p. 389)

What seemed to separate the blockers from the nonblockers in Rose's interviews and observations was not an emotional factor, such as fear of evaluation, but rather cognitive style. Stated simply, blockers were stymied by their use of rigid or inappropriate rules for writing such as "I won't go on until I get that first paragraph down." Compared to nonblockers, blockers paused longer, produced shorter drafts, got lower evaluations by readers, did more prewriting, expressed four times as many nonfunctional rules, and were twice as likely to edit prematurely (Rose, 1981).

Although Rose's reports do not include actual treatment of blocks, he offers this advice to composition teachers faced with blocked students:

> Rather than get embroiled in a blocker's misery, the teacher or tutor might interview the student in order to build a writing history and profile: How much and what kind of writing was done in high school? . . . How does the student compose? . . . How would he or she define "good" writing? . . . This sort of interview reveals an incredible amount of information about individual composing processes. Furthermore, it often reveals the rigid rule or the inflexible plan that may lie at the base of the student's writing problem. . . . Dysfunctional rules are easily replaced with or counterbalanced by functional ones if there is no emotional reason to hold onto that which simply doesn't work. Furthermore, students can be trained to select, to "know which rules are appropriate for which problems." (1980, pp. 399–400)

Flower and Hayes (1977), whose problem-solving strategies are probably the best-known among composition researchers, offer an approach related to Rose's for helping problem writers. Part of their strategy reflects the contemporary move away from traditional beliefs that good writing must be the result of forces like inspiration that are outside the writer's control (Flower & Hayes, 1977). Instead, Flower and Hayes argue, writers would do better to learn that good writing is dependent on mental preparation. For example, writers should learn to use "heuristics" (i.e., cognitive processes that help find problems to be solved) and to build "stored problem representations" (i.e., set formulas for organizing certain types of writing, such as a critique that begins with a compliment and then settles into main problems).

Flower and Hayes have not reported work with blocked writers, but they have delineated differences between skilled and novice writers: (a) Poor writers overattend to relatively minor details in the assignment like the required number of pages while underattending to major concerns such as audience. (b) Poor writers derive too many of their ideas for writing directly from superficial aspects of a task (e.g., concern with how many pages it must comprise); conversely, good writers create a rich network of ways to express ideas. (c) Poor writers tend to stick with an unimaginative plan, whereas good writers continually redevelop their representation of the problem.

One study outside of composition research qualifies as a cognitive-psychological treatment of writer's block. It is Barrios and Singer's (1981) comparison of two imagery techniques in relieving a variety of creative blocks, including writing blocks. Subjects were exposed to either a control condition (discussion group) or to systematic sessions of guided "waking imagery" (i.e., daydreaming) or hypnotic dreaming. According to subjects' self-ratings, the two imagery techniques were most effective in helping them unblock. Moreover, certain kinds of subjects were most amenable to treatment: those with good attentional control (because both imagery techniques made hypnotic-like demands) and those with low levels of "dysphoric" (negative) daydreaming before treatment began. Barrios and Singer offer almost no explanation of why their imaginal techniques worked except to note that successful authors like Joan Didion report working from pictures in their heads. Because they made no attempts to induce cognitions obviously relevant to writing or, apparently, to record what images were evoked, it is difficult to specify the unblocking agent. The agent may have been a simple one—for example, the establishment of momentum in producing images (cf. Mandel, 1980).

Anecdotal Information as a Source of Ideas for Treatments

A final source of ideas about treatments is informal but potentially valuable. Writers are not generally shy about expressing their tribulations with writing; and so we have an enormous store of information, some of which pertains to blocking. Accounts of Ernest Hemingway, for instance, include several references to what he thought made writing so difficult.

> "The hardest thing to do," said he, "is to write straight honest prose on human beings. First you have to know the subject; then you have to know how to write. Both take a lifetime to learn. . . ." (Baker, 1980, p. 353)

One problem with this sort of information is that we have yet to systematize it. Only a few students of writing, notably Gould (1980), have made the effort to draw reliable impressions about what contributes to success or at least to fluency in writing. Among Gould's conclusions are these: that good writers do lots of revising; they try not to let distracting thoughts interfere with their composing; they rarely dictate; and they are uniquely preoccupied with writing. A second problem with these potentially valuable sources is that we may be able to place little direct reliance on anecdotes about creative processes. Perkins (1981) has shown that creators typically distort accounts of discovery and success so that writing appears to be much more the product of spontaneity and sudden inspiration than it really was.

Another source of anecdotal information about writing blocks is the self-help literature for blocked writers. The best and most inclusive of these works is *Overcoming Writing Blocks* by Mack and Skjei (1979).

Their presentation of unblocking techniques is arranged in a linear fashion, in parallel with that they view as the sequential stages of the writing process. Thus, Mack and Skjei begin with antidotes for procrastination and for fear of criticism (internal and external). Solutions include breaking writing tasks down into manageable steps (e.g., prewriting steps including organizational schemes, rough drafts, and revision). Mack and Skjei have achieved popularity because of tactics presented as clearly as this "purpose statement":

> You may think you already know what you want to say, or the objective your writing is intended to accomplish, but trust us, it will help no end in the unblocking process for you to take a few minutes now to set forth a simple, clear summary of what you want to say and why you need to say it. (1979, p. 77)

I don't doubt the correctness of this advice or of most other techniques and advice proposed by Mack and Skjei. My concerns are much the same as those that I have with most self-help books: *Overcoming Writing Blocks* offers an almost overwhelming array of techniques, none of them evidently proven effective; and it takes little account of individual differences or of environmental or political factors in treating blocks. Consider this example of the problems inherent in basing advice for treatment entirely on anecdotal accounts. Mack and Skjei advise putting a first draft away in a drawer and coming back to it later. I agree that this can be good advice, perhaps for writers without a tendency to block. But for the blockers in my studies, the longer away from a project, the greater the likelihood of reblocking.

Conclusions about Treating Writing Blocks

In over a decade of work with blocked writers, I have tried a variety of treatment interventions, all of them reasonably successful. Does this mean, then, that the type of technique—say analytic versus cognitive modification—makes little difference? Not in my view. I conclude, albeit somewhat warily before an audience of humanists, that behavioral techniques are the most effective because, though other techniques seem sufficient to help get writers started and to elicit sporadic writing, only behavioral approaches seem to keep writers unblocked. It appears that writers must establish regular and moderate writing habits if they are to remain productive and contented.

Does the therapist make a difference? Perhaps. I think that my success in treating blocked writers owes in part to my own writing habits; I enjoy writing, I believe that it is my most valuable medium of self-education, and I make it a priority activity that cannot be interrupted except in emergencies or when I have scheduled vacations (Boice, 1982b). Add to the foregoing an expectancy factor. I enthusiastically expect that my clients will get over their blocks—and rather quickly and painlessly. Sometimes, I suspect, they write only to avoid disappointing me (cf. Hatterer, 1965); for I always share with them the sentiment regularly expressed by my Dutch relatives: "Talk is cheap." Translated, that means I encourage clients to talk as much as necessary but to then move on to action in place of complaints. Academicians, I have discovered, are gifted talkers—especially when explaining why they can't write.

One important thing I have learned by working with well over 100 blocked writers is that there is nothing mysterious about writing blocks. That is, they can be treated in much the same way as any common clinical problem requiring insight about causative factors and self-management skills to build new habits. Blocked writers are, in many respects, like phobics whose real fear is of public embarrassment; like overeaters who simply haven't learned to arrange their environment to ensure that they consume less; and like socially unskilled clients who need to learn to calm down, observe, and model the habits of others in threatening situations. The difference is that with, say, an agoraphobic (the person who fears leaving home for public places like supermarkets), we rarely attribute the cause of fear to some mystical force like lack of inspiration.

The second important lesson I have learned is to take an ever-broadening view of writing blocks. I am just beginning to appreciate many of the factors involved in blocking and the variety of sources that can provide more information about them. Sources include literature on technical writing (Horowitz & Curtis, 1982), computer-based editing (Gould, 1980; Osborne, 1983), reading (Hartley, 1980), motivation (Nixon, 1928), feminism (Valian, 1977), and writing apprehension (Daly & Miller, 1975).

THE FOUR P'S OF WRITING-BLOCK TREATMENTS

As research accumulates, we will be able to speak with more confidence about therapeutic and teaching interventions for writing blocks. We should also be better prepared to deal with the whole complex of factors that influence blocking. I propose categorizing those factors, and extending the categories beyond the two factors already popular with composition researchers, process and product in writing. The wholistic picture presented here adds two aspects of writing and blocking: "productivity" (i.e., writing habits that result in finished copy), and "politics" (the environmental and societal forces that encourage or discourage writing).

Process and Product. The contemporary inclination among composition researchers to value the importance of process might result in neglect of the finished product. But aspects of the product are also relevant in teaching people how to write with ease and effectiveness. Research on reading, for instance, demonstrates how important the mere formatting of writing can be in eliciting favorable reader responses (Hartley, 1980). Skilled readers prefer clear headings that help organize topics, and they like salient indications in the text that act as signposts. Writers who do not learn to present information so as to satisfy readers may find their manuscripts misunderstood and unappreciated.

Productivity. I emphasize productive writing habits when treating blocked academicians (Boice, 1982b), and therefore I join Hull (1981) in criticizing composition teachers who fail to instill good attitudes toward writing that will persist outside of classrooms and beyond term paper assignments. Habits of productivity may, in the long run, be just as important as habits of good process (Boice, 1983a). A regular regimen of writing does much more than produce copy; it instills a sense of self-control and competence (Wason, 1980a, 1980b), and it can help teach better writing via experience (Elbow, 1981).

Politics. In presenting psychotherapies for writing blocks I have said little about political factors such as gender or social networks that can discourage writing and thus engender blocking. Psychology, which has traditionally focused on "subjects" in isolated laboratory conditions (Boice, 1981), has been slow to appreciate political factors. So have I.

Working with some clients over the course of several years has taught me the importance of changing their environmental conditions as well as their writing habits. Consider some of the things that make writing and publication easier (Boice & Jones, 1984): (a) Being a male, of course, is one. Olsen (1977), among others, has helped raise our sensitivity to the societal factors that discourage and distract women who want to write. Women in the academy seem to be caught in a vicious circle; they are apparently discriminated against by male gatekeepers (Spender, 1981) who have low expectations for them, and so they tend to maintain work habits that favor other activities such as committee work over writing. (b) "Connections" are paramount. Doing graduate work and then teaching in high-status departments greatly increase the chances of writing for publication and of having one's publications cited by others. (c) Mentoring is probably more important than most of us realize. Working with successful writers who can model good prose, good writing habits, and savvy in dealing with the publication process seems to be an antidote for blocking.

What can be done to help change these political conditions? A few writers (e.g., Scarr, 1981; Stolz, 1981) have begun to share the secrets of the publication process with their culturally disadvantaged peers. Some (e.g., Orne, 1981) give specific directions on how to prepare manuscripts to please reviewers. My efforts in what will be a long-term project are taking two related directions. I hope to show that graduate students, male and female, who learn to write habitually and painlessly will persist in writing, even if they take jobs where writing is not encouraged. The second effort is an objective study of the publication process in academic journals. My colleagues and I are painstakingly examining the files of journals to see what factors in submitting papers correlate with success. We have an opportunity to go beyond the usual conjectures of how unfair and unreliable the publication process is (Boice, Pecker, Zaback, & Barlow, 1983). If, in fact, male reviewers do give female authors crueler comments and more rejections than they direct to male authors, the evidence can be used to demand changes. Reviewers might, in such an outcome, be subjected to more extensive education and supervision. Authors, similarly, who fail as writers because of naïveté about stylistic and ritualistic niceties could be given feedback in those dimensions, and not in vague terms that do little to promote constructive change.

My decade of work with blocked writers, then, has taken me far beyond my initial interests. I still work with distressed and blocked writers, and I continue to experiment with clinical techniques that help unblock and maintain writing. But now I am equally interested in the larger issues of writing problems. Why do so *few* of us write, so few even of those of us who teach and treat writing problems? Why does our society perpetuate myths that make writing seem so mysterious and difficult? What is lost, to individuals and to society, by the silence of so many nonwriters?

REFERENCES

Applebee, A. N. (1981). *Writing in the secondary schools*. Urbana, IL: National Council of Teachers of English.

Asimov, I. (1979). *In memory yet green*. New York: Avon.

Baker, C. (1980). *Ernest Hemingway: A life story*. New York: Avon.

Ballard, E. D., & Glynn, T. (1975). Behavioral self-management in story writing with elementary school children. *Journal of Applied Behavior Analysis, 8*, 387–395.

Barrios, M. V., & Singer, J. L. (1981). The treatment of creative blocks: A comparison of waking imagery, hypnotic dream, and rational discussion techniques. *Imagination, Cognition and Personality, 1*, 89–109.

Bergler, E. (1950a). Does "writer's block" exist? *American Imago, 7*, 43–54.

Bergler, E. (1950b). *The writer and psychoanalysis*. Garden City, NY: Doubleday.

Bergler, E. (1955). Unconscious mechanisms in "writer's block." *Psychoanalytic Review, 42*, 160–168.

Boice, R. (1981). Captivity and feralization. *Psychological Bulletin, 89*, 407–421.

Boice, R. (1982a). Increasing the writing productivity of "blocked" academicians. *Behaviour Research and Therapy, 20*, 197–207.

Boice, R. (1982b). Teaching of writing in psychology. *Teaching of Psychology, 9*, 143–147.

Boice, R. (1983a). Clinical vs. experimental treatments of writing blocks. *Journal of Consulting and Clinical Psychology, 51*, 183–191.

Boice, R. (1983b). Observational skills. *Psychological Bulletin, 93*, 3–29.

Boice, R. (in press). The neglected third factor in writing: Productivity. *College Composition and Communication*.

Boice, R., & Jones, R. (1984). Why academicians don't write. *Journal of Higher Education, 55*, 567–582.

Boice, R., & Myers, P. E. (1983). *Automaticity & writing*. Manuscript submitted for publication.

Boice, R., Pecker, G., Zaback, E., & Barlow, D. H. (1983, August). *An examination of reviewer bias, reliability, and harshness in the files of a clinical journal*. Paper presented at the convention of the American Psychological Association, Anaheim, CA.

Bois, J. (1907). *Le miracle moderne*. Paris: Ollendorf.

Börne, L. (1958). *Gesammeltè Schriften*. Milwaukee: Bickler.

Boudin, M. H. (1972). Contingency contracting as a therapeutic tool in the deceleration of amphetamine use. *Behavior Therapy, 3*, 604–608.

Brande, D. (1934). *Becoming a writer*. New York: Harcourt, Brace.

Crisp, A. H., & Moldofsky, H. (1965). A psychosomatic study of writer's cramp. *British Journal of Psychiatry, 111*, 841–858.

Daly, J. A., & Miller, M. D. (1975). The empirical development of an instrument to measure writing apprehension. *Research in the Teaching of English, 9*, 242–249.

DeBeaugrande, R. (1982). Cognitive processes and technical writing: Developmental foundations. *Journal of Technical Writing and Communication, 12*, 121–145.

Domash, L. (1970). The therapeutic use of writing in the service of the ego. *Journal of the American Academy of Psychoanalysis, 4*, 261–269.

Earle, B. V., & Theye, F. W. (1968). Automatic writing as a psychiatric problem. *Psychiatric Quarterly, 42*, 218–222.

Edwards, B. (1979). *Drawing on the right side of the brain*. Los Angeles: J. P. Tarcher.

Elbow, P. (1973). *Writing without teachers*. New York: Oxford University Press.

Elbow, P. (1981). *Writing with power*. New York: Oxford University Press.

Ellenberger, H. (1970). *The discovery of the unconscious*. New York: Basic Books.

Erickson, M. H. (1937). The experimental demonstration of unconscious mentation by automatic writing. *Psychoanalytic Quarterly, 6*, 513–529.

Erikson, E. H. (1964). *Insight and responsibility*. New York: Norton.

Erikson, E. H. (1974). *Dimensions of new identity*. New York: Norton.

Fine, R. (1979). *A history of psychoanalysis*. New York: Columbia University Press.

Flower, L., & Hayes, J. R. (1977). Problem-solving strategies and the writing process, *College English, 39*, 449–461.

Freud, S. (1913). *The interpretation of dreams* (A. A. Brill, Trans.). New York: Macmillan. (Original work first published 1900)

Galbraith, D. (1980). The effect of conflicting goals on writing: A case study. *Visible Language, 14*, 364–375.

Gardiner, N. H. (1908). The automatic writing of Mrs. Holland. *Journal of the American Society for Psychical Research, 2*, 595–626.

Goldiamond, I. (1977). Literary behavior analysis. *Journal of the Applied Behavior Analysis, 10*, 527–529.

Goodman, P. (1952). On a writer's block. *Complex, 7*, 42–50.

Gould, J. D. (1980). Experiments on composing letters: Some facts, some myths, and some observations. In L. W. Gregg & E. R. Steinberg, (Eds.), *Cognitive processes in writing* (pp. 97–127). Hillsdale, NJ: Erlbaum.

Gregg, L. W., & Steinberg, E. R. (Eds.). (1980). *Cognitive processes in writing*. Hillsdale, NJ: Erlbaum.

Harriman, P. L. (1951). Automatic writing as a means for investigating experimentally induced conflicts. *Personality, 1*, 264–271.

Harris, M. B. (1974). Accelerating dissertation writing: Case study. *Psychological Reports, 34*, 984–986.

Hartley, J. (1980). Introduction. In J. Hartley (Ed.), *The psychology of written communication* (pp. 11–15). London: Kogan Page.

Hatterer, L. J. (1965). *The artist in society: Problems and treatment of the creative personality*. New York: Grove.

Haym, R. (1870). *Die romantische Schule*. Berlin: R. Gaertner.

Henning, L. H. (1981). Paradox as a treatment for writer's block. *Personnel and Guidance Journal, 60*, 113–114.

Hocevar, D. (1981). Measurement of creativity: Review and critique. *Journal of Personality Assessment, 45*, 450–454.

Horowitz, I. L., & Curtis, M. E. (1982, April). The impact of technology on scholarly publishing. *Scholarly Publishing*, pp. 211–228.

Hull, C. S. (1981). Effects of self-management strategies on journal writing by college freshmen. *Research in the Teaching of English, 15*, 135–148.

Janet, P. (1889). *L'automatisme psychologique*, Paris: Alcan.

Janet, P. (1919). *Les médications psychologiques*, Paris: Alcan.

Jones, A. C. (1975). Grandiosity blocks writing projects. *Transactional Analysis Journal, 5*, 415.

Kronsky, B. J. (1979). Freeing the creative process: The relevance of Gestalt. *Art Psychotherapy, 6*, 233–240.

Linder, R. M. (1944). *Rebel without a cause: The hypnoanalysis of a criminal psychopath*. New York: Grune & Stratton.

LeCron, L. M. (Ed.). (1956). *Experimental hypnosis*. New York: Macmillan.

Liversedge, L. A., & Sylvester, J. D. (1960). Conditioning techniques in the treatment of writer's cramp. In H. J. Eysenck (Ed.), *Behaviour therapy and the neuroses* (pp. 327–333). Oxford: Pergamon.

Mack, K., & Skjei, E. (1979). *Overcoming writing blocks*. Los Angeles, J. P. Tarcher.

Mahoney, M. J., & Thoreson, C. E. (Eds.). (1974). *Self-control*. Monterery, CA: Brooks/Cole.

Mandel, B. J. (1980). The writer writing is not at home. *College Composition and Communication, 31*, 370–377.

McKeachie, W. J. (1979). Perspectives from psychology: Financial incentives are ineffective for faculty. In D. R. Lewis & W. E. Becker (Eds.), *Academic rewards in higher education* (pp. 3–20). Cambridge, MA: Ballinger.

Meichenbaum, D., & Cameron, R. (1974). The clinical potential of modifying what clients say to themselves. In M. J. Mahoney & C. E. Thoresen (Eds.), *Self-control.* Monterey, CA: Brooks/Cole.

Mellgren, A. (1976). Hypnosis and artistic creation. *Journal of the American Society of Psychosomatic Dentistry and Medicine, 23,* 133–135.

Menks, F. (1979). Behavioral techniques in the treatment of a writing phobia. *American Journal of Occupational Therapy, 33,* 102–107.

Meyer, L. (1953). A new fear in writers. *Psychoanalysis, 2,* 34–38.

Minninger, J. (1977). "Reteachering: Unlearning writing blocks. *Transactional Analysis Journal, 7,* 71–77.

Muhl, A. M. (1930). *Automatic writing.* Dresden: Theodor Steinkopff.

Muhl, A. M. (1956). Automatic writing and hypnosis. In L. M. LeCron (Ed.), *Experimental hypnosis* (pp. 422–438). New York: Macmillan.

Nixon, H. K. (1928). *Psychology for the writer.* New York: Harper.

Nurnberger, J. T., & Zimmerman, J. (1970). Applied analysis of human behavior: An alternative to conventional motivational inferences and unconscious determination in therapeutic programming. *Behavior Therapy, 1,* 59–60.

Oliver, L. J. (1982). Helping students overcome writer's block. *Journal of Reading, 25,* 162–168.

Olsen, T. (1977). One out of twelve: Women who are writers in our century. In S. Ruddick & P. Daniels (Eds.), *Working it out* (pp. 323–341). New York: Pantheon.

Orne, M. T. (1981). The why and how of a communication to the literature. *International Journal of Clinical and Experimental Hypnosis, 29,* 1–4.

Osborne, A. (1983, February/March). Will micros eliminate "typing phobia"? *The Portable Companion,* p. 11.

Passman, R. (1976). A procedure for eliminating writer's block in a college student, *Behavior Therapy and Experimental Psychiatry, 7,* 297–298.

Pear, J. J. (1977). Self-control techniques of famous novelists. *Journal of Applied Behavior Analysis, 10,* 515–525.

Perkins, D. N. (1981). *The mind's best work.* Cambridge, MA: Harvard University Press.

Prince, M. (1905). *The dissociation of a personality.* New York: Longmans, Green.

Quaytman, W. (1969). Psychotherapist's writing block. *Voices, 4,* 13–17.

Quaytman, W. (1973). Ego factors in psychotherapist's writing block. *Journal of Contemporary Psychotherapy, 5,* 135–139.

Rainer, T. (1978). *The new diary.* Los Angeles: J. P. Tarcher.

Rank, O. (1934). *Art and artist.* New York: Knopf.

Reavley, W. (1975). The use of biofeedback in the treatment of writer's cramp. *Journal of Behavior Therapy and Experimental Psychiatry, 6,* 335–338.

Rose, M. (1980). Rigid rules, inflexible plans, and the stifling of language: A cognitivist analysis of writer's block. *College Composition and Communication, 31,* 389–401.

Rose, M. (1981). *The cognitive dimension of writer's block: An examination of university students.* Unpublished doctoral dissertation, University of California, Los Angeles.

Rosenberg, H., & Lah, M. I. (1982). A comprehensive behavioral–cognitive treatment of writer's block. *Behavioural Psychotherapy, 10,* 356–363.

Rosenberg, M. (1976). Releasing the creative imagination. *Journal of Creative Behavior, 10,* 203–209.

Sanavio, E. (1980). A wider model of writer's cramp. *Behavior Analysis and Modification, 4,* 17–27.

Scanlon, L. (1979, September). Writing blocks in an interdisciplinary program or getting around the professional block. *RTE Report*, pp. 1–3.

Scarr, S. (1981). *An editor looks for the perfect manuscript*. Paper presented at the conference of the American Psychological Association, Los Angeles.

Schuman, E. P. (1981). A writing block treated with psychoanalytic interventions. *Psychoanalytic Review, 68*, 113–134.

Sears, P. (1979, September). A technique for treating writer's block, *RTE Report*, pp. 1–2.

Silverman, L. H. (1976). Psychoanalytic theory: "The reports of my death are greatly exaggerated." *American Psychologist, 31*, 621–627.

Skinner, B. F. (1934, January). Has Gertrude Stein a secret? *Atlantic Monthly*, pp. 359–369.

Skinner, B. F. (1972). *Cumulative Record*. New York: Appleton-Century-Crofts.

Spender, D. (1981). The gatekeepers: A feminist critique of academic publishing. In H. Roberts (Ed.), *Doing Feminist research* (pp. 186–202). London: Routledge & Kegan Paul.

Stein, G., & Solomons, L. (1896). Normal motor automatism. *Psychological Review, 3*, 492–512.

Stolz, S. (1981). *Overcoming common barriers to publishing psychological work*. Paper presented at conference of the American Psychological Association, Los Angeles.

Suler, J. R. (1980). Primary process thinking and creativity. *Psychological Bulletin, 88*, 144–168.

Upper, D. (1974). An unsuccessful self-treatment of a case of "writer's block." *Journal of Applied Behavior Analysis, 7*, 497.

Valian, V. (1977). Learning to work. In S. Ruddick & P. Daniels (Eds.), *Working it out* (pp. 162–168). New York: Pantheon.

Wallace, I. (1971). *The writing of one novel*. New York: Simon & Schuster.

Wason, P. C. (1980a). Conformity and commitment in writing. *Visible Language, 14*, 351–361.

Wason, P. C. (1980b). Specific thoughts on the writing process. In L. W. Gregg & E. R. Steinberg (Eds.), *Cognitive processes in writing* (pp. 129–137). Hillsdale, NJ: Erlbaum.

Wohlberg, L. R. (1945). *Hypnoanalysis*. New York: Grune & Stratton.

Worth, P. (1917). *The sorry tale: A story of the time of Christ*. New York: Holt, Rinehart & Winston.

Zoellner, R. (1969). Talk-write: A behavioral pedagogy for composition. *College English, 30*, 267–320.

10

The Essential Delay: When Writer's Block Isn't

DONALD M. MURRAY

Morison isn't writing. He's a professional writer, published and anthologized, but he's not writing. He goes to his typewriter and jumps up to find more paper. He organizes and reorganizes his notes, makes a third cup of tea, visits the stationery store to buy a new pen, hunts through the library for that one elusive reference. He makes starts and notes and more notes and folders and outlines, but he does not produce a draft.

He wonders if he has writer's block. He clears writing time on his schedule, shuts the door to his study, and watches a tree grow. Slowly. He makes neat work plans, types them up, pins them above his desk, and doesn't follow them. He drafts letters—in his head—telling the editor he cannot deliver the piece. He considers going into real estate, or advertising, or becoming a hit person. He composes suicide notes—in his head—that are witty, ironic, publishable. He grumps at his wife and lies awake at night wondering if there is treatment for writer's block.

But Morison knows he doesn't have writer's block. He's been writing for almost 40 years. He is passing through the normal, necessary, always terrifying delay that precedes effective writing.

"Delay is natural to a writer," E. B. White states. "He is like a surfer—he bides his time. Waits for the perfect wave on which to ride

Donald M. Murray. The English Department, University of New Hampshire, Durham, New Hampshire.

in." Virginia Woolf reminds herself in her diary, "As for my next book, I am going to hold myself from it till I have it impending in me: grown heavy in my mind like a ripe pear; pendant, gravid, asking to be cut or it will fall."

To understand writer's block, we have to discover what is not writer's block, what forms of delay are essential for good writing. Again and again we hear our best writers—perhaps whistling in the dark—counseling themselves not to worry as they wait for writing. Ernest Hemingway said, "My writing habits are simple: long periods of thinking, short periods of writing." Franz Kafka had one word over his writing desk: "Wait." Denise Levertov says, "If . . . somewhere in the vicinity there is a poem . . . I don't do anything about it, I wait.

Recently Carol McCabe, a prizewinning journalist, explored this period of waiting. "The time just before I begin to write is the most important time I spend on a piece. By now the piece is there, waiting inside the notebook, tape or transcripts, clip files and photos, like a sculpture, waiting for release from a block of limestone. I just have to figure out how to get it out of there."

"As I begin, I turn on my own switch before the machine's," McCabe continues. "I put myself into a fugue state, a sort of hypnotic trance in which I am sensitive to blips of idea and memory, receptive to the voices of my characters whom I begin to hear as I write."

There is, of course, no certainty for McCabe, Kafka, or any other writer that the waiting will be productive. It may be a pregnancy without issue. Each writer fears that writing will never come, yet the experienced writer knows it may take days, weeks, and months to produce a few hours of text production.

I kept an unscientific account of my writing time for the first 43 weeks of 1982. I wrote the introductory material for a collection of my articles on writing and teaching, responded to the editing of a collection of pieces on writing journalism, edited a journal article, drafted and revised chapters for two different collections, completed a newspaper editorial, wrote several poems, finished a freshman text and revised it once, worked on a novel. Yet I did formal drafting, revising, or editing for only 206 hours.

I had 43 weeks, or 301 days in which to write, yet I averaged far less than an hour a day, less than five hours a week. And my working pace wasn't that even. One week I wrote for more than 22 hours, and in 10 different weeks I wrote nothing. I had more than adequate time for panic and terror, doubt that I would ever write again, fears of writer's block, and plenty of time for the necessary incubation that precedes writing. My middle name is Morison.

The more I observe the writing patterns of my students, my colleagues, and professional writers; the more I study the testimony of respected writers in published interviews, journals, essays, letters, biographies and autobiographies; the more I study my own writing processes—the more convinced I become that we not only can state the importance of delay but also can begin to comprehend those conditions or kinds of knowledge the writer waits for. There appear to be five things the writer needs to know—or feel—before writing.

Information

Amateurs try to write with words; professionals write with information. They collect warehouses full of information, far more than they need, so much information that its sheer abundance makes the need for meaning and order insistent. "One of the marks of the true genius is a quality of abundance," says Catherine Drinker Bowen. "A rich, rollicking abundance, enough to give indigestion to ordinary people." The writer turns over this compost of information in the file, in the notebook, in the head, seeking what Maxine Kumin calls the "informing material" that produces meaning.

The writer also knows it is dangerous to start writing too soon when all the writer has on hand are ideas, concepts, theories, abstractions, and generalizations. Good writers learn to fear the vague and general, to seek the hard-edged and precise. Maxine Kumin says, "What makes good poetry for me is a terrible specificity of detail." "The more particular, the more specific you are, the more universal you are," declares Nancy Hale. Vladimir Nabokov testifies, "As an artist and scholar I prefer the specific detail to the generalization, images to ideas, obscure facts to clear symbols, and the discovered wild fruit to the synthetic jam."

Specifics give off meaning. They connect with each other in such a way that two plus two equals seven—or eleven. Writers treasure the informing detail, the revealing specific, the organizing fact; and their notebooks are filled with sentences, test paragraphs, diagrams, as they connect and disconnect, order and reorder, building potential significance from their abundant fragments.

Insight

"Whenever the special images and phrases that are always criss-crossing in a poet's mind begin to stream in a common direction, rhythmically and distinctly, he will begin to write a poem," says James Emanuel. That streaming, or insight, is a single vision or dominant meaning that will be tested by the writing of the draft.

The insight is not often a thesis statement; it is less formed than that. It is a figure seen in a fog, a fragile relationship between facts, a sketch, a hint, a feeling, a guess, a question.

Mary Lee Settle says, "I start my work by asking a question and then try to answer it." But it may take a long time of fiddling around with notes, starting and discarding opening paragraphs, searching and researching, and just plain waiting for the key question to appear. Anton Chekhov says, "An artist observes, selects, guesses, and combines." Virginia Woolf speaks in her diaries of "the power of combination." And the writer has to find a way to combine the elements into a single vision before beginning a draft.

One of the most effective forms of insight is a problem that may be solved by the writing. Eugene Ionesco says, "That's what a writer is: someone who sees problems a little more clearly than others." The problem is what motivates the writer, for the best writers do not want to solve those problems they have already solved, to write what they have written before. Joubert says, "To write well, one needs a natural facility and an acquired difficulty." Experienced writers are suspicious of ease, and wait for challenge. As James Wright says, "the writer's real enemy is his own glibness, his own facility; the writer constantly should try to discover what difficulties there truly are inherent in a subject or in his own language and come to terms with these difficulties."

When the writer has achieved this difficulty, or found the question, or defined the problem, the writer may be able to begin the draft. It is important, however, for the writer seeking insight not to expect precision. Exactness comes after the final draft, after revision and re-revision, reading and rereading, editing and re-editing. Before the first draft the writer is seeking possibility. As Donald Barthelme says, "At best there is a slender intuition, not much greater than an itch."

Order

Barbara Tuchman tells us that "writing blocks . . . generally come from difficulty of organization." John McPhee says, "I want to get the structural problems out of the way first, so I can get to what matters more. After they're solved, the only thing left for me to do is to tell the story as well as possible."

Experienced writers refuse to leave on a trip through a draft without a map. The map may be in the head or on paper, but the writer needs a sense of destination. "A novel is like getting on a train for Louisiana," says Ernest J. Gaines. "All you know at the moment is that you're getting on the train, and you're going to Louisiana, but you don't know who you're going to sit behind, or in front of, or beside; you don't know what the weather is going to be when you pass through certain areas of the country; you don't know what's going to happen south; you don't know all these things, but you know you're going to Louisiana."

A significant number of writers wait until they have the ending before they begin. "I don't know how far away the end is—only *what* it is," states John Irving. "I know the last sentence, but I'm very much in the dark concerning how to get to it." Katherine Anne Porter says, "If I didn't know the ending of a story, I wouldn't begin. I always write my last line, my last paragraph, my last page first." Eudora Welty agrees, "I think the end is implicit in the beginning. It must be. If that isn't there in the beginning, you don't know what you're working toward. You should have a sense of a story's shape and form and its destination, all of which is like a flower inside a seed."

An even greater number of writers wait for the lead or first few lines that will set the draft in motion, and they are willing to spend a great deal of time waiting for those lines or worrying them into place. "Leads, like titles, are flashlights that shine down into the story," says John McPhee. "With novels it's the first line that's important," says Elie Wiesel. "If I have that, the novel comes easily. The first line determines the form of the whole novel. The first line sets the tone, the melody, then I have the book."

Need

Writers often delay beginning a draft until they feel a need to write. This need usually has two parts: the internal need of the writer to speak, and the perceived need of readers to listen.

The best writing usually comes from a need that precedes the entire process of writing. The writing comes in a climate of need created by the experiences and obsessions of the writer. The writer has an itch that must be scratched. If the writer does not have that need, then it must be achieved during the waiting period.

We delay writing until we can find the need to write. This is especially true of that writing that comes by assignment or invitation. When the need is initiated outside of the writer, the experienced writer will find a way to discover a personal need that parallels the external need.

Donald Graves writes of the importance of ownership in teaching writing. He argues that the teacher should not take over ownership of the draft, but the student must maintain ownership of what is being written. The struggle for ownership between writer and teacher, or writer and editor, is normal. But the writer must win. The writer must feel as Louise Nevelson does when she says, "My work is a feast for myself."

I almost lost the struggle with the editor of this book while drafting this chapter. When writing the first draft I was too conscious of the editor's suggestions, which I read as instructions. After I completed the draft, the editor responded with a long letter of criticism. I congratulated him for it, since it was perhaps the most impressive editorial response I've ever received. But when I came to rewrite the draft, it was lifeless. I was bored, and felt as if I were painting a picture by number. It was *his* draft, not mine. I had to put his letter aside, put away my notes based on his suggestions, put aside my earlier drafts, and start anew.

The writer has to create the illusion that the writing is his, or hers, that only this writer can deliver this message. Such arrogance is essential. I had to internalize the editor's suggestions and make them mine. And, of course, the editor has to have his own illusion. He watches me dance and knows he pipes the tune.

The writer also must have a sense of a need outside of the writer, that there is a reader who has to know what the writer says. In waiting to begin a draft, the writer is also waiting to see a reader, a person who needs what will be written. But we write for ourselves first, and others afterward; we must need to write and need to be read.

Voice

Morison waiting, staring out the window, pacing the floor, slumped in a chair, is listening, trying to hear the voice that may be able to write the draft. Morison scribbling, crossing out, drafting, crumpling paper into a ball and hurling it near the wastebasket, then writing again and moving his lips as he reads what is written, is listening. Writers know not to write until they can hear the voice that will run through the draft.

An effective piece of writing creates the illusion of a writer speaking to a reader. The language, although written, sounds as if it were spoken. Speech is the glue that holds the piece together. The writing voice provides the intensity that captures the reader; the voice provides the music and grace and surprise that keeps the reader interested; the voice communicates the emotion and the mood that makes the reader involved.

Each writer, of course, has an individual voice. But the writer learns how to extend that voice so it is appropriate for the particular piece of writing. "The most difficult task for a writer is to get the right 'voice' for his material; by voice I mean the overall impression one has of the creator behind what he creates," says John Fowles. Wright Morris adds, "The language leads, and we continue to follow where it leads."

Morison draws an angry line through the top page of a draft and hurls the stack of paper across the floor. He has written too soon. He forces himself to sit quietly in his Morris chair, to stare into that blurred middle territory between intent and realization, to wait and listen for the essential accumulation of abundant information, for a guess of a potential meaning he may call insight, for an order that may lead him toward that meaning, for a need that makes it necessary for him to write, for the sound of the draft's voice.

This waiting may be the hardest part of writing. "It's a matter of letting go," Walker Percy points out. "You have to work hard, you have to punch a clock, you have to put in your time. But somehow there's a trick of letting go to let the best writing take place." It is essential to let the writing grow within the writer, accepting the doing nothing that is essential for writing. "You have to be willing to waste time," counsels Robert Penn Warren. "When you start a poem, stay with it and suffer through it and just think about nothing, not even the poem. Just *be* there." The writer has to accept the writer's own ridiculousness of working by not working. "I spend a great deal of time simply walking around," says Joyce Carol Oates, "sitting, day-dreaming, going through the motions of an ordinary life with—I suspect—an abstracted, dreaming, rather blank expression on my face."

Morison has completed the chapter. It is in the mail. He sits down to write the next book. He is a Puritan; he makes a work schedule on Sunday, and keeps to it on Monday. Not on Tuesday. On Wednesday he reads Simone de Beauvoir: "A day in which I don't write leaves a taste of ashes." He smiles bitterly. The following Monday he forces a draft of the first chapter. It doesn't even come close. He lies awake that night and wonders if he has writer's block. But then he remembers what he has just written the week before. There is an essential delay; he must be patient; he must wait for information, insight, order, need, voice. He must not write to write.

11

Complexity, Rigor, Evolving Method, and the Puzzle of Writer's Block: Thoughts on Composing-Process Research

MIKE ROSE

I.

When I first became interested in writer's block as a dissertation topic, several influential faculty at my school tried to dissuade me. They said the problem was too complicated, too messy, or, to be a little more precise, too uncontrollable to be explored with the tools of traditional educational research. I ignored them, went my way, and now six years later must admit that they were right. As the contributors to the present volume make very clear, a writer can be stymied for all sorts of reasons; and any one of those reasons, if isolable, would itself be difficult to explore. And then there's the thorny problem of definition. As Donald Murray warns (Chapter 10), "not writing can be writing." There are all sorts of necessary mulling and rehearsing periods in our composing processes; differentiating them from true blocks is difficult, perhaps in some cases impossible. And there's a related issue: Writing blocks are usually defined in negative terms. Should they be? Donald Graves in Chapter 1 suggests that some blocks are a necessary by-product of growth. Should we then even approach writer's block as a difficulty? Questions like these make clear that writer's block is one

Mike Rose. Freshman Writing Program, University of California, Los Angeles, California.

messy problem or, more likely, a web of problems. The temptation, of course, is to render it manageable, reduce it, define it in reductive ways (as, for example, the psychoanalyst Edmund Bergler did by labeling it a breakdown of unconscious defenses against oralmasochistic conflicts) or examine it in reductive ways (for example, by recording its behavioral manifestations—time spent pausing, number of words produced, etc.). Now, certainly, some delimiting, some selecting, some excluding of cases is necessary for any inquiry to proceed—whether the inquiry be ethnographic, cognitive-process tracing, or classically experimental. All research sets limits. But there comes a point past which the limiting of a problem changes the problem. The question, then, was how to explore this very real and thus very messy problem without unduly sacrificing its complexity. The rest of this chapter will be an attempt to provide—through example as well as speculation—some answers to this question.

Clearly, whatever formal research decisions I made in planning my study had to grow out of the preliminary, to a large extent "soft," information about writing blocks I already had: observations as a teacher, anecdotes, hunches, and simple pilot studies. This information was revealing a number of problems that seemed to be primarily cognitive rather than primarily emotional. The more I read in cognitive psychology—and the more I adapted and analogized it to the writing process—the more sense I was making of some of my students' behaviors (Rose, 1980). These early investigations were instructive, but a truly comprehensive exploration of the cognitive dimension of writer's block would require more scope and more rigor. Now, the issue of rigor raises the problem about reductive limiting I mentioned earlier. Rigor in traditional educational investigation is often equated with experimental designs; but, at this early stage of investigation, I didn't have enough information to enable me to effectively use such designs. Furthermore, even with richer information, traditional designs alone—though they offer more latitude than is often thought[1]—might have proved to be too constraining to illuminate the richness of a multifaceted composing problem. Was there another kind of rigor that wouldn't sacrifice complexity? The answer that my chairman, Richard Shavelson, and I arrived at was to use multiple methods that, since they would all be focused on the same problem, might reveal different dimensions of the problem or provide multiple readings of the same dimension, each reading confirming or qualifying the other. This strategy provided the kind of rigor one attains with multidiagnostic procedures in clinical medicine, with "triangulation" in sociology (Denzin, 1970; Webb, Campbell, Schwartz, & Sechrest, 1966), and with the more eclectic interpretive approaches in literary criticism. A rigor of multiple sightings rather than a rigor of singular constraints.

Let me now briefly summarize the study to illustrate the kinds and sequence of methods we used and suggest ways that the various methods enhanced each other. This summary will provide a starting point for my proposal of a comprehensive composing-process research framework.

We began by framing a questionnaire from information gained during my preliminary observations and pilot studies. One reason we needed a questionnaire was to enable us to identify large numbers of stymied or fluent writers, but we had other reasons for framing the questionnaire as well. First of all, we had to arrive at some identifying behavioral characteristics of writer's block. How else would we (or other teachers and researchers) know what to look for? Since I had conducted a number of conferences with students who reported themselves (or were referred) as being stymied or fluent writers, I had a sense of what general behaviors accompanied writer's block and also a sense of the variety of ways that students themselves used the term. For example, one student was bored with school; her assignments—in or outside of composition class—didn't spark much interest, and she didn't spend much, if any, time one them. Out of the blue she said, "I guess I've got a writing block." Responses like this gave me some sense of the term's popular usage but also made me realize that some delimiting boundaries had to be established. Otherwise "writer's block" would mean everything—and nothing. The pilot interviews revealed some broad behavioral indicators of writer's block (e.g., a number of stymied writers seemed to spend a good deal of time editing a sentence before going on to the next sentence). These indicators would allow us to identify students who fit our consensus of what "writer's block" meant and exclude cases, like that of the disenchanted student, that seemed more rooted in lack of motivation, boredom, uncertainty about one's career goals, and so on.

Another reason for framing a questionnaire was to gain further information about the cognitive dimension of writer's block. If we created subscales (subcategories of questionnaire items) that tapped behaviors and attitudes that provided further clues about cognition, then our questionnaire inquiry could be a bit more refined. That is, we could say more than "the student reports blocking behaviors like spending long periods of time without getting words on paper." We could also say, for example, "The student reports problems with organizing complex discourse or with evaluating his/her own writing." Via statistical analyses, we would then be able to explore the relationships among blocking behaviors and these other difficulties.

We administered the questionnaire over the year to six different groups of undergraduates at the University of California (Los Angeles), who ranged in English experience, class standing, and major. After each administration, we interviewed a small subsample of students and, as well, conducted statistical analyses. We used both sources of information to refine the instrument. (A much fuller discussion of the questionnaire as well as other artifacts and procedures of the study can be found in Rose, 1984.)

But questionnaires, no matter how refined, provide only one kind of report on behavior and attitude. We needed to find out what lay behind these responses. We chose 10 students from extreme ends of the 351 undergraduates who took the fifth version of the questionnaire. The 10, 6 high-blockers and 4 low-blockers, varied in English experience, class standing, major, and response to the different subscales. I closely explored the writing behaviors of these students via a technique adapted from decision-making research, "stimulated recall." The way I used it, stimulated recall worked as follows: Each student was presented with a university-level writing topic and was given some time to become familiar with it. Each was then given one hour to compose, and while composing each was alone. Two videotape cameras—one partially concealed across the room, another behind the student—respectively recorded the student from the waist up and the student's text emerging on the page. When the hour was over, I returned to the room and played the tapes to the student. What the student saw was a split screen: he or she on one side, the emerging text on the other. I stopped the tape at every pause, lining out, rescanning, and so on, and questioned these behaviors. The student, too, could stop the tape and comment. Our entire series of questions and answers was recorded on audiotape and later transcribed. The transcription, called a "protocol," could then be analyzed.

With the assistance of an independent rater, I analyzed the protocols, identifying and tallying, among other things, composing rules; plans used to interpret the assignment; assumptions about composing; instances of conflict among rules, plans, and assumptions; instances of editing at inappropriate times during composing; and, finally, positive and negative evaluations voiced by the student about the text he or she was creating.

We further decided that the fullest picture of blocking would emerge if we computed additional quantitative measures from the videotapes and from the students' written productions, measures that, taken alone, are pretty reductionistic, but that could provide one more perspective on blocking or fluency: We recorded time spent prewriting and planning and time spent in various kinds of pauses; we tallied words written and deleted on assignment materials, scratch paper, and drafts. Finally, we had the essays evaluated by two independent raters.

In the final, comprehensive analysis, then, we brought all our data to bear on the puzzle of writer's block. In summary, the data included questionnaire self-reports; tallies of prewriting, pausing, and planning time; tallies of words produced and deleted; reader evaluations of essays; the tracing and tabulation of a variety of cognitive–behavioral entities and processes, including rules, plans, assumptions, premature editing, conflict, and self-evaluations; and, finally, observations of mannerisms and other behaviors that would not be caught by the more circumscribed quantitative analyses. These data were presented in tabular as well as discursive formats and also were written up as case studies. The variety of methods and presentations checked and complemented each other. Tallies of pauses and of words produced and deleted helped make precise the qualitative observations, and observations fleshed out simple tallies as well as measures of cognitive processes. Empirical counts confirmed or checked questionnaire self-reports. Observations of the writers at work provided context for what the writers produced and for what the readers said about those productions. And so on. One single method would have been inadequate to reveal the complexities of writer's block or to verify, qualify, or reject our speculations about it. But multiple methods enabled us to gain a rich array of perspectives on a complicated composing problem and allowed us to formulate a theory about certain kinds of blocking.

The above narrative gives a sense of what we did, of how we used a varied methodology to reveal a dimension of a complex writing behavior. But the narrative, it seems to me, raises two concerns. First, it appears that we treated all methods as equals, picked them happily out of the researcher's bag of tricks as we needed them. Yet it is common knowledge that methods carry with them particular assumptions about reality and knowledge. Did we consider the philosophical roots of the methods we combined? This question is important and is central to one of the conclusions of this chapter, so I'll save it for the final section. The second concern, and I'll address it now, involves the limited focus of my study.

II.

The study was successful in that it demonstrated a complex dimension of blocking that was primarily cognitive, mapped that dimension, modeled it, and derived from it practical implications for instruction. But, clearly, no complex composing behavior is purely cognitive; so, while this study was broad in scope, it was still constrained in that its primary purpose was to explore the heretofore neglected cognitive dimension of writer's block. Affective and sociocultural data were recorded and briefly discussed but were not fully explored. Further studies or networks of studies would have been required to investigate these dimensions. Now, this recognition implies more than the obvious fact that a single study can accomplish only so much; it also suggests that, where writer's block or any other complex writing behavior is concerned, a broad conceptual research framework (as well as an array of methods) is needed. This framework should have both structural value (it can assist in the organization of studies and of information gained from those studies) and heuristic value (it can serve as a reminder about kinds of information that must be sought out). I suggest that one such powerful framework would be the cognitive/affective/social–contextual trinity that organizes the present volume. This framework contains the traditional two domains of human mental reality and the social context that influences and is influenced by that reality. Let me quickly describe each of these dimensions, orienting each brief description in a direction consonant with the aims of this book. I will then qualify the framework's use and demonstrate its utility with a preliminary case study.

THE SOCIAL-CONTEXTUAL DIMENSION

Because writing can be such a private act, we tend to forget that it is also, paradoxically, a social act. Writing is learned; it isn't naturally acquired as is speech (though speech, too, needs a social context to develop). And as it's learned, learned as well are the myriad explanations, opinions, and biases of the immediate societies of teachers and family and the larger societies of institutions and communities that teach and receive writing. Even the solitary diarist manifests vestiges of the environment in which he or she learned to write: stylistic turns, images of past audiences, and so on.

The social sphere provides, in most cases, the prompt to write: school essays, business reports, editor's proposals, letters of request or complaint, personal letters. And any prompt carries with it specific constraints (e.g., deadline, mode) as well as general atmosphere (e.g., supportive, critical). Then the social sphere again has its say by responding to the writing that is produced. Response is critical. What Donald Graves tells us in Chapter 1 about the young writer's life remains true, in different guises, throughout a writer's growth: The responses of others can foster or limit the development of mechanical, grammatical, and rhetorical competence. And social influences do not begin or end with the immediate responses. There exist institutionally based criteria and expectations (tacit or articulated) like those discussed by David Bartholomae in Chapter 7; and there exist, as well, broad cultural expectations that might well find expression within a particular setting—for example, the notions about women and the academy that seem to hamper the female graduate students that Lynn Bloom discusses in Chapter 6.

In an attempt to arrive at an understanding of general mental processes, many traditional psychological/educational studies try to remove or control for social and environmental interferences. Yet, though situational variables can obscure or be mistaken for individual cognitive or emotional effects, they can also be powerful determiners and shapers of those effects. "Human behavior is complexly influenced by the context in which it occurs," notes Stephen Wilson (1977, p. 253); and Elliot Mishler boldy asks, "'Meaning in context'—is there any other kind?" (Mishler, 1979). Even those who were major figures in the development of traditional social science experimental designs now question the attempt to exclude context from the derivation and interpretation of experimental data (Campbell, 1974, 1979; Cronbach, 1975). It seems, then, that composing-process researchers need to keep in mind the fact that the situation—both the immediate writing context as well as the larger school and social environment—plays into a study's results, needs to at least be acknowledged as part of the data.

AFFECT AND COGNITION

Because of the fundamental interplay of mind and social context, the elements of one's setting interact with, are filtered through, modify or are modified by, one's knowledge of and beliefs, assumptions, and theories about the world: one's skills and one's fears, one's predilections and one's interpretations. We now, of course, enter the realm of individual differences.

One longstanding Western convention for talking about mental reality has been to separate cognition from affect, intellect from feeling. Certainly, this convention has not gone without its philosophical and literary challenges. And a number of contemporary personality and clinical theorists have proposed a complex interweaving of cognition and affect (see, e.g., Ellis, 1959; Kelly, 1963; and Shapiro, 1965); several have even argued for the cognitive bases of emotional states (see Beck, 1976, on depression; and Lazarus & Averill, 1972, on anxiety) and for the emotional dimension of acts usually thought to be cognitive (Maslow, 1968, 1969). Such complex interweaving certainly manifests itself in composing. A fear of taking chances with one's writing, for example, might well stem from the way one assesses one's skills; and rigid planning strategies could be tied to feelings of inadequacy as a writer. Still, there is value, both theoretical and pedagogical, in speaking of some mental activities as being *primarily* cognitive (e.g., planning strategies) and others as *primarily* affective (e.g., fearing writing), as long as it is remembered that emotion cannot always be neatly stripped away from the way we deal with information.

THE AFFECTIVE DIMENSION

Writers don't simply process information in computer-like fashion. Professional writers often speak of the emotionally charged core of material that they then shape into the literature we read (see, e.g., the interviews in Cowley, 1977; Plimpton, 1977, 1981). And all of us have had the experience of being excited or dispirited as we've produced a piece of writing. The topic, setting, and constraints of a writing task each has the potential to arouse a variety of feelings (see, especially, Larson, Chapter 2). And there are times when these feelings can be overpowering. A few examples of such negative effects: Robert Boice in Chapter 9 details the ways in which a writer's conflicts and fears can subvert the composing process. John Daly and Cynthia Selfe (in Chapters 3 and 4 respectively) present evidence to demonstrate that some students get apprehensive when facing school-based writing assignments. Peitzman (1981) found that an emotionally loaded topic stymied one of her student writers. A very competent student writer whom I studied (Rose, 1981) got anxious during the study and reduced her normally complex planning and organizing strategies to an associational stream of ideas. Writers, then, can experience some level of discomfort—of anxiety, anger, or depression; and, if sufficiently pronounced, the discomfort can lead to a variety of observable responses: an agitated or flat style; an inability to get anything on paper; even, as Daly's (Chapter 3), Boice's (Chapter 9), and Holland's (1980) work suggests, an avoidance of certain writing tasks altogether.

These reactions, to borrow an important distinction of Spielberger's (1972), can be "state-specific," that is, particular to a given environment, kind of writing task, or kind of topic, or can be more generalized, or a "trait" of the individual's personality—a wide variety of writing tasks trigger a negative response. This distinction is extremely important, for we have a tendency to make generalizations about people's emotional responses from limited observations. The case of a student of Sondra Perl's (1979) serves as a good reminder here. Though Louella did get apprehensive about school-based writing assignments, she wrote letters easily enough. Emotional reactions are more often than not specific to the situation and are not evidence of general affective traits. This recognition should be central to our theory-building as well as to our teaching.

THE COGNITIVE DIMENSION

Writing involves the shaping, structuring, refining, and evaluating of thought. To affirm this complex and deliberate series of processes is not to deny the fact that some composing also involves flashes of insight, seemingly unconscious connections, and the feel of rightness or wrongness. It is simply to say that composing, particularly the shaping of thought to utterance (Britton, 1980) and whatever subsequent refining of that utterance that may occur, involves conscious linguistic–cognitive behaviors: planning and rehearsing, organizing and structuring according to various formal conventions, weighing the fit of formal or lexical options, reading with an attention to graphic–mechanical errors, and so on. Bereiter (1980), Graves (1982), and Scardamalia (1981) have shown how these complex abilities, and a higher level ("metacognitive") awareness of them, develop. Cooper and Matsuhashi (in press) have outlined some of the linguistic and cognitive decisions writers make during the production of sentential and extra-sentential discourse. D'Angelo (1979) has suggested that the enactment of basic rhetorical strategies is related to the enactment of fundamental patterns of thinking. Flower and Hayes (1980, 1981) have mapped the planning processes of adult writers. Bridwell (1980) and Sommers (1980) have demonstrated the different ways that professional and student writers conceive of and enact revision.

When writing proceeds fluently, cognitive and linguistic processes interact in complex, productive ways. But there are times when a writer's cognitive and linguistic repertoire comes up short or when that writer's composing rules or planning strategies or assumptions about writing don't match the constraints of a particular task. In the study of mine summarized at the beginning of this chapter, students who reported a high degree of blocking, versus those who did not, displayed a number of rigid composing rules (e.g., "You're not supposed to have passive verbs"), and some of the rules conflicted with others. They also tended to plan rigidly or inadequately, and half of them expressed assumptions about writing that were inappropriate or inaccurate (e.g., that planning subverts spontaneity and thus "sacrifices truth and real feelings"). It is possible, then, that some of our rules, strategies, assumptions, decision sequences, and so on can impede writing as well as make it possible. Stan Jones and Muriel Harris in Chapters 5 and 8 respectively, discuss some of these primarily cognitive difficulties.

Some theorists attempt to generalize beyond specific cognitive processes and pose broad orientations to problem solving. These orientations are usually discussed in terms of extremes at either end of a continuum; for example, some people seem to depend on the field surrounding an object when perceiving that object, others tend to perceive the object independently of the field (Witkin, Moore, Goodenough, & Cox, 1977); some people tend to approach intellectual problems impulsively, others reflectively (Kagan, Moss, & Sigel, 1963); some serially, others holistically (Pask & Scott, 1972); and so on. There may be value in posing general cognitive orientations to composing, and my studies led me in fact to speculate about composing styles: Several writers seemed to compose cautiously, reflectively, while others wrote much more spontaneously; and each group expressed rules and assumptions that were consonant with their different approaches. Asked how typical these orientations were of their writing on other assignments, they said they were fairly typical (Rose, 1984). Now, if (and this is a very big "if") a number of other observations in varied settings with varied tasks over time were to confirm these preliminary observations and self-reports, then perhaps we could posit a notion like "composing styles," general orientations to writing that are based on fundamental assumptions and broad composing strategies. One would have to make such assessments cautiously, however, since writing behavior, like any complex behavior, is tremendously variable and can play itself out in different ways, given different settings, tasks, materials, constraints, and moods.

In one sense, the above research framework presents the obvious. It doesn't reveal anything other than what we've already learned from day-to-day living: People act and react intellectually and emotionally and do so in situations that trigger, shape, and quell those behaviors. But I would suggest that it is precisely this "obviousness," this commonsense validity that gives the framework its value as a *research* paradigm. We are forced to at least acknowledge in our research projects the complexity that we live by. The framework reminds us to be alert to the possibility of interactions of the cognitive, the affective, and the situational.

There is good reason, then, to believe that the cognitive/affective/contextual framework could inform and enrich composing-process research; but, before going further, I must attach two qualifiers to its application, both of which stem from a fundamental characteristic of systematic inquiry. "All research," Egon Guba reminds us, "sets constraints" (Guba, 1978, p. 6). While the comprehensiveness of the cognitive/affective/contextual framework forces us to honor complexity, it would, if *fully* played out, make most research efforts impossible. There are two reasons why this would be so, one practical, the other conceptual.

1. Perhaps the ideal composing-process research project would be one that extended over years; involved large and diverse numbers of subjects; fully explored the cognitive, affective, and situational dimensions of their writing across a wide sample of public and private writing tasks; involved multiple researchers and studies to reduce experimenter bias and methodological limitations; and so on. But, of course, no investigation—from the artistic and literary to the scientific—has attained such comprehensiveness. The costs, the demands on personnel, the sheer bulk of data would be prohibitive. So, for the most practical of reasons, we must "set constraints"—focus our research, make strategic decisions about what to include and what to exclude.

2. But there are also conceptual reasons for setting limits. A good deal of research, from the literary to the scientific, involves the analysis of constituent elements. Such analysis derives from the notion that a

complex system—whether of language or organic compounds—may need to be explored, at least initially, by attempting to focus on the separate pieces of its puzzle. This strategy becomes especially compelling when one faces a problem whose components are so intertwined that one cannot get even a moderately clear sense of their nature or of how they interact. The strategy exposes us again, of course, to the danger of reductionism that I have been discussing. The interplay of elements within a system helps define these elements and, ultimately, the system itself. Thus one can misrepresent a system by envisioning it as a mere aggregate of constituent parts. But if componential analysis is carried out with the awareness that elements of most systems are not neatly isolable, then the examination of constituents can more likely be conducted and reported in a way that is appropriately qualified, that admits the possibility of modification via involvement in the system, and that suggests what, ultimately, to look for in less artificial settings (Cronbach, 1975). The analysis, to borrow and adapt a distinction made by the mathematician Ralph Strauch (1976), becomes a perspective on the phenomenon rather than a surrogate for it.

With these two qualifiers about necessary limits in mind, we can consider the utility of the cognitive/affective/contextual framework. It reminds us that any composing act could result from and be shaped by intellect, feeling, and setting. When our research projects necessitate a focus on one of these dimensions, the framework would make us mindful of possible influences and interactions of other dimensions: We could note such influences and interactions when they occur, even though we couldn't explore them fully; or we could speculate on how our present data might be interpreted if we were to consider them in the light of another of these perspectives. And, then, there would be circumstances where the framework could serve as more than a conceptual check and balance. It could inform an entire study, become a complex lens that brings cognitive, affective, and situational dimensions equally into focus. Let me illustrate the value of the latter—the use of the framework to fully inform investigation—with a brief case study, that of Stephanie, taken from the research project of mine described earlier.

Stephanie's case was interesting from the beginning, for as her writing process unfolded via stimulated recall and as she sketched out her writing history, it became clear that, for her, a cognitive paradigm alone had limited explanatory power. Her writing problems were resulting from a complex interplay of cognitive, affective, and situational factors. I'll begin her brief case study with some general data and with the essay she wrote during the composing session. Then I'll offer a descriptive overview of what transpired during that session. I'll follow the description with an analysis of selected problems in her composing process.

III: The Case of Stephanie

Stephanie was a freshman who had not decided on a major. Her verbal score on the Scholastic Aptitude Test was 400 and her grade point average was 2.18. Her scores on our university's written placement test had exempted her from the university's remedial English requirement. She had not yet taken the standard composition course. Her questionnaire results suggested that she did have trouble with writer's block and that she tended to turn in papers late. The results also suggested some, though not dramatic, tendencies to overedit her papers and a good deal of trouble structuring written responses to complex topics. (A fuller analysis is provided in Rose, 1981.)

For the stimulated-recall phase of the study, Stephanie had to work with the following assignment: She was given a three-page case history of a man named Angelo Cacci who visited a counseling center with complaints of depression. Her task was to interpret the man's situation in light of a passage from Karl Jaspers's *Man in the Modern Age*, a passage attributing the cause of contemporary malaise to alienating work. (The entire assignment can be found in the Appendix.) She was given time to adjust herself to the artificial writing setting and to read the materials; she was then asked to write for 60 minutes. The (unfinished) essay she produced is reprinted here. Nothing is corrected, though words Stephanie lined out are not included. Some of these deletions will be discussed in the upcoming overview of her writing session. The overview will contain a number of quotations. Most will be Stephanie's comments from the stimulated-recall protocol, though my questions, passages from the essay, and readers' comments will also be incorporated.

STEPHANIE'S ESSAY

In the case history of Angelo Cacci it's rather obvious that he hasn't ever been and isn't now very fulfilled or satisfied with his life. His occupation is that of an average middle-class man, a job where you do the same thing over and over again, not very exciting. Carl Jaspers quotation seems to describe this sort of lifestyle but this is only one part of a life. It is true that people seem to be shuffled together but this is inevitable in the society in which we live, for survival is the first priority. It isn't because Angelo is put in this situation that he should suffer of the "blues" as he does. If the other parts of Angelos life were more fulfilling then perhaps his discription of his job would not be settling for something he doesn't want.

In everyones life there are things we must do that we don't really want to do; having a job of unimportance or having a job at all may be one of them. But what we do with the rest of our time is more important, having a relationship, keeping family ties . . . In Angelos case he doesn't have a fulfilling relationship with anyone and he never got or gave much love in his family. There is always time for those things after the work is done. The memories of his grandfather were the only thing that didn't have anything to do with working and surviving. After his grandfather died he didn't experience this kind of love, of doing things outside of the mechanical life of the city. His occupation seems to be the main stream of his life because there isn't much else, and since what Jasper says about being pushed together with others without much meaning in part of your life is true, then anyone would have the "blues" in his position. However, what Jasper says about not having any time left for thinking about life isn't true. If people don't have

STEPHANIE'S SESSION

Stephanie began the session by slowly rereading the Jaspers quotation. She then shifted to the case history, mentally rephrasing its events "as if [she] were telling someone about this case history of Angelo Cacci, so [she] could explain it to [her]self better." But her retelling of Angelo's life was not comprehensive; she sidestepped the dream because "it didn't make much sense" to her, and, keeping Jaspers in mind, was "trying to pick out . . . more important points, trying to separate the points that related to the quotation from those that didn't." Stephanie intermittently spoke aloud while reading, and later while writing. Though she claimed she had a "lousy memory," she left the assignment materials virtually unmarked. (She underlined a string of five words in the case history: "grandfather. The old man used to"). Asked why, if she considered her memory so poor, she did not gloss or underline the Jaspers quotation and the case history she explained, "the ideas are put so clearly that I can just refer back" to the materials. After 8 minutes and 44 seconds of rereading, Stephanie began to write.

But Stephanie's first sentence did not come without some difficulty: "I'm trying to think of something to start with. I'm never satisfied with much. . . . I hate starting out papers, you know, in the usual." Though she "was trying to think of something better," she finally did rely on a stock opening because "it's easier for [her] to just put something down and start and then come back later." Halfway through her first sentence, however, she did pause 45 seconds to make a rhetorical change (she was going to write "that he hasn't had a fulfilling life" but instead wrote "that he hasn't ever been and isn't now very fulfilled or satisfied with his life"). "It was just another way of wording it," she explained; but it was clear that once started, she was trying to give her sentence the flair she earlier decided to forgo: "See, my . . . parents are both good writers and my brother's a good writer, and so I want that something, you know, that something a little extra that doesn't just make it a . . . clear sentence, but makes it a good, clear sentence."

Completing her first sentence, Stephanie paused for 58 seconds and rescanned what she had written, wondering if it was "irrelevant or not." Asked if she had a general idea of what was to come, she explained, "No. I don't really, because I'm writing, hoping that the more I write, the more it will come together . . . I never get the whole idea before I start writing."

Stephanie began her second sentence with "He is," paused, crossed it out, and wrote the existing version ("His occupation is . . ."). She wanted to "phrase it a different way." After writing, "His occupation is that of an average middle-class man," Stephanie paused and scanned the case history to verify her labeling of Angelo as middle-class: "I was checking back to see what his job was, and a lot of times I'm not sure if the word I'm using is right to describe something." At three other junctures in the protocol, Stephanie similarly checked the accuracy of her descriptions of Angelo's life.

Commenting on the production of her third sentence, Stephanie said she "wanted to bring the quotation into it somehow" in order to anchor her discussion in the assignment materials. She began her sentence ("Carl Jaspers quotation seems to") and paused, then came up with "describe." "I couldn't think of a word to put down," she explained; "my vocabulary is not that large." She continued the sentence—"describe this sort of lifestyle"—and paused for 60 seconds before completing the sentence with a clause that would qualify her agreement with Jaspers: "but this is only one part of a life." She then scanned the Jaspers quotation: "Some things, I think, in the quotation were right, and some I don't . . . I'm just trying to interpret it right because . . . that's where my biggest problem is, interpreting information." As she continued, a fundamental difficulty in dealing with complex information emerged: "I have a hard time knowing exactly what I'm thinking . . . I would rather write about something that only has one subject instead of having to give my opinion, because whenever it comes to giving my opinion, my opinion always goes two ways."

Through sentences four, five, and six, Stephanie continued to express disagreement with Jaspers—the crux of her argument being that mechanical work alone does not automatically result in alienation, for there are other factors (particularly that of family) in one's life that could allay or intensify that alienation. But Stephanie did not forge a solid direction for her disagreement, and at several points she said she was confused about "exactly what she wanted to say." Stephanie's drafting of the sixth and final sentence in the first paragraph revealed the semantic and conceptual difficulties she was having. She had originally written, "If the other parts of Angelos life were more fulfilling then perhaps this robot-like"; she paused, deleted "this robot-like," and continued, "perhaps his discription of his job would have more"; she paused again, deleted "have more," and continued, "not be so robot-like"; she paused once more, scanned the case history, deleted "so robot-like," and continued, "settling for something he doesn't want," a phrase that she enclosed in parentheses—her way of indicating that she believed her language was not quite right. Stephanie's trails with writing about "robot-like" behavior and her parenthesizing of "settling for something he doesn't want" suggest that she was having trouble clarifying her argument, mentally and scribally. She put it this way:

STEPHANIE: The job was bad, but that wasn't his reason for feeling blue. . . . It was that he was lacking something else that caused his life to be like that.

RESEARCHER: Why didn't you say it the way you just said it to me?

STEPHANIE: Well, 'cause what I just said wasn't even that clear . . . some things you can say, but they just don't sound right on paper.

Asked what would happen if she were at home and found herself in the just-witnessed difficulty, she said she "might ask my Mom to . . . rephrase the sentence for me."

Before beginning her second paragraph, Stephanie rescanned her first paragraph "just to keep the idea fresh in [her] mind." Except for its last few sentences, the construction of this second paragraph proceeded fairly uneventfully, though three behaviors are worth noting: (a) The rhetorical play of the first sentence's second clause ("having a job of unimportance or having a job at all may be one of them") resulted in a positive self-evaluation: "I know when you read a paper, you look to see if it sounds good. If I come up with something like that . . . it's pleasing." (b) Questioned about omitted apostrophes, Stephanie replied, "I always have that problem . . . so I just leave them out and then ask my mom." (c) After completing her sixth sentence of the second paragraph, Stephanie wrote, "His family worried about," paused, deleted the clause, and reread her entire essay: "Just to get the stream of it because sometimes when I can't think of anything to write, I'll just . . . read it back and forth. . . . It'll trigger off something hopefully, eventually." Though Stephanie's rationale for rescanning is legitimate, the reason for the pause is telling: She was going to continue discussing Angelo's family, making the point that "all his family worried about was survival." But "if I had said that, it would've been putting too much of my opinion, making a judgment, too much of a judgment on the [case history] because I didn't really have enough information to say it." Her vigilance about including her opinion is interesting because, as she said a few minutes prior to the last comment (and echoing a much earlier explanation), she read the case history in a way that recast it in somewhat personal terms: "I read the case history, and I just sort of changed it into my own, you know, just as if I could see the person and so on. And that [way it's] not so hard to remember."

I don't have enough direct information on Stephanie's reading and memorizing strategies to say what follows with certainty, but it seems that her method of interpreting and of committing to memory did not lead smoothly to her composing. Angelo's history was, perhaps, a little too selectively read and personalized to make it accessible for an assignment that Stephanie perceived as demanding some sort of academic objectivity.[2] Maybe this conflict contributed to the fact that her second paragraph was part rehash, part loose development of previously stated ideas. In one reader's words:

> The student has shot [her] bolt rather early and has set up a structure of dreadful repetition. . . . Since the student is really offering an opposing theme, [she] needs to be more precise about her area of attack or emphasis.

Stephanie might not have been aware of her repetitiousness, but she did believe that her "main part . . . the idea [she] wanted to work on" was still not precisely stated; so, oddly enough, she generated two more repetitive sentences in an attempt to clarify. These last two sentences gave her more trouble than any other sentences in the essay and revealed the difficulty she was having structuring her disagreement with Jaspers. Of her second to last sentence, she said, "If I said everything I wanted to say, the sentence would just be too long; it wouldn't make sense . . . I put three ideas in one sentence [and] I didn't succeed . . . In my mind . . . everything [got] so confusing." She untangled herself by "writing one word . . . and [taking] it from there"; but, by her own admission, her rambling sentence "is sort of unclear." The confusion she noted in the production of her penultimate sentence was also present as she drafted her final sentence—she parenthesized "isn't true" and put a question mark in the margin: "I didn't want to say that it's not true, because it's his opinion." She was writing another sentence, a further elaboration on the previous two, when the clock ran out.

DISCUSSION

I must begin this section by emphasizing the fact that, in the contextual realm particularly, I am speculating from very limited data. I did not observe Stephanie at home and did not study her production of a variety of kinds of writing. Furthermore, for practical reasons, I will focus this discussion on only two aspects of Stephanie's composing: her difficulty in structuring complex discourse and her feeling of discomfort in doing so. This investigation, then, is a preliminary rather than a definitive one and is intended as a sketch rather than a full illustration of the kind of analysis the cognitive/affective/contextual framework can help produce. The particular value of the framework here is that it enables us to see the way Stephanie's cognitive and linguistic difficulties (e.g., inadequate argumentative structure; reliance on relatively uncomplex syntactic structures) were intertwined with emotional issues (e.g., her reluctance to assert her opinion) and to further see how these problems may have been more or less pronounced, depending on the nature of the writing situations she found herself in. But the framework also allows us to ponder the successful play of Stephanie's skills. Despite her conflicts and limitations, she did not stare at a blank page but produced the beginnings of a decent enough essay and, as I'll suggest, did so because of a particularly empowering interplay of cognitive, affective, and contextual factors.

It would be difficult to understand Stephanie's compositional difficulties without considering her relationship *as a writer* with her family. She mentioned her family at nine different junctures in the protocol. At each point, she commented on the superior skills of her father, mother, or brother; or on how one of them could help her out of the particular grammatical, stylistic, or structural jam she was presently in; or on how she would like to match their prowess on a particular composing task before her. Two of her comments are particularly revealing:

> All the time I was growing up, I depended on my parents a lot, and my parents . . . are rather bright. . . . And my mother is an excellent writer, and she loves to help out. It's something I sort of got used to in elementary school and high school, and whenever I'm mixed up about something, I'll always ask my parents to explain it to me. And then maybe I'll go from there because I'm sort of insecure with my own idea about something, even like how to interpret a quotation. . . . I know whatever my father interprets is going to be correct.

> In high school a lot of times . . . at the last minute I would ask my mom to help me with something. It's hard to get out of that pattern because my mom puts it [in] her typewriter and . . . she types an essay for me in about 15 minutes.

But Stephanie was no longer at home. She was in the midst of her third quarter at UCLA and, as her mediocre grade point average (2.18) suggests, was moving through her classes without much distinction. She put off papers and missed deadlines. Now that Stephanie was on her own and her writing assignments (e.g., for classical art history) were more research-oriented and more ambitious than those she grew up with, she could not as easily rely on her family and, as her essay suggests, lacked the discourse strategies and perhaps the self-confidence needed to structure and take a position on complex information. I couldn't get much data on her schooling, but the home writing environment Stephanie grew up in didn't sufficiently guide her toward engaging in the kind of independent thinking and framing of complex discourse her new environment demanded. Given this conflict, the present writing task, based as it was in the academy, might well have sparked feelings of inadequacy and some of the kinds of blocking behaviors she had reported on the questionnaire.

But the interesting thing is that, though Stephanie may have felt inadequate and though while composing she displayed some of the behaviors that she had reported stymie her during other assignments, she did nonetheless write. I'd suggest three general reasons for her relative fluency. The first reason is cognitive: She had a variety of techniques to help spark the flow of prose. She would test a few words ("I'll start writing maybe one word"); place parentheses around inadequate language, in hope of returning to it ("I would work towards [that] later"); scan what she had already written ("It'll trigger off something, hopefully); or follow alternatives ("I can't think of the right way to say it, so [I'll] move to something else"). These behaviors suggest the presence of a powerful and multifaceted heuristic rule that presents a number of options to the stymied writer. This rule seems associated with and potentiated by an assumption about discovery: "The more I write, the more it will come later."

The second reason, and this one is more guesswork on my part than are the other two, has to do with her feelings and beliefs about Karl Jaspers's passage. Though Stephanie felt uncomfortable disagreeing with Jaspers, she did disagree, taking issue with the focus on work and alienation in his analysis. She objected on the grounds that routine work alone cannot explain alienation; she found more explanation for Angelo's dilemma in his family situation. (I think it is interesting that the only words Stephanie underlined in Angelo's case history were "grandfather. The old man used to.") Stephanie often spoke of her family and of her closeness to it. It is possible, then, that Angelo's situation combined with Jaspers's theory sparked feelings strong enough to impel her to write.

The third reason concerns an artifact of the present writing context: the deadline. Stephanie reported that she normally procrastinated and thus produced rushed, inadequate essays. (Her high "lateness" score on the questionnaire and her low grade point average lend some credence to this report.) Though Stephanie produced a relatively flawed essay for the present study, she did not block. She attributed her fluency to the time limit; if she had been at home it would have taken her "hours and hours and hours," for she would not have been "satisfied" with her ideas. The pressure of the deadline, however, seemed to help her override her insecurities, dissatisfactions, and mechanical and structural limitations. She produced a two-paragraph essay of 300 words.

Stephanie's performance on this study's assignment, then, suggests that, if she did feel inadequate to frame complex arguments or to interpret information, there were—at least in this case—cognitive, affective, and situational variables that could help her overcome her reservations. The problem that remained, though, was primarily a cognitive–linguistic one. Stephanie constructed a first paragraph that inductively led to a thesis, but her second paragraph did little to develop it. Though she did use some argumentative conventions (e.g., granting Jaspers's thesis some legitimacy before taking issue with it), she seems to have had trouble with the overall structure of the argument. The thrust of the essay dissipates into repetitive, loosely connected sentences that don't hypotactically subordinate issues one to the other but paratactically string together issues of varied relevance with simple connectives. As protocol excerpts have illustrated, Stephanie was most confused and conflicted when writing the particular sentences that embodied her not-quite-honed, sometimes rambling disagreement with Jaspers. Though she could occasionally turn a few nice rhetorical tricks, she had trouble with larger rhetorical concerns.

William Perry (1970) has suggested that college students develop along a series of "positions," the first few being characterized by difficulty in dealing with ambiguity, with multiple acceptable answers to a problem, and with intellectual and moral complexity. Stephanie doesn't neatly fit into Perry's early positions, for she was able to accept Jaspers's viewpoint as one opinion and put hers forth as another. But she was not comfortable with this complexity and with asserting her position within it ("whenever it comes to giving my opinion, my opinion always goes two ways") or with the interpretive activity that was central to it ("that's where my biggest problem is, interpreting information"). These struggles were complicated by her apparent lack of skill in working complex information and opinion into appropriately complex syntactic structures and in framing an argument. Her uncertainties, her conceptual dilemmas with Jaspers, and her discourse limitations all interacted to vex her composing. Picture this web of difficulties against the backdrop of a home writing environment that, if her reports are accurate, had protected her from rather than aided her through the intellectual and linguistic difficulties that attend academic development. This protection, as we've seen, had both affective and cognitive consequences. Simon and Simon (1978) discuss the confidence that experienced problem-solvers acquire and the way that that confidence aids them in understanding a problem and executing a solution. Stephanie lacked such confidence. She was able to disagree with Jaspers but seemed trapped within his framework and tended to waffle and repeat herself, never bringing her argument to a clear focus. Hand in glove with the foregoing was her paucity of the syntactic and global discourse skills that would have enabled her to adequately structure the disagreements she was able to articulate.

It is possible, though this is speculation based on her commentary, that Stephanie's difficulties with writing could have been leading to a general distrust in or avoidance of writing. She preferred speaking to writing. For example, she said she "enjoys reading case histories" but would "rather talk about them than write about them"; she used to keep a journal, but it was "too time-consuming." "If I could put it on tape it would be a lot easier." And, most pervasively, she preferred speech because she could always qualify what she believed would be irreversible in print. It is valuable here to consider one reader's remarks.

> The writer is good at commenting at first, but [she] draws back. Probably she thinks [her] reader will disagree. She needs, I think, more courage to stick to [her] argument.

Place this evaluation alongside two comments of Stephanie's.

> A lot of times the reason I'd rather . . . sit and talk out loud about a topic is because then I can say something, and can say, "No. That's not right." But you can't do that on paper.

> I'm sort of insecure with my own idea about something. . . . I wait to see what the teacher's thing is or my parents' opinion is . . . so I'll know what's good of mine. 'Cause a lot of times I can't tell myself.

Stephanie might well have preferred speaking to writing because she could continually amend the ideas she had never been taught to trust. She preferred speaking to writing as well because she did not have to wrestle with internalized parental standards that she was never given the painful freedom to confront and possibly go beyond. And finally, in informal speech, Stephanie was freed from the complex syntactic and formal conventions that are so central to academic writing.

IV.

I began this chapter with the suggestion that we can rigorously yet nonreductively investigate complex composing-process problems by using multiple and converging methods. I then suggested that we can further honor the full scope of writing behavior by espousing a broad research framework that interweaves the cognitive, affective, and situational dimensions of composing. Then came the case of Stephanie. One of the things that I hope her story illustrates is the complementarity of a multipronged methodology and a cognitive/affective/contextual framework, for in fact each implies the need for the other. The various dimensions of the framework cannot be adequately explored by any single method. And the presence of the framework reminds the researcher of cognitive, affective, and contextual variables that a single method would probably not reveal. There is one issue I have yet to deal with, one I raised earlier and temporarily set aside: the philosophical foundations of methodology.

People in composition studies are beginning to seriously examine the methods that are available to them and are particularly concerned with the historical and philosophical traditions that certain orientations and methods represent (see, e.g., Berthoff, 1981; Bizzell, 1979; Connors, 1983; Emig, 1982). The issue is this: Research methods develop out of particular historical and philosophical contexts and thus are defined by, or at least are associated with, particular sets of assumptions about human nature and human knowledge. This truism often leads people to embrace or reject methods because of the origins of those methods. Classical experimental designs smack of positivism and are held at arm's length by some humanists, just as some behavioral scientists question ethnographic investigations as being unrigorous, fuzzy phenomenology.

While admitting the legitimacy of an historical critique of the origins of method (one would be philosophically naive to reject such examination), I would like to suggest that certain methods, anyway, might not be as constrained by their origins as at first seems to be the case and that methods that are constraining or reductive with certain kinds of problems or at certain stages of research might be used to good effect with other problems, at other stages. Let me illustrate these assertions.

- Some methods are less constrained by their origins and their structures than are others. Pre–post experimental designs and procedures involving the tallying and classifying of observed behaviors both grew out of the empiricist–behaviorist tradition. Yet the first set of methods is much more constrained, historically and structurally, than the second. The process of recording and classifying behaviors has been readily adapted by ethnographers working in a phenomenological–anthropological, rather than a behaviorist, tradition.
- Some methods lend themselves to the earlier stages of particular

research endeavors, others to later stages. Naturalistic observation, as has often been noted (see, e.g., Guba, 1978; Kantor, Kirby, & Goetz, 1981; Reichardt & Cook, 1979), can provide enough information to develop hypotheses that might then be explored by more controlled procedures. And, in turn, more controlled techniques might assist in identifying problems, the play of which can then be observed in more natural settings. Stephanie provides a good case in point. She was identified by a questionnaire (a pretty contrived research device), and then her writing process was studied in a relatively artificial setting. The results of these investigations, though, suggest a complex interaction of processes, feelings, and settings that could now be fruitfully explored by naturalistic observation techniques.

• It can be instructive to use several methods simultaneously or in close sequence, even (perhaps especially) methods traditionally seen as uncomplementary. Methods used in this way can check and enhance each other. A nice example of the successful fusion of two fairly disparate methods can be found in David Bartholomae's study of the error patterns of basic writers (1980). He blends error analysis from applied linguistics with literary theory's hermeneutics in a way that allows each to empower the other. Error analysis lends precision to the examination of a student's text, but also underscores the places at which linguistic analysis falls short and must be supplemented by the methods of literary interpretation.

Methods from behavioral science, anthropology, and literary studies, then, need not be seen as incompatible, for it is possible that some of them in some settings can be combined in creative ways.[3] But even as I write that last sentence, I realize that to speak in primarily combinatorial terms of the selection and application of methods leaves out a further, very important dimension of the process. Methods are not only combined, even combined innovatively; they can also evolve. Methods stem from one period of history but, like any artifact of culture, become part of historical processes; thus the possibility is always there that they may be modified and changed by new concerns, new environments, new definitions of knowledge. Let me make this point more concrete with an example from the work of the Russian psychologist, Lev Vygotsky.

Vygotsky reacted against the predominate behaviorist experimental method of his time by insisting on the importance of exploring the mental processes that people go through while solving problems versus simply quantifying some end product of that problem-solving. In reaction he created a number of new methods, one of which was really a modification of a standard experimental design: He kept the trappings of behaviorist method (set tasks, systematic controls on stimuli, manipulable conditions) but freed up the outcome constraints. For example, subjects had to perform certain tasks that tested memorial strategies and capacity but could solve these tasks in whatever way they wanted. Their attempts to solve the memory problems—their processes—became the data. This approach, termed "experimental-developmental" by Vygotsky, fused the situational control of the experimental design with the open-ended data collection of more naturalistic methods. He created methods to suit the questions he was asking, and some of those creations were in fact evolved from older, more rigid procedures.

I want to be very clear here. I am not denying the fact that research methods develop out of particular historical contexts nor that some of those contexts pose a model of human beings and definitions of knowledge that some of us in composing-process research find very troubling. I also don't want to deny that some methods are close to being procedural incarnations of these bothersome assumptions (or as Vygotsky put it, "Experimental procedures become surrogates for psychological processes"; 1981, p. 67). What I am arguing is that some methods from psychology and anthropology (and literary criticism, which, lest we forget, has had its own moments of philosophical and procedural narrowness) are not necessarily limited to the constraints of their origins and can be adopted and even revamped to serve other problems built on models of human beings and definitions of knowledge different from those that gave birth to such methods. To return to an earlier example, tallying and classifying observable behaviors becomes epistemologically reductionistic in the behaviorist paradigm because such quantification is defined as the only legitimate knowledge from which to build theory. In other paradigms—for instance, the phenomenological-ethnographic—this method, combined with others, serves a less restricted model of knowledge.

A discipline is defined by the problems it embraces and the questions it asks of those problems. And questions, in turn, result in investigative action when methods are incorporated into them. We in composing-process research, though we draw on the rich traditions of rhetoric and psychology, are really just beginning to identify the problems and formulate the questions by which we will define ourselves. But this development could be cut short or narrowed if we constrain our questions by a too early dismissal of methodological options. Such a limiting of disciplinary growth could easily happen; in some ways, I fear it has already begun. There is some division among us into literary and social science camps: The literary camp attributes to itself philosophical and interpretive sophistication, while the other congratulates itself on its empirical rigor. This separation—the exaggerated separation of polemics—falsely dichotomizes ways of thinking about writing. It threatens to rarify our theories and trivialize our observations.[4]

More than most other fields, ours—because of the complexity of the phenomena it studies and because of its many connections with both theoretical and applied concerns—demands the convergence of insight and method from multiple disciplines. This convergence can be simplistic, a mechanical overlay of one discipline's methods onto another's problems; or, as I've tried to suggest in this chapter, the convergence can be enlightening and generative, can lead to the creation of new investigative procedures. As researchers ask new and increasingly ambitious questions about the composing process, methods from philosophical, rhetorical, and literary study, psychology and cognitive science, anthropology and sociology will combine and fuse in special ways. And new methods, new research frameworks will emerge as they must when unique problems are investigated in ways that don't sacrifice their complexity.

Appendix: Assignment Materials for Stimulated Recall Study

INSTRUCTIONS

1. Read the case history of Angelo Cacci and the quotation from Karl Jaspers printed below.
2. Write an essay in which you discuss Angelo Cacci's situation in terms of the quotation from Jaspers. That is, does Jaspers's passage shed any light on Angelo's situation? If it does, explain how. If it doesn't, explain that as well. Supply evidence from the case history and the quotation to support your assertions.

FROM *MAN IN THE MODERN AGE* BY KARL JASPERS

It has been said that in modern times man has been shuffled together with other men like a grain of sand. He is an element of an apparatus in which he occupies now one location, now another. . . . He has occupation, indeed, but his life has no continuity. What he does is done to good purpose, but is then finished once and for all. The task may be repeated after the same fashion many times, but it cannot be repeated in such an intimate way as to become, one might say, part of the personality of the doer; it does not lead to an expansion of the selfhood. . . . Love for things and human beings wanes and disappears. The machine-made products vanish from sight as soon as they are made and consumed; all that remains in view is the machinery by which new commodities are being made. The worker at the machine, concentrating upon immediate aims, has no time or inclination left for the contemplation of life as a whole.

THE CASE OF ANGELO CACCI

A young man visited a local counseling center because he was feeling "very down in the dumps." Angelo Cacci was 32 years old, lived alone, and was employed as a clerk in a large insurance company. The counselor noted that Angelo was fairly good looking, clean-shaven, and dressed nicely, though not expensively. He spoke articulately, though not with any particular flair; however, the lack of emphasis in his speech could have been related to his depression. He seemed to be willing to discuss his history and his feelings.

Angelo stated that he had had passing periods of the "blues" before, but that his present feelings of depression were more severe. Several months earlier, Angelo had broken up with his girlfriend. "It just wasn't working out," he explained. "We used to go out—go to the park, a ball game, the movies—but after a while it fizzled. I just didn't feel that much for her anymore." He added that a similar event had occurred with a different woman five years earlier.

Angelo talked a great deal about his past. He came from an Italian, working-class family. He had a brother and sister but doesn't see either one any longer. His brother was transferred to another large city because the automotive industry was booming there. His sister moved out west after she got married. When Angelo was younger, the Cacci family lived in a predominately Italian neighborhood. Both of the paternal grandparents died when Angelo was quite young. Still, some of Angelo's fondest memories were of his grandfather. The old man used to take him fishing outside the city. Angelo's father, on the other hand, didn't have much time for his children. Mr. Cacci supported the family as a dockworker, but he left when Angelo was 11. After the separation, Mrs. Cacci got a job in the clock factory, and she has worked there ever since.

Angelo explained that his childhood was a very unhappy period. His father was seldom home; and, when he was present, he was constantly fighting with Mrs. Cacci. Mrs. Cacci usually became sullen and withdrawn after an argument, refused to speak to her husband, and became uncommunicative with her children. Angelo remembered that many times as a child he was puzzled because it seemed that his mother was angry with him too. Sometimes after an argument, Mrs. Cacci told her children that she ruined her life by marrying a "truckdriver." Angelo went on, explaining that his mother rarely smiled or laughed and did not converse very much with the children. When she came home from work, she would usually put on her robe, cook dinner, and spend the evening watching television. This pattern continued well into Angelo's young adulthood.

After high school, Angelo went into the army where he developed good typing, clerical, and basic accounting skills. He describes the army as being uneventful. He put in his time and was honorably discharged.

Angelo characterized his job as being, "OK. It pays the bills and leaves me a decent amount for entertainment." His particular task is to certify damage claims by checking customer estimates against insurance investigator reports. This provides the company with the information it needs to challenge possibly exaggerated or even fraudulent claims. On an average day, Angelo said he examines and registers 20 to 25 estimates and reports. The counselor noted that Angelo's work record must be a good one. He has been with the company for ten years and regularly gets the raises afforded employees in good standing.

The reason for Angelo's visit to the counseling center, his depression, puzzled him. He recounted a dream he has had several times in the last month, wondering if it is connected to his depression. The counselor described the dream in Angelo's case history, but, though she might have offered an interpretation, she didn't write it down. In the dream Angelo and a man from another department in the insurance firm are walking in an open field. Horses are roaming the area as are several large dogs. One of the dogs seems to be injured and limps by Angelo and his friend. A third man appears and begins attending to the dog. Here either the dream fades or Angelo wakes up. Angelo then turned to other aspects of his life, but didn't see any immediate connection between them and his situation. "Sure I broke up with my girl," he speculated, "but I wasn't in love with her. Besides, I've been through this before." As for his job, "like I explained, it's all right. I've got a good record and the pay is satisfactory." As for his mother, "I go to see her now and then. She's still gloomy as always, but I realize there's little I can do about it. She's been that way for a long time."

ACKNOWLEDGMENTS

I would like to thank Michael Havens, Linda Flower, and Richard Shavelson for their generous comments on earlier versions of this chapter. Along the way, I also had helpful conversations with Peggy Atwell, Al Hutter, Karin Mack-Costello, Sondra Perl, and Sandy Thompson.

NOTES

1. My experience is that many people in humanities and composition studies are not familiar with the range of research methods available to the educational and social science researcher. Though a footnote is hardly the place to attempt a survey of those methods, it might prove helpful to at least sketch out a few of the options.

Fundamental to certain kinds of social science investigation is the experimental design, and the most celebrated—and perhaps most notorious—experimental design is the "pretest-posttest control group design." An experimental design, like the "pre-post design," is defined by two characteristics: (a) It has one or more experimental groups (groups receiving some treatment) and one or more control groups (similar groups not receiving the treatment); and (b) people are randomly assigned to each of the groups. Some social scientists consider the experimental design the ultimate research design because it provides them with the most assurance in making causal interpretations from data. The reasoning is straightforward: Similarity of subjects is assured by randomly assigning people to experimental groups (for example, groups receiving training in sentence-combining) and to control groups (similar groups not receiving sentence-combining instruction); if the experimental group subjects display some statistically significant outcome effect that the control group subjects do not (e.g., increased syntactic maturity), then it seems probable that, all other things being equal, outcome effects resulted from the treatment.

The proper use of an experimental design depends on the reseacher's ability to exercise a good deal of control over the people and the phenomenon her or she is studying. But such control isn't easily obtained, especially for researchers interested in complex educational phenomena. More latitude is provided by a further set of designs called "quasi-experimental designs." These designs, like the classic experimental designs, rely on one or more experimental and one or more control groups; but, unlike the classic designs, they do not involve random assignment of subjects. Two examples: In the "nonequivalent control group design," the researcher conducts a pre-post experimental and control group study using subjects who have *not* been assigned randomly but are naturally assembled—as in a classroom. In the "time-series design," the researcher uses the same group of subjects as, so to speak, both a control and an experimental group. A series of measurements is taken over time to provide a baseline (say, to stick with my earlier illustration, of syntactic maturity); then a treatment is given (say, instruction in sentence-combining), and the series of measurements continues. The researcher notes whether, after treatment began, any changes occurred in the phenomenon in question (e.g., the syntactic complexity of sentences) and tests their significance via statistical analysis. Though they must do so with caution, those using quasi-experimental designs can posit causal relationships between treatments and effects. (See Campbell & Stanley, 1963, for the classic treatment of experimental and quasi-experimental designs; and see Filstead, 1979, and Guba, 1978, for critical assessment of these designs.)

Experimental and quasi-experimental designs are appropriate for probing certain kinds of questions about phenomena that can be delimited and controlled. Survey research methods provide a very different set of procedures for probing different sorts of questions. The survey researcher uses questionnaires (either administered orally or in writing) to gain information on attitudes, habits, and behavioral patterns. Large samples are used, and questionnaires typically go through multiple stages of refinement. The researcher uses the data to describe specific attitudes, opinions, or habits of a particular population. It is not uncommon for the researcher to then correlate his or her findings with other measures of opinion, achievement, or behavior. (See, e.g., John Daly's reports in Chapter 3 of relations between writing apprehension and grades,

English courses taken, general anxiety, teacher assessment of ability, and so on. For an introduction to survey research, see Babbie, 1983.)

Single correlational studies, like those resulting from survey research, do not allow the researcher to make statements about causality, only about co-occurring phenomena. However, one can examine patterns of relationships in a number of correlational studies and, given an appropriate theory, derive possible causal relationships between variables. The procedure for doing this, "causal modeling" or "structural equation modeling," involves systems of correlations (or regression coefficients) in formal statistical models that allow one to test a particular causal intepretation against other, competing interpretations. (For a discussion of causal modeling, see Pedhazur, 1982.)

One criticism of experimental and quasi-experimental designs (and, by implication, of survey research and correlational studies) is that they provide some measure of a behavioral outcome, or attitude or opinion, or pattern of relationships, but they typically do not allow exploration of the mental processes that lead to them. Thus it is that an increasing number of cognitively oriented psychologists and educational researchers are relying on what has come to be called "process-tracing." The goal of process-tracing is to render the nature and sequence of the mental processes a subject goes through while solving a problem rather than simply to record, as one would in experimental and quasi-experimental designs, the end result of that problem-solving. (See Shavelson, Webb, & Burstein, in press, for further discussion.) One popular process-tracing technique is speaking-aloud protocol analysis: The researcher trains a person to speak aloud while solving problems, records that speech, and then analyzes the resulting transcript (called a "protocol") for traces of mental processes. The researcher follows guidelines for determining the validity of the person's reports and attempts to render an approximation of what happened cognitively as that person engaged in problem solving. (See Ericsson & Simon, 1980, for a theoretical defense of this procedure, and Hayes & Flower, 1983, for an application of the procedure to composition studies.)

Other social science researchers, particularly those in anthropology, wish less intrusion into the lives of their subjects than results from either experimental or quasi-experimental designs or from process-tracing procedures; furthermore, such researchers wish to observe their subjects' behavior in natural rather than research settings. These researchers rely on various naturalistic inquiry procedures: They live with their subjects over time, develop and refine various methods to categorize the behaviors they observe, ask questions of the subjects to determine their perception of the events being observed, and so on. The results are often, though by no means always, written up as case studies. (See Guba, 1978, for an overview of these naturalistic observation methods; Stake, 1978, for a theoretical defense of the case study; and Kantor, Kirby, & Goetz 1981, for an application of naturalistic inquiry to composition studies.)

2. Allow me to play out this speculation a bit further. As Stephanie commented throughout the protocol on her reading of the case history, three comprehension strategies emerged: (a) She read the case history with the Jaspers quotation in mind to develop links between the two; (b) she tried to imagine the history's events in terms of her own life; and (c) she imagined she was telling Angelo's story to others "to explain it to [her]self better." All three strategies represent effective ways to actively engage in the reading of a text, and the last two—which seem related—could certainly have enhanced comprehension and recall by incorporating the case history's events into Stephanie's own experience. The use of these last two strategies, combined with the fact that the case history's events are fairly vivid, could explain why—though she felt that

she had a "lousy memory"—Stephanie didn't underline the text of the history. The events were clear, and she tried to make them her own. Anything that was hazy, she could double-check. (And in fact she did refer back to the case history four times during the session.)

But it's possible that the way she read the case history, while active and involving, was also problematic. Though schema theorists are right to insist that we best comprehend and remember that which we can relate to prior knowledge (Rumelhart, 1980; Spiro, 1977, 1980), the nature of that prior knowledge and the manner in which we relate new knowledge to old are important variables in determining the quality and appropriateness-to-task of our comprehension and recall. It is possible that Stephanie so incorporated the history's events into her own experience—saw them so much in terms of her own life—that she felt conflicted when she had to present those events "objectively." Thus she kept "wanting to bring a quotation" into her discussion. She knew she had to be faithful to the text of the history but also knew she had recast the history in personal terms. Perhaps in the heat of the timed assignment, her conflict intensified and fed into her more general uncertainty about her stance toward Karl Jaspers.

3. I have spoken so far about the conceptual-investigative advantages of selecting from and combining a variety of methods. There is, of course, another advantage to such methodological flexibility, a political-rhetorical one. Whenever evaluation is a goal of a research project, the investigator has to consider the audience who will receive the data, for, as Ernest House reminds us, evaluation is an "act of persuasion" (House, 1977, p. 5). An evaluator of programs and curricula must use methods that are most sensitive to that which is being evaluated, but must also consider what kinds of methods will have the most persuasive impact on those who have requested the investigation. (Or the evaluator has to persuade the recipients to accept the methods he or she has chosen.) Where evaluation is a concern, then, methods cannot be adopted or rejected without considering the political-rhetorical context of a particular investigation.

4. One current variation of this battle finds some humanists embracing the phenomenological-ethnographic paradigm and rejecting all other approaches as intrusive and artificial. Any research involving set tasks and/or procedural constraints is counterposed to naturalistic inquiry which is thought to preserve the integrity of the phenomena being studied and which is admired for being built on philosophical underpinnings compatible with humanistic study. While there is little doubt that naturalistic inquiry provides a much-needed balance to traditional quantitative approaches and thereby greatly enriches composition research, there are problems with the way this particular saga of methodological heroes and villains is playing itself out. First of all, there is potential danger in elevating any method. The fascination with naturalistic inquiry can lead, on the part of some, to a habit of uncritical acceptance (not unlike the unquestioning acceptance of experimentalism in the American academic psychology of a generation ago). In such uncritical embrace, naturalistic methods are trivialized and are used to legitimize work that, in one ethnographer's words, is "poorly conducted and ill-conceived" (Rist, 1980, p. 8). Second, not all methods using set tasks and procedural constraints are equally limiting (see footnote 1); and the distinction between "qualitative" and "quantitative" paradigms might not be as neat as it seems, for the approaches share more characteristics than the polemicists would have us believe (see Reichardt & Cook, 1979, for further discussion). Third, when it comes to the study of cognitive processes, naturalistic methods alone will most likely come up short. It is important to keep in mind the fact that the two most influential researchers of cognitive development in our time, Vygotsky and Piaget, found it necessary to tamper with their subjects' natural settings in order to gain their rich data on the way children solve problems.

One last thought. This polarization of naturalistic and quantitative methods also results in a limiting of the ways we can write about writing. The naturalistic camp champions interpretation, rich detail, "thick description," while the more experimentally oriented camp insists on measurements, numerical analysis, the discussion grounded in statistics. The ideal text for the first group becomes the case study; for the second, it's the research article with its attendant tables and charts. But why must these be the two primary choices—two extremes pitted against each other? I would suggest that the most enlightening and comprehensive writing about writing would fuse these two approaches, would weave statistics into descriptions and provide interpretive human contexts for measurements. We in composing-process research need a way to write about our findings that blends the interpretive and metaphoric with the baldly referential and notational. How else will we render the richness of the writing act?

REFERENCES

Babbie, E. R. (1983). *The practice of social research.* Belmont, CA: Wadsworth.

Bartholomae, D. (1980). The study of error. *College Composition and Communication, 31*, 253–269.

Beck, A. T. (1976). *Cognitive therapy and the emotional disorders.* New York: International Universities Press.

Bereiter, C. (1980). Development in writing. In L. W. Gregg & E. R. Steinberg (Eds.), *Cognitive processes in writing* (pp. 73–93). Hillsdale, NJ: Erlbaum.

Berthoff, A. E. (1981). *The making of meaning.* Montclair, NJ: Boynton/Cook.

Bizzell, P. (1979). Thomas Kuhn, scientism, and English studies. *College English, 40*, 764–771.

Bridwell, L. S. (1980). Revising strategies in twelfth grade students' transactional writing. *Research in the Teaching of English, 14*, 197–222.

Britton, J. (1980). Shaping at the point of utterance. In A. Freedman & I. Pringle (Eds.), *Reinventing the rhetorical tradition* (pp. 61–65). Conway, AR: Language and Style Books.

Campbell, D. T. (1974). *Qualitative knowing in action research.* Paper presented at the meeting of the American Psychological Association, New Orleans, LA.

Campbell, D. T. (1979). "Degrees of freedom" and the case study. In T. D. Cook & C. S. Reichardt (Eds.), *Qualitative and quantitative methods in evaluation research* (pp. 49–67). Beverly Hills, CA: Sage.

Campbell, D. T., & Stanley, J. C. (1963). *Experimental and quasi-experimental designs for research.* Chicago: Rand McNally.

Connors, R. J. (1983). Composition studies and science. *College English, 45*, 1–20.

Cooper, C., & Matsuhashi, A. (in press). A theory of the writing process. In E. Martlew (Ed.), *The psychology of writing.* New York: John Wiley & Sons.

Cowley, M. (Ed.). (1977). *Writers at work* (1st Series). New York: Penguin.

Cronbach, L. J. (1975). Beyond the two disciplines of scientific psychology. *American Psychologist, 30*, 116–127.

D'Angelo, F. J. (1979). Paradigms as structural counterparts of topoi. In D. McQuade (Ed.), *Linguistics, stylistics, and the teaching of composition* (pp. 41–51). Arkon, OH: University of Akron Press.

Denzin, N. K. (1970). *The research act.* Chicago: Aldine.

Ellis, A. (1959). Rationalism and its therapeutic applications. *Annals of Psychotherapy, 1*, (Monograph No. 2), 55–64.

Emig, J. (1982). Inquiry paradigms and writing. *College Composition and Communication, 33*, 64–75.

Ericsson, K. A., & Simon, H. A. (1980). Verbal reports as data. *Psychological Review, 87,* 215–251.

Filstead, W. J. (1979). Qualitative methods: A needed perspective in evaluation research. In T. D. Cook & C. S. Reichardt (Eds.), *Qualitative and quantitative methods in evaluation research* (pp. 33–48). Beverly Hills, CA: Sage.

Flower, L. S., & Hayes, J. R. (1980). The dynamics of composing: Making plans and juggling constraints. In L. W. Gregg & E. R. Steinberg (Eds.), *Cognitive processes in writing* (pp. 31–50). Hillsdale, NJ: Erlbaum.

Flower, L. S., & Hayes, J. R. (1981). Plans that guide the composing process. In C. H. Frederiksen & J. F. Dominic (Eds.), *Writing: The nature, development, and teaching of written communication* (Vol. 2, pp. 39–58). Hillsdale, NJ: Erlbaum.

Graves, D. (1982). *A case study observing the development of primary children's composing, spelling, and motor behaviors during the writing process.* Washington, DC: Educational Resources Information Center. (ERIC Document Reproduction Service No. ED 218 653)

Guba, E. (1978). *Toward a methodology of naturalistic inquiry in educational evaluation* (Monograph Series in Evaluation, No. 8). Los Angeles: University of California, Center for the Study of Evaluation.

Hayes, J. R., & Flower, L. (1983). Uncovering cognitive processes in writing: An introduction to protocol analysis. In P. Mosenthal, L. Tamor, & S. Walmsley (Eds.), *Research in writing: Principles and methods* (pp. 207–220). New York: Longman.

Holland, Morris. (1980, July). *The state of the art: The psychology of writing.* Paper presented at the Inland Area Writing Project's summer writing conference, University of California, Riverside.

House, E. R. (1977). *The logic of evaluative argument* (Monograph Series in Evaluation, No. 7). Los Angeles: University of California, Center for the Study of Evaluation.

Kagan, J., Moss, H. A., & Sigel, I. E. (1963). Psychological significance of styles of conceptualization. In J. C. Wright & J. Kagan (Eds.), *Basic cognitive processes in children* (pp. 73–112). *Monographs of the Society for Research in Child Development, 28.*

Kantor, K. J., Kirby, D. R., & Goetz, J. P. (1981). Research in context: Ethnographic studies in English education. *Research in the Teaching of English, 15,* 293–309.

Kelly, G. A. (1963). *A theory of personality.* New York: Norton.

Lazarus, R. S., & Averill, J. R. (1972). Emotion and cognition with special reference to anxiety. In C. D. Spielberger (Ed.), *Anxiety: Current trends in theory and research* (Vol. 2, pp. 241–283). New York: Academic Press.

Maslow, A. H. (1968). *Toward a psychology of being* (2d ed.). New York: Van Nostrand Reinhold.

Maslow, A. H. (1969). *The psychology of science.* Chicago: Henry Regnery.

Mishler, E. G. (1979). Meaning in context: Is there any other kind? *Harvard Educational Review, 49,* 1–19.

Pask, G., & Scott, B. C. E. (1972). Learning strategies and individual competence. *International Journal of Man–Machine Studies, 4,* 217–253.

Pedhazur, E. J. (1982). *Multiple regression in behavioral research* (2d ed.). New York: Holt, Rinehart and Winston.

Peitzman, F. (1981). *The composing processes of three college freshmen: Focus on revision.* Unpublished doctoral dissertation, New York University.

Perl, S. (1979). Unskilled writers as composers. *New York University Education Quarterly, 10,* 17–22.

Perry, W. G., Jr. (1970). *Forms of intellectual and ethical development in the college years.* New York: Holt, Rinehart and Winston.

Plimpton, G. (Ed.). (1977). *Writers at work* (2d, 3d, 4th Series). New York: Penguin.

Plimpton, G. (Ed.). (1981). *Writers at work* (5th Series). New York: Penguin.

Reichardt, C. S., & Cook, T. D. (1979). Beyond qualitative versus quantitative methods. In T. D. Cook & C. S. Reichardt (Eds.), *Qualitative and and quantitative methods in evaluation research* (pp. 7–32). Beverly Hills, CA: Sage.

Rist, R. C. (1980). Blitzkrieg ethnography: On the transformation of a method into a movement. *Educational Researcher 9*, 9–10.

Rose, M. (1980). Rigid rules, inflexible plans, and the stifling of language: A cognitivist analysis of writer's block. *College Composition and Communication, 31*, 389–401.

Rose, M. (1981). *The cognitive dimension of writer's block: An examination of university students.* Unpublished doctoral dissertation, University of California, Los Angeles.

Rose, M. (1984). *Writer's block: The cognitive dimension.* Carbondale: Southern Illinois University Press.

Rumelhart, D. E. (1980). Schemata: The building blocks of cognition. In R. J. Spiro, B. C. Bruce, & W. F. Brewer (Eds.), *Theoretical issues in reading comprehension* (pp. 33–58). Hillsdale, NJ: Erlbaum.

Scardamalia, M. (1981). How children cope with the cognitive demands of writing. In C. H. Frederiksen & J. F. Dominic (Eds.), *Writing: The nature, development, and teaching of written communication* (Vol. 2, pp. 81–103). Hillsdale, NJ: Erlbaum.

Shapiro, D. (1965). *Neurotic styles.* New York: Basic Books.

Shavelson, R. J., Webb, N. M., & Burstein, L. (in press). Measurement of teaching. In M. Wittrock (Ed.), *Handbook of research on teaching* (3rd ed.). New York: Macmillan.

Simon, D. P., & Simon, H. A. (1978). Individual differences in solving physics problems. In R. S. Siegler (Ed.), *Children's thinking: What develops?* (pp. 325–348). Hillsdale, NJ: Erlbaum.

Sommers, N. (1980). Revision strategies of student writers and experienced adult writers. *College Composition and Communication, 31*, 378–388.

Spielberger, C. D. (Ed.). (1972). *Anxiety: Current trends in theory and research* (Vols. 1 & 2). New York: Academic Press.

Spiro, R. J. (1977). Remembering information from text: The "state of schema" approach. In R. C. Anderson, R. J. Spiro, & W. E. Montague (Eds.), *Schooling and the acquisition of knowledge* (pp. 137–165). Hillsdale, NJ: Erlbaum.

Spiro, R. J. (1980). Constructive processes in prose comprehension and recall. In R. J. Spiro, B. C. Bruce, & W. F. Brewer (Eds.), *Theoretical issues in reading comprehension* (pp. 245–278). Hillsdale, NJ: Erlbaum.

Stake, R. E. (1978). The case study method in social injury. *Educational Researcher, 7*, 5–8.

Strauch, R. (1976). A critical look at quantitative methodology. *Policy Analysis, 2*, 121–144.

Vygotsky, L. S. (1981). *Mind in society* (M. Cole, V. John-Steiner, S. Scribner, & E. Souberman, Eds.). Cambridge, MA: Harvard University Press.

Webb, E. J., Campbell, D. T., Schwartz, R. D., & Sechrest, L. (1966). *Unobtrusive measures.* Chicago: Rand McNally.

Wilson, S. (1977). The use of ethnographic techniques in educational research. *Review of Educational Research, 47*, 245–265.

Witkin, H. A., Moore, C. A., Goodenough, D. R., & Cox, P. W. (1977). Field-dependent and field-independent cognitive styles and their educational implications. *Review of Educational Research, 47*, 1–64.

Name Index

Abbott, R. D., 47, 53, 79*n*.
Adams, V. A., 65, 76*n*.
Aldrich, P. G., 61, 76*n*.
Applebee, A. N., 174, 180*n*., 205, 215*n*.
Aristotle, 163*n*., 164*n*.
Arora, M., 75*n*., 76*n*.
Asimov, I., 188, 215*n*.
Atlas, M. A., 93, 94*n*., 169, 180*n*.
Auman, W. W., 65, 76*n*.
Auten, A., 174, 180*n*.
Averill, J. R., 19, 41*n*., 92, 95*n*., 234, 259*n*.

Babbie, E. R., 256*n*., 258*n*.
Bailey, N., 100, 117*n*.
Baker, C., 210, 215*n*.
Ballard, E. D., 203, 215*n*.
Barlow, D. H., 214, 215*n*.
Barrios, M. V., 209, 215*n*.
Barthes, R., 142, 143, 164*n*.
Bartholomae, D., 65, 76*n*., 120, 132*n*., 135–162, 163*n*., 164*n*., 165*n*., 250, 258*n*.
Basile, D. D., 64, 76*n*.
Basowitz, H., 92, 94*n*.
Bechtel, J., 93, 94*n*.
Beck, A. T., 234, 258*n*.
Beech, H. R., 75*n*., 76*n*.
Belcher, G. L., 163*n*., 165*n*.
Bell, E., 65, 76*n*.
Bell, R. A., 49, 78*n*.
Bereiter, C., 144, 163*n*., 165*n*., 235, 258*n*.
Berger, E. M., 49, 76*n*.
Bergler, E., 184, 185, 215*n*.
Berkenkotter, C., 132*n*.
Berthoff, A. E., 249, 258*n*.
Bisanz, J., 61, 79*n*.
Bizzell, P., 146, 147, 156, 163*n*., 164*n*., 165*n*., 249, 258*n*.
Blake, R. W., 47, 77*n*.
Bloom, L. Z., 53, 60, 65, 77*n*., 119–133, 123, 124, 127, 132*n*.
Bloom, M., 119, 131, 132*n*.
Boice, R., 53, 75*n*., 77*n*., 182–214, 189, 191, 193, 200, 203, 205, 212–214, 215*n*.
Bois, J., 189, 215*n*.
Book, V., 57, 77*n*.
Boozer, R. W., 47, 57, 74*n*., 81*n*.
Borne, L., 193, 215*n*.
Boudin, M. H., 198, 215*n*.
Brande, D., 184, 193, 215*n*.
Bridwell, L. S., 236, 258*n*.
Britton, J., 235, 258*n*.
Burgoon, J., 48, 49, 56, 57, 74*n*., 77*n*.
Burstein, L., 256*n*., 260*n*.
Burt, M., 100, 117*n*., 118*n*.
Burton, J. K., 48, 55, 80*n*.

Calkins, L., 10, 18*n*., 120, 133*n*.
Callewaert, H., 43, 77*n*.
Cameron, R., 206, 217*n*.
Campbell, D. T., 229, 233, 255*n*., 258*n*., 260*n*.
Carroll, B., 101, 117*n*.
Cattell, R. B., 92, 94*n*.
Chomsky, N., 116*n*., 118*n*.
Clark, E., 103, 118*n*.
Clark, H., 103, 118*n*.
Claypool, S. H., 47, 52, 77*n*.
Cohen, A., 99, 114, 118*n*.
Coles, W. E., Jr., 163*n*., 165*n*.
Connors, R. J., 249, 258*n*.
Conry, R. F., 47, 50, 59, 79*n*.
Cook, J. A., 75*n*., 80*n*.
Cook, T. D., 250, 257*n*., 260*n*.
Cooper, C., 235, 258*n*.
Cornelio, R., 75*n*., 77*n*.

Covitt, G., 99, 113, 118*n*.
Cowley, M., 234, 258*n*.
Cox, P. W., 236, 260*n*.
Craven, J., 64, 77*n*.
Crisp, A. H., 43, 75*n*., 77*n*., 195, 215*n*.
Cronbach, L. J., 233, 238, 258*n*.
Csikszentmihalyi, M., 20, 21, 28, 32, 36, 41*n*.
Curtis, M. E., 212, 216*n*.

Daly, J. A., 20, 41*n*., 43–82, 45, 47–52, 54, 55, 56, 58, 59, 61, 62, 65, 66, 70, 72, 74*n*., 75*n*., 77*n*., 78*n*., 79*n*., 80*n*., 81*n*., 83, 84, 93, 94*n*., 95*n*., 123, 133*n*., 212, 215*n*.
D'Angelo, F. J., 235, 258*n*.
Davis, B., 104, 118*n*.
Davis, D. M., 75*n*., 78*n*.
DeBeaugrande, R., 197, 208, 215*n*.
Deen, R., 163*n*., 165*n*.
Denzin, N. K., 230*n*., 258*n*.
Diamond, I. M., 65, 78*n*.
Dickson, F., 48, 54, 58, 78*n*., 80*n*.
Domash, L., 194, 215*n*.
Dreussi, R. M. E., 65, 78*n*.
Duke, C. R., 61, 78*n*.
Dulay, H., 100, 117*n*., 118*n*.
Durrell, L., 43, 78*n*.

Earle, B. V., 190, 215*n*.
Easterbrook, J., 23, 41*n*.
Edwards, B., 194, 205, 215*n*.
Elbow, P., 189, 191, 193, 194, 213, 215*n*.
Ellenberger, H., 183, 184, 189, 191, 215*n*.
Ellis, A., 234, 258*n*.
Emig, J., 249, 258*n*.
Erickson, M. H., 190, 215*n*.
Ericsson, K. A., 169, 180*n*., 256, 259*n*.
Erikson, E. H., 187, 188, 215*n*., 216*n*.

Faigley, L., 55, 58, 59, 78*n*.
Federn, P., 43, 78*n*.
Feltz, D., 179, 180*n*.
Fenichel, O., 28, 41*n*.
Filstead, W. J., 255*n*., 259*n*.
Fine, R., 187, 216*n*.
Fish, S., 163*n*., 164*n*., 165*n*.
Flower, L. S., 60, 69, 79*n*., 93, 95*n*., 138, 140, 142, 165*n*., 168, 176, 180*n*., 205, 208, 209, 216*n*., 236, 256*n*., 259*n*.
Fowler, B., 55, 79*n*.
Fox, R. F., 64, 79*n*.
Freud, S., 92, 95*n*., 183, 216*n*.
Furukawa, M. J., 179, 180*n*.

Galbraith, D., 194, 216*n*.
Garcia, R. J., 57, 59, 79*n*.
Gardiner, N. H., 189, 216*n*.
Garrido, M., 55, 79*n*.
Gere, A. R., 47, 53, 79*n*.
Getzels, J., 28, 41*n*.
Gibson, H. B., 75*n*., 79*n*.
Glynn, S. M., 55, 79*n*.
Glynn, T., 203, 215*n*.
Goetz, J. P., 250, 256*n*., 259*n*.
Goldiamond, I., 199, 216*n*.
Goodenough, D. R., 236, 260*n*.
Goodman, P., 185, 216*n*.
Gorrell, D. K., 65, 79*n*.
Gorsuch, R., 48, 81*n*.
Gould, J. D., 204, 210, 212, 216*n*.
Graef, R., 20, 41*n*.
Graves, D., 1–18, 119, 120, 133*n*., 235, 259*n*.
Gregg, L. W., 208, 216*n*.
Grinker, R. R., 92, 94*n*.
Guba, E., 237, 250, 255*n*., 256*n*., 259*n*.

Haar, M., 48, 59, 81*n*.
Hailey, J. L., 66, 72, 74*n*., 75*n*., 78*n*.
Hairston, M., 94, 95*n*., 139, 165*n*.
Hale, J. L., 48, 49, 56, 57, 74*n*., 77*n*.
Harriman, P. L., 190, 216*n*.
Harris, M., 166–181, 175, 180*n*.
Harris, M. B., 75*n*., 79*n*., 198, 216*n*.
Hartley, J., 212, 213, 216*n*.
Harvley-Felder, Z. C., 47, 62, 79*n*.
Hatch, E., 113, 118*n*.
Hatterer, L. J., 212, 216*n*.
Haugen, N. S., 65, 78*n*.
Hayes, C. G., 60, 79*n*.
Hayes, J. R., 60, 69, 79*n*., 140–142, 165*n*., 168, 176, 180*n*., 205, 208, 209, 216*n*., 236, 256*n*., 259*n*.
Haym, R., 193, 216*n*.
Hearn, G. W., 163*n*., 165*n*.
Hecker, B., 22, 32, 39, 42*n*.
Hemingway, E., 43, 79*n*.
Henning, L. H., 196, 203, 216*n*.
Herzberg, B., 164*n*., 165*n*.
Hocevar, D., 203, 216*n*.
Hogan, T., 20, 41*n*.

Holland, M., 235, 259*n*.
Horowitz, I. L., 212, 216*n*.
House, E. R., 257*n*., 259*n*.
Hull, C. S., 205, 213, 216*n*.
Hunt, J., 23, 41*n*.

Isherwood, C., 43, 79*n*.
Izard, C. E., 23, 36, 41*n*.

Jaccard, J., 74*n*., 75*n*.
Jacklin, C. N., 126, 127, 133*n*.
Janet, P., 190, 195, 216*n*.
Jeroski, S. F., 47, 50, 59, 79*n*.
Jones, A. C., 53, 75*n*., 79*n*., 197, 216*n*.
Jones, R., 189, 205, 213, 215*n*.
Jones, S., 96–118, 96, 105, 115, 117*n*., 118*n*.

Kagan, J., 236, 259*n*.
Kail, R. V., 61, 79*n*.
Kant, I., 19, 41*n*.
Kantor, K. J., 250, 256*n*., 259*n*.
Kean, J. M., 65, 78*n*.
Kelly, G. A., 234, 259*n*.
King, B., 47, 79*n*.
Kirby, D. R., 250, 256*n*., 259*n*.
Korchin, S. J., 92, 94*n*.
Korinek, J., 49, 78*n*.
Krashen, S., 97–99, 100, 112–114, 115*n*., 117*n*., 118*n*.
Kroll, B. M., 47, 55, 64, 79*n*., 80*n*.
Kronsky, B. J., 196, 216*n*.

Lah, M. I., 198, 217*n*.
Lally, T., 47, 57, 74*n*., 81*n*.
Landers, D., 179, 180*n*.
Lane, J. C., 61, 82*n*.
Larson, R., 19–42, 20–22, 32, 39, 41*n*., 42*n*.
Lazarus, R. S., 92, 95*n*., 234, 259*n*.
LeCron, L. M., 190, 216*n*.
Lehr, F., 174, 180*n*.
Levine, B. A., 75, 77*n*.
Lewin, K., 119, 133*n*.
Lilly, R., 49, 80*n*.
Linder, R. M., 190, 216*n*.
Liversedge, L. A., 75*n*., 80*n*., 81*n*., 195, 216*n*.
Lunsford, A. A., 164*n*., 165*n*.
Lushene, R., 48, 81*n*.

Maccoby, E. E., 126, 127, 133*n*.
Mack, K., 43, 80*n*., 210, 211, 216*n*.
Madden, C., 100, 117*n*.
Maggitti, P., 64, 82*n*.
Mahoney, M. J., 206, 216*n*.
Maimon, E. P., 163*n*., 165*n*.
Mandel, B. J., 194, 210, 216*n*.
Maslow, A. H., 234, 259*n*.
Matsuhashi, A., 102, 104, 118*n*., 235, 258*n*.
Matthews, J. L., 55, 79*n*.
May, R., 92, 95*n*.
McGroskey, J. C., 45, 78*n*.
McKeachie, W. J., 203, 217*n*.
McLaughlin, B., 115*n*., 118*n*.
McLeod, B., 115*n*., 118*n*.
Meichenbaum, D., 206, 217*n*.
Mellgren, A., 193, 217*n*.
Menks, F., 75*n*., 80*n*., 199, 217*n*.
Meyer, L., 186, 217*n*.
Meyer, P., 65, 72, 78*n*.
Meyer, R., 75*n*., 80*n*.
Meyers, G. D., 48, 51, 64, 81*n*.
Miller, M. D., 20, 41*n*., 45, 47, 48, 50, 51, 54, 56, 65, 74*n*., 75*n*., 78*n*., 80*n*., 83, 84, 95*n*., 212, 215*n*.
Miller, T., 47, 72, 78*n*.
Minninger, J., 75*n*., 80*n*., 196, 197, 217*n*.
Mishler, E. G., 119, 124, 133*n*., 233, 259*n*.
Moldofsky, H., 43, 75*n*., 77*n*., 195, 215*n*.
Moore, C. A., 236, 260*n*.
Moss, H. A., 236, 259*n*.
Muhl, A. M., 189, 190, 217*n*.
Murray, D. M., 219–226
Murthy, R. S., 75*n*., 76*n*.
Muth, K. D., 55, 79*n*.
Myers, I. B., 50, 80*n*.
Myers, P. E., 189, 191, 215*n*.

Nathanson, C. A., 127, 133*n*.
National Assessment of Education Progress, 47, 80*n*.
Newmeyer, F., 116*n*., 118*n*.
Nietzsche, F., 19, 42*n*.
Nixon, H. K., 212, 217*n*.
Nodine, B. F., 163*n*., 165*n*.
Nold, E., 104, 118*n*.
Norem, J., 22, 32, 39, 42*n*.
Nurnberger, J. T., 198, 217*n*.

O'Connor, F. X., 163*n.*, 165*n.*
Offir, C., 124, 125, 133*n.*
Oliver, L. J., 208, 217*n.*
Olsen, T., 123, 133*n.*, 213, 217*n.*
Olson, D. R., 155, 156, 163*n.*, 165*n.*
Orne, M. T., 214, 217*n.*
Osborne, A., 212, 217*n.*

Pai, M. N., 75*n.*, 80*n.*
Pappas, P., 115, 118*n.*
Pask, G., 236, 259*n.*
Passman, R., 75*n.*, 80*n.*, 198, 217*n.*
Pear, J. J., 198, 217*n.*
Pecker, G., 214, 215*n.*
Pedhazur, E. J., 256*n.*, 259*n.*
Peitzman, F., 234, 259*n.*
Perkins, D. N., 144, 165*n.*, 205, 210, 217*n.*
Perl, S., 60, 69, 80*n.*, 178, 180*n.*, 235, 259*n.*
Perry, M., 179, 180*n.*
Perry, W. G., Jr., 247, 259*n.*
Persky, H., 92, 94*n.*
Pervin, L., 49, 80*n.*
Pfeifer, J., 49, 80*n.*
Pianko, S., 93, 95*n.*, 102, 118*n.*, 168, 181*n.*
Plimpton, G., 234, 259*n.*
Pon, P., 99, 112, 114, 118*n.*
Ponsot, M., 163*n.*, 165*n.*
Powell, B. J., 55, 80*n.*
Powers, W. G., 75*n.*, 80*n.*
Price, A., 65, 76*n.*
Prince, M., 189, 217*n.*
Pringle, I., 112, 118*n.*

Quaytman, W., 186, 189, 217*n.*

Raeder, U., 179, 180*n.*
Rainer, T., 190, 191, 194, 216*n.*
Rank, O., 184, 217*n.*
Reavley, W., 195, 217*n.*
Reece, S. C., 65, 80*n.*
Reed, W. M., 48, 55, 80*n.*
Reichardt, C. S., 250, 257*n.*, 260*n.*
Richardson, E. M., 59, 80*n.*
Richmond, V. P., 58, 80*n.*
Rist, R. C., 257*n.*, 260*n.*
Robbins, M., 99, 114, 118*n.*
Rodriguez, R., 142, 165*n.*
Rose, M., 53, 68, 80*n.*, 96, 102, 112, 114, 115*n.*, 118*n.*, 122, 133*n.*, 163*n.*, 165*n.*, 167, 168, 171, 175, 181*n.*, 208, 209, 217*n.*, 227–258, 228, 230, 234, 236, 239, 260*n.*
Rosen, R. D., 43, 80*n.*
Rosenberg, H., 198, 217*n.*
Rosenberg, M., 49, 81*n.*, 183, 193, 217*n.*
Ross, D., 55, 79*n.*
Rossman, T., 115*n.*, 118*n.*
Rumelhart, D. E., 257*n.*, 260*n.*

Said, E. W., 142, 165*n.*
Salovey, P., 48, 59, 81*n.*
Sandilands, B., 115, 118*n.*
Sanovio, E., 75*n.*, 81*n.*, 195, 217*n.*
Scanlon, L., 196, 218*n.*
Scardamalia, M., 144, 163*n.*, 165*n.*, 235, 260*n.*
Scarr, S., 214, 218*n.*
Schuessler, B. R., 47, 53, 79*n.*
Schultz, L. M., 48, 51, 64, 81*n.*
Schuman, E. P., 186, 218*n.*
Schwartz, R. D., 229, 260*n.*
Scott, B. C. E., 236, 259*n.*
Sears, P., 194, 218*n.*
Sechrest, L., 229, 260*n.*
Selfe, C. L., 51, 60, 81*n.*, 83–95, 169, 181*n.*
Shamo, W., 51, 78*n.*
Shapiro, D., 234, 260*n.*
Shaughnessy, M. P., 120, 133*n.*, 160, 163*n.*, 165*n.*
Shavelson, R. J., 256*n.*, 260*n.*
Sigel, I. E., 236, 259*n.*
Silverman, L. H., 187, 218*n.*
Silverman, R., 47, 64, 82*n.*
Simon, D. P., 247, 260*n.*
Simon, H. A., 169, 180*n.*, 247, 256*n.*, 259*n.*, 260*n.*
Singer, J. L., 209, 215*n.*
Skinner, B. F., 190, 197, 202, 218*n.*
Skjei, E., 43, 80*n.*, 210, 211, 216*n.*
Smith, R., 28, 42*n.*
Solomons, L., 190, 218*n.*
Sommers, N., 60, 69, 81*n.*, 236, 260*n.*
Sowers, S., 120, 133*n.*
Spender, D., 214, 218*n.*
Spielberger, C. D., 48, 81*n.*, 93, 95*n.*, 235, 260*n.*
Spiro, R. J., 257*n.*, 260*n.*
Stacks, D. W., 47, 57, 74*n.*, 81*n.*

Stafford, C., 99, 113, 118*n*.
Stafford, L., 49, 61, 81*n*.
Stake, R. E., 256*n*., 260*n*.
Stallard, C., 168, 181*n*.
Stanley, J. C., 255*n*., 258*n*.
Stein, G., 190, 218*n*.
Steinberg, E. R., 208, 216*n*.
Stolz, S., 214, 218*n*.
Strauch, R., 238, 260*n*.
Strouse, J., 123, 133*n*.
Suler, J. R., 184, 218*n*.
Sylvester, J. D., 75*n*., 80*n*., 81*n*., 195, 216*n*.

Tavris, C., 124, 125, 133*n*.
Tetroe, J., 96, 105, 117*n*., 118*n*.
Thackray, R. I., 28, 42*n*.
Theye, F. W., 190, 215*n*.
Thompson, M. O., 47, 48, 64, 81*n*.
Thoreson, C. E., 206, 216*n*.
Tibbetts, A., 167, 181*n*.
Toth, D., 59, 81*n*.

Updike, J., 43, 81*n*.
Upper, D., 43, 81*n*., 198, 218*n*.

Valian, V., 212, 218*n*.
Vandett, N., 48, 55, 80*n*.
Veit, R., 65, 82*n*.
Vygotsky, L. S., 250, 251, 260*n*.

Wagner, E. N., 65, 82*n*.
Walker, J. R, 43, 82*n*.
Wallace, I, 199, 218*n*.
Walters, S. A., 64, 82*n*.
Warters, S., 93, 95*n*.
Wason, P. C., 213, 218*n*.
Webb, E. J., 229, 260*n*.
Webb, N. M., 256*n*., 260*n*.
Weil, B. H., 61, 82*n*.
Weiner, B., 66, 82*n*.
Weiss, R. H., 64, 82*n*.
Wilson, D., 47–49, 52, 70, 78*n*.
Wilson, S., 233, 260*n*.
Winterowd, R., 169, 181*n*.
Witkin, H. A., 236, 260*n*.
Witte, S. P., 47, 52, 55, 58, 59, 78*n*.
Wohlberg, L. R., 190, 218*n*.
Wolfe, T., 40
Wolpe, J., 75*n*., 77*n*.
Woolf, V., 123, 133*n*.
Worth, P., 189, 218*n*.

Zaback, E., 214, 215*n*.
Zamel, V., 115, 118*n*.
Zimmerman, J., 47, 64, 92*n*., 198, 217*n*.
Zoellner, R., 204, 218*n*.

Subject Index

ABAB design, 200–202
Ability, and attributions, 66, 67
Academic context
  discourse of, 134–164
  writing effect, 123
Academic journals, 214
Acquired linguistic competence
  definition, 97–99, 115*n*., 116*n*.
  versus learned competence, 116*n*., 117*n*.
  second language learning, 97–115
Adolescents, and affect, writing, 18–41
Aesthetic problems, children, 3–5
Affective states, 19–41, 233–235
Alice James: A Biography (Strouse), 123
American College Testing, 54, 55
Anxiety (*see also* Writing apprehension)
  apprehension similarity, 92, 93
  context effects, 119–132
  definition, 23, 74*n*.
  and overarousal, adolescents, 21–27
  psychoanalytic interpretation, 43, 183–186
  sex differences, 48, 127
Apathy, 27–31
Apprehension (*see* Writing apprehension)
Argumentative assignments, 58, 59
Arousal, 21–31, 34–41
Artistic factors, 122
Attention
  and anxiety, 23
  and boredom, 28
  and integrated emotions, 32, 33, 39
Attitude Toward Writing Scale, 47, 48, 50, 59
Attitudes
  as construct, 70
  educational program impact, 64
  personality correlates, 48
  sex differences, 47, 48
  of teachers, and anxiety, 52, 53
  toward writing, 65–74
    questionnaires, 65
  and writing apprehension, 50–54
"Attitudes toward written products" construct, 70
Attributions, 66, 67, 76*n*.
Audience
  children's writing, 15–17
  and composing process, 142
  and situational effects, 72
  student writing, universities, 139, 140
  unskilled writers, 93
Authority, and women, 126
Automatic writing, 189–193
Awareness, writing, 67, 68

Barthes's paradox, 143
"Basic writers"
  academic discourse, 146, 147, 158, 159
  curriculum recommendations, 158, 159
Beginnings (Said), 142
Behavior therapy, 197–208
  case studies, 198, 199
  and creativity, 202–205
  versus psychoanalysis, 187–189
  writer's block, 197–208
  writer's cramp, 195
Behavioral correlates
  blocked writers, 53, 54
  and writing disposition, 70, 71
Behavioral dispositions, 70, 71
Behavioral indicators, with writer's block, 229
Behaviorism, 249–252, 255–258

Beliefs
  blocked writers, 53, 54
  questionnaires, 65, 69
  about writing, 65–74
  writing process, 69
Bergler's theory, 184, 185
Biofeedback, writer's cramp, 195
Biological factors, 122
Boredom, and writing process, 27–31
Brainstorming, 193
Breton's technique, 190, 191
Business settings, 132*n*.

Causal modeling, 256
Children, 1–18
  audience, 15–17
  order of blocks, 3–6
  revision process, 10, 11
  writing process, 2–18
Cognition
  anxiety effect on, 23, 24
  apprehension correlates, 59–61
  and audience, 141, 146
  boredom effect on, 28
  dispositions, 66–69
  emotional processes interrelationship, 20–41
  and goal-setting, audience, 141
  inner- versus outer-directedness, 146, 147
  questionnaire measures, 229–231
  and stress, 56
  writer's block, research, 233–258
"*Cognition, Convention, and Certainty*" (Bizzell), 146
Cognitive-behavior modification, 205–208
Cognitive dispositions, 66–69
Cognitive psychology, 208–210
Cognitive stress, 56
Commonplaces, 137–139, 149–153
"Communication seeking behaviors," 62
Comparison deficiency explanation, 63
"Complexity," 57
Composing
  apprehensiveness in, 83–94
  inner- and outer-directed writers, 146, 147
  and monitor theory, 114
  process of, activities, 141–143
  process of, research, 227–258
  research in, 227–258
    application, 166, 167
  second language, 96–118
  speaking aloud protocols, 166–181
  strategies, 178, 179
  styles of, 236, 237
Composing styles, 236, 237
Computer-based editing, 212
Conceptual sequences, 2–7
Conferencing role, 115
Confidence (*see* Self-confidence)
Consciousness, 67, 68
Context effects
  academic discourse, 134–164
  anxious writers, 119–132
  writer's block, research, 232, 233
  writing, 71–73
Contingency management
  versus automatic writing, 192, 193
  versus cognitive therapy, 207, 208
  in writer's block, 198–205
Control groups, 255, 256
Conventions, in children, 3–5
Conversational memory, 61
Counterattitudinal writing task, 60
Creativity
  and behavior therapy, 202–205
  and context, 148–164
  Freudian interpretation, 183, 184
  in writing, limitations, 141–143
Cultural context, 120, 121

Daly–Miller Writing-Apprehension Scale, 57, 58
  dimensionality, 74*n*.
  reliability, 45, 47
  26-item version, 46*n*.
Deadlines, 246
Decision-making, 172–174
Descriptive-narrative assignments, 58, 59
Developmental factors, 2–18
Diary writing, 194
Discourse, academic community, 134–164
The Discourse on Language (Foucault), 134
Dispositional attitudes
  versus situational attitudes, 65, 66, 76*n*.
  about writing, 66–71
"Dispositional feelings," 44

Dissertation writing, women, 124–132
Dogmatism, 49
"Domain-specific" schemata, 144

Editing, apprehensive writer, 91, 92
Educational programs, 64
Egocentricity, children, 9, 12, 15
Ego psychology, 187, 188
Emotions (*see also* Anxiety)
  and cognition, integration, 33
  order and disorder in, 31, 32
  overarousal, 21–27
  versus rationality, writing, 19, 20
  underarousal, 27–31
  writer's block, research, 234, 235
  writing context, 122
  in writing process, 19–41
Empirical-behaviorist tradition, 249–252
English Composition Test, 55
Enjoyment, and arousal, writing, 36–40
Environmental conditions, 213, 232, 233
Error analysis, 120, 121
Errors and Expectations (Shaughnessy), 120
Ethnography, 249–252, 257
"Evaluating", composing process, 141
Expectations, and apprehension, 50–54
Experimental designs, 227–258
  description, 255, 256
"Experimental writing" technique, 190

Factor analysis, 45, 46
Fear, and writing process, 23, 24
Feedback, and emotion, 33
Females (*see* Women)
Field dependence–independence, 236
"Field-specific" schemata, 144
Field Theory in Social Science (Lewin), 119
First draft, 83–94
Fixed-ratio schedule, 199
Forced writing, 203–205
Fragmentation, and anxiety, 26
Free writing technique, 89, 189–195
Frequency, writing, 70, 71
Freudian interpretation, 183, 184

Gender differences (*see* Sex differences)
Gestalt therapy, 196, 197
Goal-setting
  composing process, 141
  dissertation writing, 126
Grades, and apprehension, 55
Graduate students, 119–132
Grammar, second language learning, 103–115
Grandiosity, 31
"Great man" theory, 151
Guilt, and writer's block, 184, 185

High school students, 19–41
Holistic orientation, 236
Humanistic approach, 249–252, 257
Hunger or Memory (Rodriguez), 142
Hypnotherapy, 189–191

Idiosyncracy, 164*n.*
Imagery techniques, 209, 210
Imitation, 157
Impulsive behavior
  and anxiety, 24
  and cognitive style, 236
Indecisiveness, 172–174
Individual differences, 47–48
"Inert knowledge," 163*n.*
Information problems, children, 3–6
"Inner-directed theorists," 146, 147
Inner discourse, 191
"*Inquiry Paradigms and Writing*" (Emig), 132*n.*
Insight, 222, 223
Intellectual factors, 121, 122
Intrinsic motivation, 34
Introduction, paper writing, 24–26, 37
Introversion, 50
Intuitive approaches, 194
Invention, in writing, limitations, 141–143
"Issue tree," 176

Jaspers, Karl, 239, 252, 253
Job choice, 51
Journal referee process, 214
Journal writing
  as therapeutic technique, 194
  writing apprehension impact, 65

"Knowledge-telling strategy," 144, 145

Language
  and audience, academic discourse, 145–164
  and composing process, 142, 143
  oral versus written, 155, 156

Language acquisition device, 116*n*., 117*n*.
Language intensity, 56
Language-study approach, 64
Learned linguistic competence, 97–115
  versus acquired competence, 116*n*., 117*n*.
  definition, 97–99, 115*n*., 116*n*.
  second language learning, 97–115
Learning-centered writing, 64
Letter-writing technique, 195
"Lexical diversity," 57
Lexical items, 103, 108–111
Likert scale, 117*n*.
Linguistic competence, 116*n*.
Linguistic production, 116*n*.
Linguistics, three components, 116*n*.
Locus of control, 49
Luck, and attributions, 66, 67
"ly" words, 56

Marriage, and writing, women, 128–132
Math anxiety, 48, 52
McGraw-Hill Reading Test, 55
Meaning, children's blocks, 15
Mechanical correctness, 90, 91
Men, writing apprehension, 47, 48
Mental state, 141
Methods, 227–258
Missouri College English Test, 55
"Modeling," 175
Monitor theory, 96–117
  and blocking, 114
  description, 97–100
  personality factors, 114
  second language learning, 96–117
Motherhood, and writing, 128–132
Motivation
  literature on, 212
  and writing process, 27–31, 34
Motor problems, children, 3–5
Multidimensional measures, 47
Muscle relaxation, 195
Myer-Briggs Type Indicator, 50

"Naive" discourse, 157
National Institute of Education, 2, 3
Naturalistic observation, 250, 251, 256–258
Need to write, 224, 225
Neurosis, 185
Nonequivalent control group design, 255
Novelty effects, 72

Observations
  as research technique, 250, 251
  writing process, 167–170
Occupational choice, 51
Oral communication anxiety, 48
Oral language, 155, 156
Order, in writing, 223
Orientation, 236
Outcomes, and situational attitudes, 73
"Outer-directed theorists," 146, 147
Outlines, 175, 176
Overarousal, and anxiety, 21–27
Overcoming Writing Anxiety workshops, 124
Overcoming Writing Blocks (Mack & Skjer), 210, 211

The page, children's blocks, 7, 8
Paradoxical treatment, 196
Passive voice, 57
Pauses, 102–115
Perception
  and anxiety, writing, 33
  situational effects, 72
Perfectionism, women, 127
Performance correlates, 54–59
Persona, 142
Personality factors, 47–50
Phenomenological paradigms, 249–251, 257
Philosophical assumptions, research, 249–252
Planning, composing process, 141
"*The Planning Strategies of a Publishing Writer*" (Berkenkotter), 132*n*.
Playwrights, 185, 186, 193
Poetry, 191
Positive reinforcement, 62
Post hoc questioning, 167, 168
Pretest-posttest control group design, 255
Prewriting activities, 93
Priority setting, 126
Problem-solving strategies, 176, 205, 208, 209, 236
"Process knowledge," 69, 72
Process-tracing, 256
Procrastination
  apprehensive writer, 92
  as behavioral construct, 70
  descriptions of, 43
  versus writer's block, construct, 71

"Productive avoidance" technique, 198
Productivity, 213
Protocol analysis
advantages, 169, 170
technique, 256
writer's block study, 230
writing-process problems, 166–181
Psychoanalysts, writing blocks, 186, 189
Psychoanalytic interpretation
versus behavior therapy, 187, 188
boredom, 28
writer's anxiety, 43
writer's block, 183–186
Psychoanalytic Review article (Schuman), 186
Psychohistorical interpretation, 188
Psychosomatics, 43
Psychotherapies, 182–214 (*see also specific types*)
Publication process, journals, 214
Public discourse, 142
Public speaking anxiety, 49
Punishment, 62, 63

Quality, and writing apprehension, 58, 59
Quantitative methods, 257, 258
Quasi-experimental design, 255, 256
Questionnaires, 229–232, 255

Rationality, 19, 20
Readability, and writing apprehension, 57
"Reader-based prose," 93, 138
Reading anxiety, 48, 52
Reflective orientation, 236
Reinforcement laws, 199
Relaxation techniques, 195
Rereading, 176–178
Research, 227–258
methods, in writer's block, 227–258
and practice, 166, 167
writing process observation, 167–170
Research methods, 227–258
"Reviewing", composing process, 141
Revision
in apprehensive writer, 91, 92
categories of, 10, 11
children, 3, 10
composing process, 141
monitor use, 102–115
The Right Stuff (Wolfe), 40
Role of conferencing, 115
Role conflicts, women, 124–132
A Room of One's Own (Woolf), 123
Rules
and blocked writers, 53, 54, 208, 209
graduate student, dissertation, 127
in second language learning, 113

Schiller's metaphor, creativity, 183
Scholastic Aptitude Test, 54, 55
School choices, 50–54
Science anxiety, 48
Scopophilia, 185
Second language composing, 96–117
Selection, and writing process, 14
Self-confidence
building of, 43
men versus women, 127
writing apprehension, 49, 50
and writing, women, 124–127
Self-consciousness, 114
Self-esteem, and writing apprehension, 49, 50 (*see also* Self-confidence)
Self-management techniques, 199
Self-report, 44–47
Sentence errors, 158, 159
Sentence length, 57
Serial approach, problems, 236
Seventeen magazine, 140–143, 163*n.*
Sex differences (*see also* Women)
anxiety, 127
perfectionism, 127
teacher expectations, 51, 52
writing apprehension, 47, 48
Shaping, 203
Short-term memory, 103
Silences (Olsen), 123
Single correlational studies, 256
Situational attitudes
versus dispositional attitudes, 65, 66, 76*n.*
measurement, 75*n.*, 76*n.*
toward writing, 71–74
Situational parameters, 74*n.*, 232, 233
Social anxiety, 49
Social approval seeking, 49
Social context
and error analysis, 120, 121
and writer's block, research, 232, 233
and writing, 122, 123
Solipsism, 164*n.*
Speaking-aloud protocols, 166–181, 256

"Speedwriting," 92
Spelling, in children, 3, 4, 12–15
Spontaneous writing, 203–205
"Stagefright in writers," 61
State-specific reactions, 235
Stimulated recall, 167, 168, 230, 239
Stress, 56
Structural equation modeling, 256
Structured writing, 88, 89
Students
  academic discourse learning, 134–164
  and writing apprehension, 50–54
"*The Study of Error*" (Bartholomae), 120
Surrealists, 190, 191
Survey methods, 255
Syntax
  and academic discourse, 159–162
  second language learning, 103
  and writing apprehension, 57, 58

T-units, 57, 58, 104–107
Task ambiguity, 72
Teachers
  and children, 4, 13, 14
  and composition research, 167
  expectations, 51, 52
  and student anxiety, 93
  writing apprehensiveness, 52
Technical writing, 212
Temperamental factors, 122
Tenacity, writing, 70, 71
Test anxiety, 48
Test of Standard Written English, 55
Think-aloud protocols, 101, 102
Time perception, 34
Time-series design, 255
Topic problems, children, 3–6
Topic sentences, 89
Trait anxiety, 48, 235
Transactional therapy, 196, 197
"Translating", composing process, 141

Unconscious factors, 184, 185
Underarousal, 27–31
University discourse, 134–164
"Unskilled" writers, 93
Unstructured writing, 88, 89

Verbal ability, women, 127
Videotapes, 61, 102–107, 168, 230
Voice, in writing, 225, 226
Vygotsky's methods, 250, 251

Women (*see also* Sex differences)
  versus men, apprehension, 47, 48
  political factors, 213, 214
  role conflict, graduate student, 124–132
  and writing, social context, 122, 123
Workshops, 65
"Writer-based" prose, 138
Writer's cramp
  and anxiety, 75*n.*
  four-stage model, 75*n.*
  origins, 195
  psychosomatics, 43
  therapies, 195, 196
Writing apprehension, 43–76 (*see also* Anxiety)
  anxiety similarity, 92, 93
  beliefs and behavioral correlates, 53, 54
  case study, 83–94
  changing of, 63–65
  cognitive correlates, 59–61
  correlates, 47–61
  definition, 74*n.*, 83
  development of, 61–63
  individual-difference correlates, 47–50
  measurement, 44–47
  performance correlates, 54–59
Writing-Apprehension Scale (*see* Daly-Miller Writing-Apprehension Scale)
Writing behavior, 56–59
Writing courses
  choices, and apprehension, 50–54
  writing apprehension impact, 64
Writing process
  and apprehensiveness, 60, 61
  children, 2–18
  diagnosis of, problems, 166–181
  emotional scenarios, 19–41
  knowledge of, and skill, 69
  observations, research strategies, 167–170
  and product, 213
  and situational effects, 72, 73
  speak-aloud protocols, 166–181
Writing quality, 58, 59
Written language, 155, 156